Get **more** out of libraries

Please return or renew this item by the last date shown.

You can renew online at www.hants.gov.uk/library

Or by phoning 0845 603 5631

Hampshire
County Council

# The Politics of Affect and Emotion in Contemporary Latin American Cinema

# The Politics of Affect and Emotion in Contemporary Latin American Cinema

## Argentina, Brazil, Cuba, and Mexico

*Laura Podalsky*

palgrave
macmillan

An earlier version of chapter 3 appeared as "Affecting Legacies: Historical Memory and Contemporary Structures of Feeling in *Madagascar* and *Amores perros*." *Screen* 44.3 (Autumn 2003): 277–94, and is reappearing here by permission of Oxford University Press.

An earlier version of chapter 4 appeared as "Out of Depth: The Politics of Disaffected Youth and Contemporary Latin American Cinema." In *Youth Culture in Global Cinema*. Timothy Shary and Alexandra Seibel, eds. Austin: University of Texas Press, December 2006.

A section of chapter 5 appeared as "Migrant Feelings: Melodrama, *Babel*, and Affective Communities." *Studies in Hispanic Cinemas* 7.1 (Winter 2011).

First published in 2011 by
PALGRAVE MACMILLAN®
in the United States—a division of St. Martin's Press LLC,
175 Fifth Avenue, New York, NY 10010.

Where this book is distributed in the UK, Europe and the rest of the world, this is by Palgrave Macmillan, a division of Macmillan Publishers Limited, registered in England, company number 785998, of Houndmills, Basingstoke, Hampshire RG21 6XS.

Palgrave Macmillan is the global academic imprint of the above companies and has companies and representatives throughout the world.

Palgrave® and Macmillan® are registered trademarks in the United States, the United Kingdom, Europe and other countries.

ISBN: 978–0–230–10955–1

Library of Congress Cataloging-in-Publication Data

Podalsky, Laura, 1964–
　　The politics of affect and emotion in contemporary Latin American cinema : Argentina, Brazil, Cuba, and Mexico / Laura Podalsky.
　　　　p. cm.
　　Includes bibliographical references and index.
　　ISBN 978–0–230–10955–1 (hardback)
　　　　1. Motion pictures—Political aspects—Latin America. 2. Motion pictures—Social aspects—Latin America. 3. Motion pictures—Latin America—History—20th century. 4. Motion pictures—Latin America—History—21st century. I. Title.

PN1993.5.L3P63 2011
791.43098'09051—dc22　　　　　　　　　　　　　　　2011005257

A catalogue record of the book is available from the British Library.

Design by Newgen Imaging Systems (P) Ltd., Chennai, India.

First edition: August 2011

10　9　8　7　6　5　4　3　2　1

Printed and bound in Great Britain by
CPI Antony Rowe, Chippenham, Wiltshire

# Contents

# Figures

# Acknowledgments

As this project developed over several years, I have many people I wish to thank. Luisela Alvaray, Gilberto Moisés Blasini, Marvin D'Lugo, Sergio de la Mora, Tamara Falicov, Paula Félix-Didier, Claire Fox, Juan Antonio García Borrero, Ana López, Kathleen Newman, Patrice Petro, Victoria Ruétalo, Ann Marie Stock, Dolores Tierney, Patricia Torres San Martín, Juan Carlos Vargas, and Cristina Venegas have offered insights, specific suggestions, and general encouragement for which I am extremely grateful. It is a pleasure, indeed, to work over the years with such thoughtful and provocative colleagues, all of whom have helped me think more profoundly and thoroughly about Latin American film. Dan Balderston has always been an inspiration—a mentor and friend on whom I rely for feedback, big and small.

I also have been extraordinarily lucky to find a professional home in the Department of Spanish and Portuguese at The Ohio State University and to enjoy the friendship and intellectual companionship of colleagues such as Maureen Ahern, Jonathan Burgoyne, Ignacio Corona, Lucia Costigan, Elizabeth Davis, Ana del Sarto, Salvador García, Richard Gordon, John Grinstead, Ileana Rodríguez, Eugenia Romero, Steve Summerhill, Abril Trigo, Fernando Unzueta, and Juan Zevallos Aguilar. Their smart interventions and warm collegiality over the past ten years have been greatly appreciated. Ignacio and Ana provided valuable suggestions and insightful commentary on particular aspects of this project. For his calm manner, sly sense of humor, and generous support. I am grateful to Fernando who has served as our department chair for the past eight years. Ileana, in particular, has been a provocative interlocutor keeping me on my toes and making me laugh—reminding me that intellectual inquiry is a joyous and passionate endeavor. I am likewise thankful for wise and thoughtful colleagues in the Film Studies program, among them John Davidson, Ron Green, and John

Hellmann. My appreciation goes to Theresa Delgadillo and Dana Renga for bibliographical references on specific issues, to Carol Robison at the Center for Latin American Studies for supplying me with films, and to the staff of the Humanities Information Systems office for their hard work and patient responses to my queries. Current and former graduate students have helped me to think about film and affect in new and challenging ways, among them Lina Aguirre, Mariana Lacunza, Raquel Pina, and Paco Villena-Garrido.

The Ohio State University's (former) College of Humanities provided research funding and leave-time without which this project would not have been possible. The generous backing of a Fulbright-García Robles grant allowed me to further my understanding of film and youth cultures during a year in Guadalajara, Jalisco. My thanks to the Universidad de Guadalajara's Centro de Investigación y Estudios Cinematográficos (CIEC) of the Centro Universitario de Ciencias Sociales y Humanidades (and to Eduardo de la Vega Alfaro, its director at the time), and to the Departamento de Imagen y Sonido of the Centro Universitario de Arte, Arquitectura y Diseño, that hosted my stay. My gratitude also goes to colleagues and graduate students at Notre Dame University, University of Wisconsin, Emory University, and the University of Iowa, where I presented parts of this project, for their comments and questions.

My debts to family and friends are immense. With Charlie Stuart, Kathy Stuart, Barbara Podalsky, Vicki Robinson, Steve Crider, Richard Crider, Reyhan Crider, Eva Ostrum, Martha McKnight, Rachel Buff, Joe Austin, Caroline Clark, Emma Clark, Ted Clark, Kurt Mortensen, Brenda Mortensen, Chris Evans, and Holley Wiseman, I have shared fine meals, witty conversation, and adventures to new places—the stuff that helps us weather life's difficulties and laugh at its absurdities. Finally, of course, my thanks and love, thousandfold, to John, the provacateur; Wyatt, the brave; and Alejandra, the fierce.

Portions of this book have appeared previously in the journals *Screen* (chapter 3) and *Studies in Hispanic Cinemas* (chapter 5) and in the following anthology, *Youth Culture in Global Cinema* (chapter 4).

# Introduction

La piel se convierte en una segunda forma de la conciencia, y desde ella es posible contemplar cinematográficamente el entorno: precisamente, porque el entorno se desplaza y modifica a un ritmo más parecido al del cine que al de la vieja realidad.

Martín Hopenhayn

In the mid-late 1990s, Latin American cinemas began to experience a renaissance. Box-office sensations like *O Que É Isso, Companheiro? / Four Days in September* (Brazil-United States, Bruno Barreto, 1997), *El Chacotero sentimental / The Sentimental Teaser* (Chile, Cristián Galaz, 1999), *Amores perros* (Mexico, Alejandro González Iñárruti, 2000), *Y tu mamá también / And Your Mother, Too* (Mexico, Alfonso Cuarón, 2001), and *Cidade de Deus / City of God* (Brazil-France, Fernando Mereilles, and Katia Lund, 2002) broke records on the domestic market. Popular success at home often coincided with critical (and, on occasion, commercial) success abroad. *El Chacotero sentimental* won audience awards at the Chicago Latino Festival (2000) and the Toulouse Latin American Film Festival (2000). Nominated for an Oscar, *Amores perros* won at Cannes (Critics Week Grand Prize and Young Critics Prize, 2000), the Montréal Festival of New Cinema (Screenplay), and the Tokyo International Film Festival (Best Director; Grand Prix). Nominated for an Oscar two years later, *Cidade de Deus* won top prizes at the Marrakech International Film Festival (Best Director, 2002), New York Film Critics Circle (2003), and Vancouver (2004). The controversial *Tropa de Elite / Elite Squad* (Brazil, José Padilha, 2007) won the top prize at the 2008 Berlin Film Festival.[1] Such success on the international film circuit has encouraged film critics to stress the ambition and artistic innovation of these films. Others, citing incredible box-office numbers and the global distribution of the films, celebrate the revitalization of Latin American cinema's popular appeal.

While this critical acclaim tends to celebrate the talents and achievements of selected auteurs, another factor is clearly at work. Throughout Latin America, but particularly in Argentina, Brazil, Mexico, and Chile, film industries are once again thriving after a period of stagnation, producing more films on an annual basis than in the prior decade.[2] Film scholars and critics have attributed the growth, in part, to the enactment of new state initiatives, the emergence of new forms of financing (e.g., public-private partnerships), the appearance of new funding sources like Ibermedia and the Hubert Bals fund (associated with the Rotterdam International Film Festival), and new promotional strategies (e.g., the types of synergistic marketing tactics employed by certain Mexican producers).[3] Few are as effusive as British scholar Stephen Hart who has argued that such shifts have allowed Latin American cinema to "finally come into its own."[4] Nonetheless, numerous critics characterize the contemporary era as a break from the past inaugurating a new horizon of "New Argentine Cinema," "New Brazilian Cinema," and "New Mexican Cinema."[5]

The emergence of this "new" cinema has also met with skepticism from a variety of quarters that point to its excessive preoccupation with stylistic innovation and its inadequate grasp of past traumas and current socioeconomic problems. The attacks have frequently been aimed at the most expensive and well-promoted films. In an article published in a Mexico City newspaper, the Mexican cultural critic Carlos Monsiváis denounced both *Amores perros* and *Y tu mama también* in the aftermath of their box-office success as examples of a shallow postmodern cinema, emphasizing their derivative style (taken from "*video-clips* [and] the cinema of Quentin Tarantino and Abel Ferrara...") and their portrayal of contemporary Mexican adolescents to suggest the films' collusion with neoliberal values—that is, for buying into the standards and values of globalized (youth) culture.[6] Other critics have gone beyond the denunciation of particular films to indict broader industrial trends. Brazilian film scholar Ivana Bentes has been equally doubtful about the worthiness of recent Brazilian films like *Central do Brasil / Central Station* (Brazil-France, Walter Salles, 1998), which she has critiqued for their undue preoccupation with style and their superficial engagement with socioeconomic issues. Comparing contemporary films with those of the politically militant and aesthetically experimental Cinema Nôvo of the 1960-70s (known for its "aesthetic of hunger"), she has belittled the more recent cinema for its "cosmetics of hunger."[7] Bentes dismisses the depiction of socioeconomic inequalities in recent Brazilian films because they lack an overarching political project, and criticizes their attempt to dress up Brazil's poverty in order to attract the eye of foreign consumers.

Critics like Monsiváis and Bentes respond not only to the films them-selves, but also to the pronouncements of contemporary cineastes. Younger Argentine filmmakers have been particularly vocal about their disinterest in politics. Seeing themselves as a "generation of orphans," they generally dis-avow any connection to earlier Argentine films, particularly to the explicit political engagements of both "Third Cinema" advocates like Fernando Solanas (who emerged in the 1960s alongside Cinema Nôvo) and directors of "redemocratization" like Luis Puenzo (*La historia oficial / The Official Story*, 1985).[8] For their part, Mexican filmmakers Alejandro González Iñárruti, Alfonso Cuarón, and Guillermo del Toro attribute their success to their rejection of the type of state financial support that had, until recently, sustained national film production. Generally working outside of Mexico, they underscore their interest in maintaining authorial independence and making films that respond to their personal obsessions in ways that appeal to mass audiences. In a 2006 interview with U.S. journalist Charlie Rose, Cuarón argued that one of the things his work shares with his two compa-triots is a thematic concern for how ideology is "a wall between communi-cation and people."[9] By situating themselves globally and deemphasizing national commitments, these filmmakers contribute to the characterization of contemporary Latin American cinema as a willing participant in the depoliticized, pro-market atmosphere that emerged in the region in the late 1980s and early 1990s as neoliberal administrations took power throughout the region.

While sharing some of Monsiváis and Bentes's concerns, I believe that the films they decry are more complex and call upon us to reconsider how aesthet-ics and politics intersect in today's cinema. This book contributes to that effort by offering an overview of recent Latin American film that identifies several important tendencies shared by works made in different countries. This map-ping project allows us to see how today's cinema participates in larger sociocul-tural processes and to discern the degree to which contemporary filmmaking represents a break with older traditions in the region—most notably, with the New Latin American Cinema of the 1960s and 1970s, which is often seen as the hallmark of aesthetically innovative, politically militant cinema. Unlike other books on film and politics, *The Politics of Affect and Emotion in Contemporary Latin American Cinema* pays particular attention to the sensorial and emotional appeals of recent Latin/a American films. As detailed later, it is the recent cinema's preoccupation with reaching audiences through sensation that is often read as the most potent sign of its overarching conservatism.

But what distinguishes the sensorial dynamics of today's cinema from those of previous eras? After all, as noted by film scholars Carl Platinga and Greg M. Smith, people have long gone to the movies to feel.[10] How do (certain) contemporary films invite us to feel differently? This phenomenon is clearly not isolated to Latin America. From the United States, one need only think of the unsettling affects of David Lynch's *Blue Velvet* (1986) and *Mulholland Drive* (2001) or Quentin Tarantino's *Reservoir Dogs* (1992) and *Pulp Fiction* (1994). As one of the earliest examples of this new type of cinema, *Blue Velvet* shocked audiences and critics alike with its strange appeal. From its opening sequence, the film offered viewers a disturbing vision of suburbia by juxtaposing slow-motion long shots of the residents' plastic smiles and robotic waves with regular-motion close-ups of insects undulating beneath well-groomed lawns. The shots' shifting speed and nostalgic Technicolor-like palette lent a hyper-real feel to the diegesis, endowing the white, middle-class life depicted in the profilmic space with a sense of the uncanny. Lynch's interest in discomforting audience members was equally evident in *Mulholland Drive*. In a pivotal scene, Betty and Rita, after making love for the first time, attend a late-night performance at a local theater where they listen to a singer's Spanish-language rendition of Roy Orbison's "Crying." Cutting between the singer and the women in classic shot-reverse shots, the film suggests the degree to which "Llorando" resonates emotionally and physically with the two women, who begin to weep, curling their bodies together as they listen to the seemingly incomprehensible (yet nonetheless "intuitable") lyrics. Yet, as in *Blue Velvet*, all is not as it seems. When the singer collapses on stage, her singing continues. This spectacular moment of disintegration (in which body and voice fall apart) ruptures the ties that bind the women and ourselves to the emotionally charged display. What had appeared to be the authentic correlative of the new couple's profound feelings for each other—that is, the song's emotional resonance—is revealed to be nothing more than a simulacrum. In abruptly severing the "emotional scripts" of established film forms, which anchor spectators to the profilmic event, the film sets the spectator adrift.

Tarantino is another U.S. filmmaker intensely concerned with cinema's affective possibilities. As noted by Paul Gormley, "new-brutality" films by Tarantino, Kathryn Bigelow (*Strange Days*, United States, 1995), David Fincher (*Se7en*, United States, 1995), and others share an interest in "renegotiat[ing] and reanimat[ing] the immediacy and affective qualities of the cinematic experience within commercial Hollywood...All of these films attempt to assault the body of the viewer and make the body act involuntarily..."[11] In many ways, these films are quite different from Lynch's work. Where *Blue Velvet* and *Mulholland Drive* aim for estrangement, *Reservoir Dogs* and *Pulp Fiction* promote our absorption to provoke "unseemly" responses—for example, encouraging us to laugh at immensely brutal acts of torture. Nonetheless, the films of both directors deploy affective appeals in innovative ways that encourage cognitive dissidence and shake up our senses.

Despite *Amores perros*'s quite different melodramatic tone, the film's equally visceral impact (along with its unconventional narrative structure) led many critics to compare it to Tarantino's *Pulp Fiction*. While the affective charge of Latin American films like *Amores perros* drew raves from many foreign journalists,[12] it turned off some domestic critics who, like Monsiváis, dismissed the works' hyper-emotivity as derivative and characteristic of globalized media culture. The frequently hyperbolic Jorge Ayala Blanco called *Amores perros* "a pre-fabricated success of marketing strategy" and a "stale, exasperating, tri-dramatic soap opera" with overwrought cinematography.[13] Such reactions hook into the powerful critique of the contemporary sociocultural conjuncture offered by public intellectuals like Argentine Beatriz Sarlo, who blames the broader "media culture" for facilitating the expansion of consumer capitalism and for debilitating historical sensibilities. Sarlo has offered eviscerating chronicles of the increasingly segregated urban culture of Buenos Aires, where new technologies remold subjectivities and atomize collectivities. Whether in her account of the domestic "zapper" using the remote control to obsessively switch between different channels or of young video gamers standing before brightly illuminated consoles in darkened public arcades, Sarlo takes aim at the way contemporary subjects plug into media devices and then, captured by the depthless possibilities of the screen, are overtaken/driven by the pulsating jerks of audiovisual phantasmagoria. Her essays depict isolated urban subjects who, seduced by the enticements of contemporary media culture, consume rhythmically, paying their monthly cable tithe or inserting their few hard-won coins to (re)gain access to the constantly unfolding possibilities on-screen.[14]

Sarlo's critique of Argentina's cultural ethos is echoed by Jean Franco, Nelly Richard, and other cultural critics in relation to countries like Chile, Mexico, and Perú, all of which have undergone similar neoliberal transformations.[15] Their analyses situate the contemporary media as constitutive of a "culture of immediacy" wherein informational overload prevents subjects from exercising the (distanced) cognitive skills necessary to act as citizens (i.e., political subjects). For Franco, today's free market economies bombard citizens with "images and 'information'" and the "media operate like a vast shredding machine that reduces even the most significant events to confetti."[16] Immersed in these free-floating bits/bytes, subjects cannot synthesize the sheer amount of daily data and, as a result, cannot participate in the public domain in meaningful ways.

Franco, Sarlo, and Richard's critiques of contemporary Latin American media emerge from a long-standing concern about its role in washing away the trauma of dictatorship in Argentina, Chile, and Uruguay. As acknowledged later in this introduction and in subsequent chapters, their writings about Latin American culture-scapes have been indispensable to my own work. However, I believe their overly broad depiction of media culture as a unified field of representations and practices is problematic, as is their reification of avant-garde aesthetics as the best means to adequately address the past. Summarily dismissing the media for supporting the "official version" of past state repressions (as unfortunate processes that, nonetheless, led to the current moment of reconciliation and prosperity),[17] Franco cites an essay by Argentine critic Nelly Snaith who draws a distinction between the repellant melodrama of the Argentine film *La historia oficial / The Official Story* (Luiz Puenzo, 1985) and the work of playwright Griselda Gambaro. Agreeing with Snaith, Franco argues that "films and literature that disidentify—that is, that interrupt the process of identification—are more effective in disturbing the spectator or reader."[18] In contrast, Puenzo's film allows the spectator a comfortable position from which to (re)view the Dirty War by privileging the perspective of Alicia, an "innocent" woman who discovers that her adopted daughter is the child of one of the disappeared. In focusing attention on the emotional discoveries of an individual "bystander," the film ignores the traumatic suffering of those who were tortured and killed and, one might add, handily avoids the difficult question of societal complicity.

Like Snaith, Franco and Richard suggest that an adequate exercise of historical memory cannot be conducted through such transparent narrative forms. In the words of Richard, "practicing memory" and "expressing its torments" necessarily depend on the deployment of dense "figurative language (symbols, metaphors, allegories) [that is] sufficiently moving so that they enter into a relationship of solidarity with the emotions unleashed by memory."[19] They credit Patricio Guzmán's documentary *Chile: La memoria obstinada / Chile: Obstinate Memory* (Canada-France, 1997) with doing just that. In "filming a Chilean audience while they watched parts of his seven-hour documentary *The Battle of Chile*, which had been filmed in 1973 but never released for public screening in that country," *La memoria obstinada* situates the "practice of memory" as a type of affective labor that "leads the [filmed] audience to performatively live the shock of remembering...."[20] In situating Guzmán's documentary outside the media culture that they denounce, Richard and Franco revivify Frankfurtian paradigms of critical thought predicated on polarities between high and low culture, avant-garde and mass media, and employ linguistically based models to analyze cultural production as a whole.[21] In citing Guzmán's work as an exceptional film, Richard and Franco evince nostalgia for the type of self-reflexive and overtly politicized cinematic praxis that emerged in the 1960s and became known as the New Latin American Cinema, demonstrating their affinity with the position of Brazilian scholar Ivana Bentes.

*The Politics of Affect and Emotion in Contemporary Latin American Cinema* is an effort to offer an alternate account of contemporary Latin American cinema that inventories its emergent sensorial dynamics and interrogates their significance to the political field. Drawing on recent studies on feeling from a variety of disciplines, I argue for the importance of understanding with greater precision how films solicit particular emotional responses and/ or stimulate more diffuse, affective reactions. The following chapters focus on how films invite viewers to feel through their formal properties, their modes of address, and their engagement with contemporary sociopolitical discourses. Whether discussing the dynamics of film form (understood as narrative structure and film "style") or the relationship of particular films to the larger sociocultural contexts in which they are produced and exhibited, the current study emphasizes the importance of historicization. In other words, I want to look at how film's sense-making potential has changed over time and how films contribute to the articulation of new sensibilities. The book's more general goal is to offer a richer understanding of how films "touch us" and to suggest the political potential of certain films regarded as apolitical and sensationalistic by the majority of critics.

The chapters that follow survey a wide corpus, including films of spectacular appeal like *Amores perros*, and thrillers like *O Que É Isso, Companheiro?* and *Ação Entre Amigos* (Brazil, Beto Brant, 1998), as well as detached tales of youthful alienation like *La ciénaga / The Swamp* (Lucrecia Martel, 2000). The variety of fiction films under discussion allows one to identify filmic and sociocultural trends that transcend national boundaries. Why, for example, did the thriller emerge as an important genre in the 1990s as evident in the success of films like *Johnny Cien Pesos* (Chile-Mexico-United States, Gustavo Graef Marino, 1993) and *O Que É Isso, Companheiro?* Why have filmmakers from across Latin America utilized that genre along with coming-of-age stories (*Kamchatka, Machuca*, etc.) to comment on the dictatorial past? Do formulaic narratives laced with blatant emotional appeals work like sandpaper to abrade the face of the past to be easily forgotten, as Richard, Franco, and Avelar suggest? Or might these particular genres—revolving as they do around the question of who knows what when—move us toward a heartfelt realization of the limitations of dominant epistemologies? Why have other directors eschewed narrative formulas and dominant stylistic conventions to experiment with film form in works centered on young adults living in an uncertain world like *Amores perros*, *Picado fino* (Argentina, Esteban Sapir, 1996), and *Nada* (Cuba-Spain-France-Italy, Juan Carlos Cremata, 2001)? Are Iñárruti, Sapir, and Cremata merely "downloading" the razzle-dazzle effects of U.S. films aimed at the media-savvy youth market? Or might their concern for color and texture offer a means of conveying to audiences the affective experiences of young protagonists living in unique sociocultural and historical contexts?

My interest in identifying larger, pan-regional trends is balanced by an equally adamant concern for discerning the differences between films made in specific countries. The articulation of adolescent aimlessness in the Argentine films *Vagón fumador* (Argentina, Verónica Chen, 2001) and *Hoy y mañana* (Argentina, Alejandro Chomski, 2003) is quite different from a Mexican film like *Amores perros*—despite certain similarities in theme and formal treatment. Thus, by establishing productive comparisons, I will discuss films in relation to specific industrial contexts, filmic traditions, and sociocultural particularities. It would be impossible to survey all of contemporary Latin American cinema's emotional and affective engagements. Thus, this book focuses on particular formal, thematic, and industrial tendencies that seem to characterize Latin American cinema during the past two decades, most notably, a) the reemergence of genre films, b) the preoccupation with the recent past and its relation to the contemporary moment, c) a fixation on depth and surface evident in the innovative use of cinematography, d) the proliferation of films about youth, and e) the heightened visibility of Latin/a American directors working across borders.

Drawing on recent research in a variety of disciplines about the cognitive potential of affect, *The Politics of Affect and Emotion in Contemporary Latin American Cinema* is concerned with how certain works encourage their spectators to feel in ways that acknowledge alternative ways of knowing (about) the recent traumatic past of the 1960s and 1970s. The book will also discuss how some films plug us into emergent subjectivities that vibrate with the pulsations of the globalized present while others help to instantiate new communitarian sensibilities by establishing "affective alliances." Underlying my analyses of particular films and groups of films is the belief that only by acknowledging the sociocultural work being carried out in specific geohistorical contexts by those films' affective engagements can we debate their social and political significance in a substantive way. At the same time, while concerned with the particularities of contemporary Latin American cinema, my analyses will be situated within a broader critical-theoretical framework that hopefully might stimulate productive discussions of films produced elsewhere.

## The Unbearable Lightness of Feeling

As mentioned earlier, the present study of contemporary Latin American cinema relies on theorizations of affect that emerged in the mid-1990s in a variety of disciplines in the humanities, social sciences, and sciences. In his foreword to *The Affective Turn: Theorizing the Social* (2007), Michael Hardt traces this growing interest in U.S. academic scholarship to two previously developed areas of research: studies on the body from feminist scholars like Judith Butler and Elizabeth Grosz and the "exploration of emotions, conducted predominantly in queer theory," citing the work of Eve Kosofsky Sedgwick and Lauren Berlant.[22] Of course, more intricate genealogies are possible. One might also find precursors in earlier feminist scholarship from the 1980s on sentimental literature and melodrama—the latter of particular importance for discussions of the cinema[23]— as well as in the field of trauma studies.[24] Some of these scholarly tendencies shared an interest in exploring the body as the site of alternative epistemologies; others, a preoccupation with the social and political "work" of emotion. Taken as a whole, they worked to unsettle hardened oppositions between mind/body, reason/emotion, and masculine/feminine.

As noted by Hardt, the recent focus on affect offers an opportunity to reconceive body and mind together and to understand feeling or emotion as integral to cognition, a partner to reason. To this end, scholars in the humanities have turned to the work of psychologist Silvan Tomkins and psychoanalyst André Green, as well as to the theoretical corpus of philosopher Gilles Deleuze. Each has been useful for thinking about how (Latin American) films' sensorial evocations function: Tomkins, for perceiving affect as relational; Green, for a refined understanding of the relationship between affect and language/representation; and Deleuze, for distinguishing between affect and emotion, for suggesting art's (or film's) capacity to produce affect, and for pointing toward evocative ways of approaching cinema, affect, and history. This study has also benefitted from a critical engagement with (mainly against) cognitivist film scholars such as Noel Carroll, Carl Platinga, and Greg Smith, who have offered the most substantive treatment of film and emotion to date.

For Kosofsky Sedgwick and communications scholar Elspeth Probyn, Tomkins's work offers a more productive model of the human experience than Freudian psychoanalytic theory, which privileges the drive system as the primary motor of human behavior and characterizes "emotion . . . as a vehicle or manifestation of an underlying libidinal drive." In contrast, according to Tomkins's model, the drive and affect systems are equally influential and differ (only) in terms of the instrumentality of their aims and the range of their objects; in short, whereas drives are highly constrained, affects are not. This contention that both affects and drive are "thoroughly embodied, as well as more or less intensively interwoven with cognitive processes" is highly suggestive.[25] As noted by Kosofsky Sedgwick and collaborator Adam Frank, Tomkins's model allows for the generative possibilities of affects, which "'produce bodily knowledge'" and shape human relationships.[26] This proposition has been valuable in the present study for countering the notion that the emotions called forth by works of art limit their capacity to be thought-provoking. On the other hand, Tomkins's notion of a limited number of basic affects (distress-anguish; fear-terror; enjoyment-joy; disgust-contempt; interest-excitement; surprise-startle; humiliation-shame; and anger) has a number of shortcomings. In characterizing affect as an always already given, Tomkins's model does not admit the role of language in constituting affect as a socioculturally significant phenomenon. Equally problematic is the way in which his universalist model disavows the significance of cultural and historical differences.[27] These aspects of Tomkins's work limit its usefulness for studies like my own that seek to underscore film's role in generating and circulating affective flows as well as the pertinence of specific cultural and historical contexts.

According to Lisa Cartwright, André Green's reworking of Freudian psychoanalysis offers a more productive framework for literary and filmic analysis. As a film scholar, Cartwright views Green's proposals as a means to reanimate film theory's somewhat dead-end discussion of spectatorship, identification, and representation.[28] While recognizing the usefulness of Tomkins's work for her own notion of "moral spectatorship" based on empathy, Cartwright nonetheless privileges Green for his more nuanced account of Freud's take on affect, his more developed model of psychic and intersubjective processes, and his concern for language and representation.[29] Green argues that throughout his work Freud saw affect and representation as "two registers [that were] interdependent and interconstitutive of the human subject" despite his marginalization of the former concept in favor of theorizing the more professionally palatable concept of representation beginning with *The Interpretation of Dreams* (1900).[30] For her part, Cartwright retakes Green's model to move beyond the shortcomings of Lacanian-infused psychoanalytic film theory, specifically its singular concern for language (over affect) and its conceptualization of identification that "relies on vision and psychic displacement to organize its terms" ("I see as you see, from your position").[31] Like Green, Cartwright argues that affect must be studied in concert with representation. Only then can we account for "film in terms of its place in relationship to movement—not as depicted action, but as psychic motivation—might we say, drive?"[32] Moreover, she contends, the dominant understanding of identification as an unconscious process mistakenly characterizes empathy in somewhat oppositional terms as a conscious process that is "closer to cognition." In contrast, Cartwright argues that "in empathy there is a force in that moment in which I feel that I know how you feel, a welling up and bursting forth of emotion about the object of regard, that is not held solely in the register of conscious perception and expression."[33] I want to bracket off the discussion of empathy to underscore the potential productivity of the underlying notion of affect that fuels Cartwright's discussion. Green's understanding of affect as a *psychical event linked to a movement awaiting form*[34] offers a promising model to rethink film's sensorial dynamics that is akin to the Deleuzian approach to affect employed by Brian Massumi as well as a large group of film scholars, including Steven Shaviro, Laura Marks, Barbara Kennedy, and Paul Gormley.

Before turning to the merits of a Deleuzian model and its particular theorization of affect, it will be useful to discuss the work of film cognitivists such as Noel Carroll, Carl Platinga, and Greg Smith who often prefer to talk about the sensorial appeals of film in terms of emotion. Like Cartwright's work, the cognitivists' proposals arise from a critique of psychoanalytic film theory.[35] Countering the notions of interpellation and spectatorial positioning favored by psychoanalytically based critics, they argue that "films do not 'make' people feel, [but rather] offer invitations to feel."[36] The defense of a viewer's agency is welcome and in line with arguments that have come from Black and queer studies about psychoanalytic theory's (initial) inattention to race/ethnicity; its reductive model of sexual difference (as a question of male and female); and, more generally, its structuralist determinism handcuffing the viewer to "the gaze." The cognitivists' underlying aversion to Screen theory has resulted in detailed accounts of the formal mechanisms through which films invite viewers to feel (e.g., by aligning them with characters, or through "mood-cues" and "genre microscripts" that allow the viewer to recognize the appropriate emotional tone), and these readings are often plausible.

Nonetheless, I find the cognitivists' overall approach ultimately unsatisfying. More often than not, their studies are highly textualist (frequently narratological and character-centered) and offer a weak account of film's intense appeal for spectators. In presenting close readings of how specific films or genres invite viewers to feel, the cognitivists give scant attention to understanding *why* viewers might be drawn to film and its articulation of affective flows. They discount psychoanalytic theory's propositions about film's role in subject formation and show little interest in how film's affective register might link to ongoing psychic processes. By positing emotions as universal attributes located "in" the individual, the cognitivists ignore the historical and sociocultural situatedness of feelings. Their analyses also disregard the context of production and reception that help account for many of film's affective appeals.[37]

The shortcomings of their approach are, in my opinion, the result of a singular reliance on cognitive psychology (particularly, the work of appraisal theorists), a field that views body and mind as intertwined but characterizes cognition as a somewhat autonomous, higher-level process.[38] Noel Carroll, one of the most influential film cognitivists, defines affect as a broad category of "bodily states...that involve feelings or sensations," including "hard-wired reflex reactions, like the startle response, sensations ([such as] pleasure, pain, and sexual arousal), phobias, desires, various occurrent, feeling-toned mental states—such as fear, anger, and jealousy—and moods."[39] Emotions are a "narrower subclass of affect" that involve cognition, and refer to "phenomena, such as fear, anger, patriotism, horror, admiration, sorrow, indignation, pity, envy, jealousy, reverence, awe, hatred, love, anxiety, shame, embarrassment, humiliation, [and] comic amusement."[40] In line with appraisal theorists, Carroll and others understand emotions as the result of the cognitive assessment of situational cues. In other words, cognition "selects" the emotion appropriate to the stimuli. The feedback loop can be complex; cognitivists note that emotion can, in turn, help orient one's response to a given situation. Nonetheless, the model is fairly static as it presumes that the "cooperative" relationship between body and mind leads to a finite number of already defined emotions.[41] As a consequence, when discussing film in terms of emotion, cognitivists like Carroll ignore the possibility that the medium might do something other than simply re-present known states of feeling; they overlook films' potential to mediate and shape the affective.

By contrast, Deleuzian-based accounts allow for this possibility and espouse more nuanced concepts for thinking about how and why films move us. In the essay "The Autonomy of Affect," Brian Massumi makes the following distinction between affect and emotion: whereas affect is embodied intensity, emotion is "the socio-linguistic fixing of the quality of an experience which is from that point onward defined as personal."[42] He further delineates emotion as "a qualified intensity, the conventional, consensual point of insertion of intensity into semantically and semiotically formed progressions, into narrativizable action-reaction circuits, into function and meaning."[43] This distinction acknowledges emotion as socially inscribed into an already constituted signifying network, or as a socially codified, meaningful "quality of experience" that is (nonetheless) understood as personal. At the same time, in subsuming emotion to the broader category of affect that is at once material/corporeal and immaterial (and presocial rather than asocial), Massumi (following Deleuze) allows for other qualities of experience that are as yet untethered to social and linguistic structures. Having found this distinction quite useful, I employ it throughout this book and utilize "the sensorial" and "feelings" as broader, more encompassing categories.

Cultural productions like films can certainly provide sites of insertion or torsion where affect is wrung (out) into emotion. Yet, the Deleuzian model allows for the obverse; art can invent affect. Unlike Tomkins (for whom affects are basic and universal), Deleuze and collaborator Félix Guattari propose that affects can be produced by or put into circulation through great art:

> It should be said of all art that, in relation to the percepts or visions they give us, artists are presenters of affects, the inventors and creators of affects. They not only create them in their work, they give them to us and make us become with them, they draw us into the compound.[44]

In *What Is Philosophy?*, Deleuze and Guattari invoke the work of nineteenth-century novelists and painters like Zola, Brontë, and Van Gogh. When Deleuze turns his attention to the cinema, he points to the work of post–World War II filmmakers, such as Rossellini (particularly his later films), Resnais, and Godard. During that period, Deleuze argues, a new type of film(making) emerged, responding in large part to that historical horizon and the myriad ruptures that "greatly increased the situations [to] which we no longer know how to react [...], in spaces which we no longer know how to describe."[45] The new "time-image" cinema offered a different type of encounter wherein sensorial appeals were no longer chained to narrative causality and character psychology. In Deleuze's terms, it was a cinema of "becoming" wherein "the distinction between subjective and objective...tend[ed] to lose its importance."[46]

This understanding of the cinematic encounter depends on a different notion of subjectivity and the body than that of psychoanalytic film theory. Whereas the latter is centrally concerned with how (certain) films contribute to the formation of a unitary subject and to the placement/emplotment of that subject within particular social parameters,[47] Deleuze turns his attention to how (certain) films open up conceptual-affective flows between bodies, themselves understood not as bounded or discrete units, but rather each as "a nexus of variable interconnections, a multiplicity within a web of other multiplicities."[48] His work encourages us to understand the cinema (and the subject) not in terms of scopic action(s), but rather multisensorial processes.[49] This, in turn, leads us away from the gaze as a central critical framework and also discourages the narratological and character-centric analysis favored by film cognitivists.[50] Instead of examining how films organize or fix the spectator's visual apprehension of the profilmic space or how they deploy moral distinctions to align us with particular characters rather than others, we need to acknowledge and account for the myriad touchpoints through which films and situated audiences encounter each other. This clearly includes examining the formal means by which films arouse unique and complex sensorial reactions in viewers.[51]

The Deleuzian approach to film also opens a space for interrogating the interplay between subjectivities and larger historically situated, sociocultural phenomena. By linking the emergence of time-image cinema to a particular historical horizon (post–World War II), which he does in his preface to *Cinema 2*, Deleuze encourages us in this direction.[52] Two recent studies by Laura Marks and Paul Gormley stand out as examples that extend Deleuze's insights. Marks coins the term "haptic visuality" to understand how recent intercultural cinema (often made by second-generation immigrants or those "between" cultures) promotes a "respect of difference, [and a] concomitant loss of self" by putting the viewer into contact with the surface of the image.[53] She ties the emergence of haptic visuality to a general historical horizon (the late twentieth century) and, more specifically, to a moment of epistemological crisis wherein the visual record is rendered insufficient to the task of registering past experiences and their influence on the present.[54] For his part, Gormley situates Hollywood's new-brutality film in relation to both a more circumscribed sociocultural dynamic (as an attempt within the racialized dynamics of late-twentieth-century U.S. culture to "produce an affective shock by imitating the immediate and bodily response provoked in white viewers by black bodies") and, more generally, to the postmodern era.[55]

Following Marks and Gormley, this book analyzes how a cinematic aesthetics of sensation emerging in the late twentieth century articulates larger sociocultural dynamics in the context of Latin America. For *The Politics of Affect and Emotion in Contemporary Latin American Cinema*, the Deleuzian model has been particularly suggestive in helping to trace a double movement wherein recent films help to name, codify, or channel lived intensities, which nonetheless also strain against or exceed their discursive/representational entrapment and unsettle established categories of emotion. In other words, Deleuze provides a productive conceptual framework to understand how certain films register affective flows that nonetheless share an unstable and forced relationship to language. While akin to Green's notion of affect as a "psychical event linked to a movement awaiting form," Deleuze's hydraulic model of flows allows for a more developed account of the sociocultural extension of film's visceral appeals and a more nuanced understanding of affect in the postmodern era.[56]

On the other hand, this book also significantly departs from Deleuzian-inspired studies, which have tended to limit their analyses to certain kinds of aesthetically innovative films: *Cinema 2* exhibits a singular interest in the work of particular auteurs; Marks focuses on what might be (perhaps unfairly) characterized as a type of art cinema; and even Gormley, who works on Hollywood films, distinguishes his "neo-brutality films" from the more conventional "postmodern blockbuster." In contrast, the present book deals with a more heterogeneous corpus of films. Some formally experimental works are discussed, but so are thrillers and other narrative films drawing on genre conventions, as well as documentaries. It is not my intention to analyze a specific subclass of films or identify an alternative aesthetic.[57] Rather, the chapters that follow survey a wide range of films produced and screened during a particular sociohistorical horizon and that, despite their heterogeneity, share a tendency to deploy sensorial appeals in new ways, albeit through different formal means and to different ends. This effort to detangle emotion/affect, aesthetics, and politics and to understand more fully the kind of sociocultural work carried out by such sensorial appeals necessitates an engagement with another set of contemporary cultural theorists. As recounted more thoroughly in the next section, my study draws upon theorists of globalization such as Arjun Appadurai and Zygmunt Bauman, as well as others who focus predominantly on Latin America, like Jesús Martín Barbero, Martín Hopenhayn, Beatriz Sarlo, and Nelly Richard.

## *The Politics of Situated Feeling*

In mapping cinematic feelings in specific historical and geopolitical contexts, and understanding the feedback dynamics between those contexts and new forms of subjectivity, I have benefitted from the insights of global theorists Arjun Appadurai and Zygmunt Bauman.[58] In recent works, Appadurai and Bauman have taken on the issue of the politics of emotion—specifically, the spread of fear and uncertainty among peoples living in the last decades of the twentieth century. While locating their discussion within different geographical frameworks, both theorists attribute the emergence of this collective apprehension to changing economic, political, and social structures.[59] In *Fear of Small Numbers: An Essay on the Geography of Anger* (2006), Appadurai argues that globalization has had a deeply unsettling effect not only on economic and political structures, institutions, and processes, but also on how people perceive their place in the world. The difficulty of understanding the new "invertebrate" aspects of contemporary capitalism (e.g., the workings of finance capital), the disbelief in the ability of the state to act as an effective mediator, and the seeming exceptionalism of the contemporary moment (whose "challenges...cannot be addressed with the comforts of history") have generated widespread anxiety and, at the same time, a desire for new configurations of community. According to Appadurai, these feelings have been central to the ultra-violent nationalist struggles that have emerged in the last decades in the Balkans, sub-Saharan Africa, and South Asia promising a new national unity based on ethnic purity.

Zygmunt Bauman considers a longer historical trajectory to explain the contemporary horizon, linking the emergence of these collective sensibilities to "the passage from a 'solid' to a 'liquid' phase of modernity," in which i) "social forms...can no longer (and are not expected) to keep their shape for long..." and ii) power and politics become divorced. As the state cedes its mediational role, older forms of solidarity and "collective self-defense," such as trade unions, have given way to a new, extreme individualism.[60] According to Bauman, the inadequacy of the state and the transitory malleability of social forms have produced widespread feelings of unease and trepidation that have infused all realms of social life, as people respond by withdrawing behind gated communities, driving Humvees, carrying handguns, and demanding smoke-free hotel rooms.[61]

Reading the present Latin American horizon through a Baumanian lens, one can easily recount examples of major transformations and attendant cultural reactions. Starting in the 1980s, Latin America has witnessed the rise of neoliberal administrations in Mexico, Argentina, Brazil, and Perú. Proclaiming faith in the rationality of the free market to improve the economic outlook of all citizens, the administrations of Carlos Salinas de Gotari (Mexico, 1988–94), Carlos Menem (Argentina, 1989–99), Fernando Collor de Mello (Brazil, 1990–92), and Alberto Fujimori (Perú, 1990–2000). carried out a series of reforms—including severe governmental downsizing and the privatization of many state-owned enterprises—designed to encourage foreign trade and investment and stimulate economic growth and consumer expansion. The effects of these policies were soon visible in the material transformation of cities like Buenos Aires and Mexico City where foreign companies built new deluxe hotels and occupied the floors of luxurious skyscrapers designed by world-renowned architects. Gated communities and satellite suburbs emerged near new commercial centers, featuring foreign outlets like Wal-Mart as well as locally owned franchises. The proliferation of malls was not limited to such communities, but also began to reconfigure downtown areas, sometimes through the remodeling of older buildings. Cable television spread and began to offer a wider selection of programming, often dominated by foreign imports, sometimes in English. Further abetting the foreign-domestic interweave of communication, Internet cafes mushroomed on street corners of large cities and smaller towns, providing access to the World Wide Web for a small fee. Not always as equally visible was the growing impoverishment of large sectors of the population.

Neoliberal economic policies, emerging built environments, and the increased penetration of media technologies all influenced contemporary sensibilities by i) promoting feelings of fear, uncertainty, and insecurity and ii) generating a sensation-driven experience of daily life.[62] Sarlo has characterized the proliferation of shopping malls in and around Buenos Aires as exemplary of a new sensationalist cultural logic. Offering few temporal or spatial signposts, the malls' glittery passageways encourage shoppers to immerse themselves in the pleasures of the present (the infinite, eye-catching products that promise to enhance one's life) and, at the same time, to neglect the future (the need to pay).[63] While this ebullient consumerism fosters the type of individualism noted by Bauman, it also contributes to the formation of new subjectivities based on intensifying sensorial experiences. Martin Hopenhayn has put it this way: "The skin becomes a second form of consciousness, and from the skin it is possible to contemplate the environment cinemtographically, since the environment is displaced and modified according to a rhythm closer to cinema than to old-fashioned reality."[64] According to Hopenhayn, today's accelerated life-rhythms have crippled our ability to process the emergent and unfamiliar. Echoing Jameson's critique of postmodern culture, Hopenhayn suggests that "depth" has been replaced by "surface"; with our senses absorbed in our constantly changing surroundings, we comprehend the world *as if it were* a montage sequence.

While their analyses coincide in many ways with Bauman, Latin American thinkers such as Sarlo, Hopenhayn, Martín Barbero, and Franco are particularly useful for situating this shift to a new "liquid modernity" within the trajectories of Latin American history. In his book *Al sur de la modernidad* (2001), Barbero characterizes contemporary sensibilities as a response to modernity's rationalization of the world. Involving secularization and an overarching trust in "cognitive, technological, and administrative power," this dominant logic helped shape governmental policies and public debates in nineteenth-century Latin America, and then was reinvigorated by neoliberalism at the end of the twentieth century. According to Barbero, the secularized, modern world is a rationalized world: "ya no hay un sentido a realizar sino un orden regido por la racionalidad instrumental" ["there is no longer a meaning to be realized, but instead an order governed by instrumental rationality."][65] This has at no time been more evident than today, according to Barbero, who notes that "[c]on la globalización el proceso de *racionalización* parece estar llegando a su límite: después de la economía y la política ahora es la cultura, el mundo mismo de la vida, sus coordenadas espacio-temporales, las racionalizadas" ["[w]ith globalization the *rationalization* process seems to be reaching its limit: [having conquered] the economic and political [realms], it is now culture, everyday life and its spacio-temporal coordinates that are being rationalized."][66]

For their part, Sarlo, Richard, and Franco position the shift to liquid modernity between the 1970s and the first decade of the twenty-first century. In their accounts, the contemporary culture of sensation is a necessary counterpart to neoliberal reforms, a means to fuel consumerism and depoliticize the citizenry. Sarlo's accounts of the proliferation of remote controls and video arcades point precisely to a media-driven domestication of the population. As the home has become an absorbing refuge, public spaces have become places of individual preoccupation, rather than encounters between fellow citizens, as we "tune in" to our video games, cell phones, and iPods.

The proliferation and densification of sensational cultural forms and practices must also be set against the backdrop of authoritarian legacies. In societies reemerging from decades-long military dictatorships, the mall's disorienting effects help to shift attention away from the horrors of the past toward the sensorial delights of the present. As noted by Franco, this connection was quite direct in the case of the Punto Carretas mall in Montevideo that was "built on the site of a notorious prison where, during the recent military regime, dissidents and revolutionaries were kept in solitary confinement and where some were shot."[67] Thus, today, forgetting constantly inflects the affective and the cultural. In Mexico, the "culture of immediacy" has functioned in analogous ways to ease the effects of a political transition and facilitate the shift to a new economic order. Although not dealing with the aftermath of a military dictatorship, Mexico is currently confronting its own history of top-down politics and authoritarian tendencies in the wake of the fall of the Partido Revolucionario Institucionalizado (PRI), the political party that had governed the country since the 1920s. In direct and indirect ways, this new materialism mobilizes affects in the service of the neoliberal order, inviting the population to disavow anguish (as past) and embrace the thrilling possibilities of the present.

Accounts like these emphasize the role played by the media in the emergence of the new culture of sensation. Yet only Barbero offers a nuanced account of how the rapid spread and popularity of new technologies (e.g., cable, video games, Internet, cell phones) and media have facilitated a new sort of embodied experience and a new sort of sociality. While recognizing the ways in which media technologies contribute to the atomization and privatization of society as well as the consumerist expansion denounced by Sarlo, Barbero is less inclined to merely dismiss their popularity as evidence of escapism. As a communications scholar, he sees the turn to the skin in contemporary media as a reaction to the increasing "demands of technological rationality:"

> It is not true that the penetration and expansion of technological innovations in everyday life implies an automatic submission to the demands of technological rationality, its rhythms and its languages... [W]hat is happening is that th[is] technological pressure itself is giving rise to the need to find and develop other rationalities, other rhythms of life and of relationships (with both objects and people), in which physical density and sensorial thickness are the primary value.[68]

Barbero has been particularly eloquent in his description of a "new sensorium" that "interconnects" bodies, rather than bringing them together in the same place.[69] His work encourages us to acknowledge the body (in mediation) as a site of meaningful engagement.

Taking up Barbero's challenge, this book examines the role of film as a site of articulation and projection through which affective flows are given form and direction. I pay particular attention to the ways in which contemporary Latin American films reanimate our perceptive capacities. Akin to Laura Marks's argument in *The Skin of the Film*, this study situates the affective work of these works in relation to a moment of epistemological crisis wherein the visual record is rendered insufficient to the task of registering past experiences and their influence on the present, as well as widespread uncertainties about the future. Whether in the form of tightly constructed thrillers like *Ação Entre Amigos* or meandering narratives like Lucrecia Martel's *La ciénaga*, recent films from the region work out of and respond to the current predicament by questioning how we know what we know. As noted earlier, these films do not experiment with film form as radically as the examples of "intercultural cinema" analyzed by Marks, which enable a different type of "haptic visuality" that forces the "eyes themselves [to] function like organs of touch."[70] Many new Latin American films make the limitations of the visual as the locus of knowledge apparent in ways that disrupt and interrupt, rather than rupture, cinematic conventions. Some problematize the relationship between the "knowable" and the visible by toying with the traditional treatment of the image track as transparent window onto another world—for example, through "inadequate" compositions or the careful use of off-screen space that impede the spectator's privileged view of profilmic events (as in *La ciénaga* and *Amores perros*), or by flattening or scratching the surface of film stock to bring into relief the textures of everyday life (as in *Picado fino*, *Nada*, and *Mil nubes de paz*). *La ciénaga*,

*Suite Habana*, and others unsettle the typical primacy of the visual through a multilayered soundtrack. The films' destabilization of the visual is paralleled by formal maneuvers that encourage us to acknowledge what the body knows. In characterizing contemporary films as visceral, I am referring to the way in which they labor to evoke certain intensities of experience that may be involuntary or unconscious, but are not thoughtless. In so doing, I do not want to situate them as either resistant to or complicit with the protocols of contemporary media culture, but rather to shift our framework of analysis in order to acknowledge the range and complexity of the sociopolitical work performed by films' affective appeals.

*The Politics of Affect and Emotion in Contemporary Latin American Cinema* calls into question the conclusions of Sarlo and other critics who overlook how more accessible, "middle brow" types of cultural production can encourage an embodied recognition of loss. In subsequent chapters, I will discuss the preoccupation with the 1960s and 1970s in films from Argentina, Chile, and Brazil. More particularly, I explore the ways in which such works reanimate the traumatic past and replay affective legacies deemed "excessive" by the neoliberalism's regimes of rationality by means of dramatic repetition—a feature of Patricio Guzmán's recent documentary *Memoria obstinada* as well as of the genre films of younger filmmakers like Andrés Wood (1965– ) and Beto Brant (1965– ). My analyses will pay particular attention to how these films invite spectators to feel as a means of questioning their knowledge about recent history. Whether set in the 1960s and 1970s or the contemporary moment, these films inevitably draw tantalizing connections between past and present.

Although a number of films explore the interplay between past and present, others deal with the uncertainties of the contemporary moment as their central concern. This can be seen in the growing number of "youth films" that chronicle the lives of young adults—cut off from family networks and without hope of steady employment—as they meander the streets of Mexico City, Buenos Aires, or Havana. If at times functioning as allegories about the hopelessness of a depoliticized future, many of these films forgo grand political propositions in favor of a refreshing concern for the rhythms and textures of the everyday experiences of their young protagonists. They encourage viewers to recognize other ways of experiencing the contemporary moment and ultimately problematize the facile dismissal of the sensorial aspects of today's youth cultures.

\* \* \*

Chapter 1 ("Of Passion, Aesthetics and Politics: Rethinking the New Latin American Cinema") examines the sensorial provocations of the politically militant and formally experimental films of the 1960s and 1970s. This first essay provides a crucial point of departure for subsequent chapters since much of the debate about contemporary trends in Latin American film-making revolves around explicit or implicit comparisons with the New Latin American Cinema (NLAC). Chapter 1 challenges the dominant scholarly framework that characterizes the NLAC as a movement favoring Brechtian techniques of distantiation over emotional appeals by identifying two key means by which the work of canonical directors such as Nelson Pereira dos Santos, Fernando Birri, Miguel Littín, Fernando Solanas, and Octavio Getino engaged audiences on the level of feeling: neorealist sentimentality and modernist disorientation. The first refers to the ways in which certain films and filmmakers drew upon an "archive of emotions" traceable not only to postwar Italian neorealism, but also to literary antecedents from nineteenth-century Latin America—namely, the national romances or foundational fictions that emerged in the decades after independence to stoke patriotic passions and promote an embodied, emotional commitment to the new nation-states. My discussion of neorealist sentimentality in the NLAC is grounded in a reinterpretation of Nelson Pereira dos Santos's *Rio 40 Graus / Rio, 40 Degrees* (Brazil, 1955). The second section on modernist disorientation delves into the critical writings of Fernando Solanas, Octavio Getino, and Tomás Gutiérrez Alea before analyzing the sensorial provoca-tions of two other films: *El chacal de Nahueltoro / The Jackal of Nahueltoro* (Chile, Miguel Littín, 1968) and *La hora de los hornos / The Hour of the Furnaces* (Argentina, Fernando Solanas-Octavio Getino, 1966–68). The re-reading of theoretical essays and manifestoes penned by NLAC filmmakers allows us to reassess how filmmakers from that era conceptualized the role of emotion in politically militant filmmaking. Close readings of *El chacal* and *La hora* will suggest the degree to which those theoretical propositions adequately account for the film's shocking affects. Finally, while acknowl-edging important distinctions between the previously mentioned films, the chapter also explores the significance of the suffering child as a recurrent figure deployed by all of them. The visceral power of this trope helps to reveal the humanist impulses underlying even the most aesthetically radical works from this era.

Following this initial reconsideration of the NLAC, subsequent chapters explore important currents that have defined Latin American filmmaking since the mid-1990s. The first two essays discuss the notable preoccupation of contemporary films with the tumultuous decades of the 1960s and 1970s. Observing the recent proliferation of genre films, chapter 2, "Thrilling Histories: Replaying the Past in Genre Films," examines why the armature of the thriller has been a preferential means by which to deal with the past.

The essay begins by appraising the larger sociohistorical contexts in which these films appear—in particular, how the legacies of authoritarian dictatorships have been "managed" and contained by subsequent democratic administrations in Chile and Brazil. Drawing on the work of Nelly Richard, the chapter makes note of how politics became "rationalized" by successive transitional governments in Chile. Political scientist Leslie Payne's work becomes a means to understand how and why the Brazilian military was able to dampen public discussion of its twenty-year dictatorship well into the 1990s. After surveying this historical backdrop, the essay offers a comparative analysis of three films: *O Que É Isso, Companheiro?*, *Acão Entre Amigos*, and UK-United States-France coproduction *Death and the Maiden* (Roman Polanski, 1994). Understanding the thriller as a genre built around questions of knowledge and time, my interpretation looks at how these three films promote a sense of epistemic urgency or a desire to know. The textual analysis suggests that even as they "wrap up" dictatorial legacies in familiar narrative formulas, the thrillers permit audiences to reexamine past social traumas in ways disallowed by the legalistic discourses dominating public debates about accountability. In considering a genre that has often been dismissed as incapable of critical intervention, chapter 2 helps to develop my overarching argument about the usefulness of teasing apart sensorial appeals from ideological stance.

Chapter 3, "Affecting Legacies and Contemporary Structures of Feeling," continues to explore contemporary Latin American cinema's preoccupation with the 1960s and 1970s. However, this essay moves beyond genre films to examine two aesthetically innovative films, *Amores perros* and *Madagascar*. The comparison enables the discussion of another tendency of recent films—namely, the disinterest in commenting directly on economic, political, and social structures (as was common of the NLAC) in favor of delving into individual lives and private realms. The chapter suggests how, within this framework, the works connect the legacies of the past to present-day dilemmas through narrative and stylistic innovations. Concerned with the relationship between parents and their children, *Amores perros* and *Madagascar* highlight a generational divide between adults who came of age during the political struggles of the 1960s and their children, who are growing up in a very different political, social, and economic context in the 1990s. Their unconventional plot structures and particular stylistic choices encourage audience members to recognize in visceral ways the affective legacies of the recent past as well as newer sensibilities emerging at the present moment. The chapter weighs the political significance of this type of sensemaking by turning to the work of film critic Thomas Elsaesser and to that of cultural studies scholar Raymond Williams. Elsaesser's reconsideration of films about the Holocaust helps us to consider the cognitive potential of film's affective engagements—specifically, how film's sensorial appeals can encourage viewers to consider their roles as historical actors. Williams's concept of structures of feeling helps to suggest how the sensorial dynamics of films such as *Amores perros* and *Madagascar* articulate emergent sensibilities that have not yet coalesced or become discursively recognized.

Chapter 4, "Alien/Nation: Contemporary Youth in Film," explores the proliferation of Latin American films about disaffected young adults and their place in the shifting landscape of the contemporary nation. The essay opens by situating the films in relation to recent public discussions characterizing today's youth as a lost generation, born under authoritarian regimes and growing up in a neoliberal era of frenzied consumerism. Responding to such contentions, "Alien/Nation" looks at several new films about young adults made by "youngish" directors for what they can reveal about the "death" of politics among the younger generation. The chapter is particularly concerned with how Argentine films like *Picado fino* (Esteban Sapir, 1993–96) and *La ciénaga* and Cuban works such as *Nada* (Juan Carlos Cremata, 2001) and *Un pedazo de mí* (Jorge Luis Sánchez, 1989) map the subjectivities of young adults by inscribing their affective disjuncture in terms of depth perception. Utilizing Frederic Jameson's theorization of the postmodern in terms of superficial play and the "waning of affect" as an initial point of departure, my analyses pay particular attention to aspects of the films' cinematography (e.g., their unconventional framings, interest in off-screen space, and preference for shallow or deep focus). I argue that the films' preoccupation with the surfaces of things registers what remains percolating below that plane or outside the frame. In positioning the films as the product of a young(er) generation of filmmakers working within new film industrial contexts, the chapter suggests that these films exemplify new forms of sociocultural engagement.

Chapter 5, "Migrant Feelings: Global Networks and Transnational Affective Communities," cues on Guiliana Bruno's suggestion that, in certain historical conjunctures, the visual arts have served as emotional cartographies that orient viewers and route them in particular ways. Her propositions become the means to interrogate the role of emotion and affect in the work of Latin/a American directors who regularly cross national borders. Although filmmakers from earlier eras also left their home countries to work elsewhere, today's "traveling" directors like Alfonso Cuarón, Guillermo del Toro, Alejandro González Iñárruti, Luis Mandoki, Fernando Mereilles, and Walter Salles are somewhat unique given the geographic scope of their endeavors (making films in and about Great Britain, Japan, Kenya, Morocco, Spain, and the United States as well as numerous Latin American countries).

Their movies are also singular in the context of Latin American film history given their ambition to speak of and for "other" cultures. Playing against Jameson's notion that Third World films "cognitively map" contemporary global relations, the chapter examines how two works by Latin/a American directors chart global networks through sensorial appeals: *Babel* (United States-France-Mexico, Alejandro González Iñárruti, 2006) and *Señorita Extraviada/Missing Girl* (United States, Lourdes Portillo, 2001). The films are very different, as are the filmmakers. *Babel* was a multimillion dollar, fiction film released in over 1,000 theaters, while *Señorita extraviada* was a low-budget documentary with a much more limited distribution. Iñárruti is seen as a commercial director with artistic (and perhaps political) pretensions, whereas Portillo is hailed as a politically committed filmmaker-activist. Nonetheless, the two films exhibit a similar interest in inviting "First World" audiences to feel for "Third World" peoples. Dialoguing with scholars like Lauren Berlant who critique the politics of compassion, the chapter argues that neither film is a simplistic call to empathize with someone else's suffering "over there." Instead, they encourage viewers to feel *through* (rather than feel *for*) others by "poaching" traditions of feeling that have emerged in Mexico in particular ways—namely, the melodrama and the *crónica roja*, or sensationalist crime press. By sketching out the similar tactics employed by both films, the comparison asks us to question well-established oppositions between fiction and documentary and the tendency to analyze Latin American and Latino/a films separately.

# CHAPTER 1

# Of Passion, Aesthetics, and Politics: Rethinking the New Latin American Cinema

Returning to Chile in 1996 after twenty-three years in exile, Patricio Guzmán began to shoot what would become *Chile: La memoria obstinada* (Canada-France, 1997), a moving documentary about the country's past and its present. The film is a calculated response to the repressive policies of the seventeen-year Pinochet dictatorship (1973–90) and to the politics of forgetting promoted by the subsequent transitional Concertación governments led by Presidents Patricio Aylwin (1990–94) and Eduardo Frei Ruiz-Tagle (1994–2000). Through a series of interviews with former political militants, brief scenes of massive, pro-Allende marches taken from Guzmán's earlier landmark documentary *La batalla de Chile* (Venezuela-France-Cuba-Chile, 1975–79), and interviews with young people who know little about their country's recent past, *La memoria obstinada* recalls the solidarity and social commitment of the Allende years and offers a subtle, yet harsh indictment of the social atomization of the present day. But, Guzmán's recent documentary also goes beyond sociopolitical critique to function as an emotionally charged treatise about the poetics and politics of memory. Attentive to *what* different generations remember about the Allende years, the film is equally concerned with *how* people remember, deploying Debussy's melancholic "Claire du Lune" (played in starts and stops by Guzmán's uncle) as a sonic motif to suggest how memory-work is a fragmentary, incomplete process. In addressing the audience through aural means, the refrains remind us that sorrow cannot be captured by words or visual images alone.

Emotion plays a central role in the film's depiction of the messy business of remembering the traumatic past and is a central feature of the touching testimonies that provide the documentary's organizational spine, from the sobs of the father of Jorge Müller, the cameraman of *La batalla de Chile* who disappeared in 1975, to the distanced reserve of Carmen Vivanco, the sole surviving member of her immediate family whose five loved ones disappeared during the dictatorship. Through the display of overpowering emotion or its seeming absence, such scenes record trauma as incommensurable loss, as discursive gap, or as that which evades efforts at representation and yet, nonetheless, inscribes itself on the body.

The film's interest in exploring the sensorial-laden nature of memory is also evident in the privileged position given to Ernesto Malbrán, Guzmán's college friend who appeared in Part III of *La batalla de Chile* and whom the director characterizes in a voice-over in *La memoria obstinada,* as having lived and spoken with "more passion than the rest of us."[1] In the first extended sequence of Guzmán's reencounter with Malbrán, the former militant points out that, at its root, the word "recordar" (to remember) means a return to the heart to wake up.[2] The words serve to identify the goal of *La memoria obstinada* itself, which situates emotional engagement as a meaningful and necessary instrument of social reckoning and political awakening.

According to the interpretive framework offered by trauma studies, the documentary's privileging of such testimonies might be seen as an attempt to "work through" the suffering caused and subsequently repressed by the Pinochet dictatorship.[3] Yet, this effort to "work through" the traumatic past is directed less at the older generation of militants portrayed in the film and more at (younger) spectators located both within and outside the frames of Guzman's film. Alongside the interviews with ex-militants, *La memoria obstinada* includes sequences of three different student groups watching *La batalla de Chile* and then discussing it after the screening. Through these screening sequences, the film registers when and how the past evokes strong emotional responses and interrogates who is moved by it. Therein lies the film's critique of the present. Whereas the male students from the conservative Catholic University respond with dry skepticism to the images from *La batalla* (figure 1.1), the young women at a parochial high school engage in a lively debate about the meaning of the past—their heated voices often overlapping in their urgency to respond to the film's provocations.[4] As the most diverse group, Malbrán's theater students are the audience that most thoroughly engages with the meaning of the repressed past. A young woman speaks of the pride she feels in her national community for having attempted such radical change. Others respond by questioning their own thoughtless inaction and careless ignorance. One young man expresses shame for having jumped on his bed the morning of September 11, 1973 (the date of the coup against Allende led by Pinochet), excited about not having to go to school. Another, in a breaking voice, speaks angrily of his complicity in the status quo during the dictatorship, having decided as a youth not to care, to remain detached and uncommitted to others. Yet another student is framed in a frontal medium close-up sobbing uncontrollably (figure 1.2).

Presented in *La memoria obstinada*'s final sequence, these heartfelt responses to *La batalla de Chile* suggest that the type of passionate commitment to national community evident during the Allende years can be reawakened in the younger generation of Chileans.[5] At the same time, the film also reaches out to mobilize its own audiences, both Chilean and international. *La memoria obstinada* encourages us to be transformed through the act of sympathetic witnessing as we listen to the poignant testimonies of former militants. And in observing the different groups of students discuss *La batalla*, the film asks us to compare our own reactions to those of the young people. Will we allow ourselves to be moved to think not only about what happened in the past but also to consider what it means for the present? It is in these efforts to touch the audience that Guzmán's film contests the dictatorship's anesthetizing tactics of repression.[6]

*La memoria obstinada*'s attention to personal histories and the intimate details of traumatic loss, as well as its unremitting invitation to its own

**Figure 1.1**   Students at the Catholic University in *La memoria obstinada*

**Figure 1.2**   A student from Ernesto Malbrán's class in *La memoria obstinada*

spectators to feel are quite startling when compared to Guzmán's previous work in *La batalla de Chile,* a three-part documentary about the rise of the Allende administration, its support among working-class groups, and the opposition it faced from conservative forces within Chile allied with the United States. A paradigmatic example of the New Latin American Cinema (NLAC), *La batalla* concerned itself with History—that is, with the supposedly more significant political and economic questions of the day. Who would retain control of the government? What role did the opposition parties—particularly the center-right Christian Democrats—play in the downfall of Allende? What of the unions and the grassroots organizations? How did political alliances respond to class interests? And what role did the United States have in Allende's ouster? *La batalla* was first and foremost a film-essay. Filmed in Chile and then put together in Cuba in the years following the coup, Guzmán's opus had a clear argumentative line aimed at persuading spectators about the majoritarian support for Allende (Part I), the hypocrisy of the opposition (Part II), and the vitality of grassroots organizations (Part III) by presenting an exhaustive amount of audiovisual documentation. What mattered in Parts I and II was chronicling the public history of the events leading up to the coup: the civic debates surrounding the March 1973 mid-term election that gave Allende a greater level of support in the Congress (despite right-wing predictions to the contrary), the massive pro-Allende demonstrations through downtown Santiago, the meetings of Allende's supporters to decide how to respond to the economic crisis, and the unrelenting efforts of the congressional opposition to undermine the democratically elected government. Part III documented the widespread, innovative, and democratic nature of grassroots activism during those years. Unlike *La memoria obstinada*, *La batalla* explored the public sphere and the growing clash between social classes and between political visions/ideological stances.[7]

In its concern to unmask the coup as an unreasonable response to the democratic will of the Chilean people, *La batalla* incorporated emotional displays in carefully orchestrated ways—for example, as a means to distinguish between the reasonability of the working classes and the rabid hysteria of middle sectors. Inverting long-standing characterizations of the masses as unthinking and highly volatile, *La batalla* contrasted the calm rationality of the (male) workers who effortlessly diagnose contemporary economic and political conditions to the nonsensical hostility of privileged sectors, exhibited most notably in the tirade of a middle-class woman who, when interviewed by the film crew during the lead-up to the mid-term elections, can only hiss invectives at the Allende administration (figure 1.3).[8]

Many scholars have interpreted this judicious use of emotion in films like *La batalla de Chile* as characteristic of the groundbreaking nature of the New Latin American Cinema, which did not "indulge" in sentimentalism,

**Figure 1.3**  A middle-class class woman curses Allende in *La batalla de Chile*

as did locally made studio productions and the Hollywood films that dominated the local box office. Understood as a militant and politicized cinema, the NLAC proposed a new relationship with audiences—one supposedly less dependent on emotional manipulation. Depicting a "suppressed reality," their works used formal experimentation to provoke a "toma de conciencia" among the spectators.⁹ Rather than offering an escape from reality, the NLAC confronted spectators with what it characterized as the true circumstances of national and regional society: structural inequalities, endemic poverty, and neocolonial exploitation, among other things. Scholars have understood the consciousness-raising impulse of the NLAC to be a result of the films' heightened engagement with the rational. Most accounts suggest that the NLAC favored the techniques of the documentary (even in fiction films) as well as Brechtian distantiation in order to allow for more direct access to the real and to prevent spectators from identifying with characters in ways that privileged emotional attachments over thoughtful contemplation.¹⁰

While overlooking the sensorial dynamics of the films themselves, scholarly accounts of the NLAC have emphasized the passionate commitment of the filmmakers themselves as well as the films' galvanizing effect on contemporaneous audiences. Responding in part to the fervent tone of the filmmakers' own manifestoes (particularly Glauber Rocha's *Uma Estética da Fome* [1963] and Solanas and Octavio Getino's *Hacia un tercer cine* [1969]), scholars typically underscore the artists' ardent dedication to producing an aesthetically revolutionary cinema that would contribute to the radical restructuring of their respective societies in economic, political, and social terms. To emphasize the distance between this revolutionary cinema and commercial films, the historiography of the NLAC canonically enumerates the risks and hardships faced by these directors during the production and distribution of their work under right-wing dictatorships: the dangers experienced by Solanas, Getino, and their collaborators in exhibiting *La hora de los hornos* given extant censorship laws in place during the military dictatorship of the Revolución Argentina (1966–73); the forced exile of Solanas and Getino from Argentina, Littín and Guzmán from Chile, Jorge Sanjinés and the other members of the Grupo Ukumau from Bolivia, and Glauber Rocha from Brazil; and, most horrifically, the disappearance of filmmakers like Raymundo Gleyzer, Jorge Cedrón, Jorge Müller, and many others at the hands of the military regimes in their respective countries.

Contemporary accounts of audience reactions to the films are also cited by scholars to exemplify the passionate politics of the NLAC. The most cited case is the screening at the 1968 Marcha film festival in Montevideo of Mario Handler's *Me gustan los estudiantes / I Like Students* (Uruguay,

1968), a film about student protests against the Conference of American Heads of State in the luxury seaside resort of Punta del Este in April 1967 (attended by several well-known dictators from neighboring countries) that included images of the repressive acts of police brutality. As related in the studies by John King and Julianne Burton at the 1968 screening, "Members of the audience were so indignant at the visual proof of official violence in their enlightened country that they rushed out of the theatre and staged a spontaneous demonstration in the Plaza de la Libertad across the street."[11] This embodied politicization was the type of reaction that NLAC filmmakers hoped to provoke with their works. In *Hacia un tercer cine,* when Solanas and Getino argued that the camera should be used as a gun (shooting 24 frames per second [fps]), they clearly suggested the type of explosive effects they hoped to produce with their work; their target was, in part, audience members who were told in *La hora de los hornos,* via graphic intertitle, that all spectators are traitors. As recounted in prior studies, Solanas and Getino sought to unsettle the notion of film as an object of contemplation by structuring *La hora de los hornos* as a film act, to be used by grassroots organizations (to be stopped and started at their discretion). Their goal was to facilitate discussions about the current economic and political situation of the 1960s *and* to promote political action.[12] This was a dangerous enterprise. In 1969, 200 people in Argentina put their lives in danger to attend a clandestine screening of the banned film and were subsequently detained.[13] According to Solanas and Getino, between 1970 and 1972, more than 125,000 people took a similar risk.[14] In sum, in the original writings of the filmmakers themselves and in subsequent scholarly accounts, the NLAC has been framed as a watershed enterprise that ignited passionate responses from audiences who moved from screening rooms onto the streets.

Lost in this standard critical history is any substantive account of how audiences became so stirred up or any consideration of how consciousness-raising involved (depended on?) engaging the viewer on a sensorial level.[15] What follows is an attempt to address what has been overlooked by discussing the formal mechanisms through which a variety of NLAC films –as diverse as *Rio 40 Graus* (Brazil, Nelson Pereira dos Santos, 1955), *El chacal de Nahueltoro* (Chile, Miguel Littín, 1969), and *La hora de los hornos* (Argentina, Grupo Cine Liberación/Fernando Solanas, 1966–68)—appeal to viewers through emotional and/or affective means. This chapter aims to complicate the understanding of the NLAC as a cerebral (reason-able) form of filmmaking and to shake up the standard paradigm of Latin American film historiography. Moving away from the periodization that treats the NLAC as a watershed movement, dividing Latin American film history into a "before" (the "industrial era" between the 1930s and 1950s) and an "after" (contemporary cinema dating from the 1980s to the present), I advocate for a more genealogical model that traces continuities across historical horizons. Thus, this book begins with a reassessment of that earlier cinema from the 1960s and 1970s in order to better situate and contextualize present-day Latin American cinema whose sensorial appeals have often been denigrated as indulgent and depoliticizing.[16]

An alternate historization might emphasize the interplay between emotion, affect, aesthetics, and politics. On the one hand, I want to explore how the expression of emotion depends on an archive of discursive formations whose articulation can be culturally specific. Here I am referring to the utilization of figures such as the (innocent) child and the (hysterical) woman, which have accrued a specific valence of meaning that calls for(th) particular emotional responses. Equally central to this archive are narrative modes such as melodrama that have formalized particular connections between feelings and meanings. On the other hand, the chapter will also illuminate how the sensorial charge of particular aesthetic formulations (and their political potentiality) has specific historical trajectories. As discussed in the work of Peter Brooks and others, particular narrative modes such as melodrama and gothic/horror emerge during specific historical conjunctures as a response to larger social, economic, and political dynamics. Their subsequent dissemination depends on their ability to adapt to local conditions and speak to contemporaneous needs that are not only ideological or social, but also "sensible"—for example, melodrama's ability to serve as a template in nineteenth-century Latin America to narrate the incipient nations in ways that would resonate in visceral ways with the local populace and call for(th) the primal allegiance. Over time, such formulations (e.g., the link established between righteous suffering/sacrifice and national identity in Latin America) harden to become part of the archive while others appear in response to emergent dynamics. Before their codification, these articulations have the potential to convey new sensibilities, or what Deleuze might call affects. One might think here of Walter Benjamin's discussion of the privileged ability of film, as a new technology, to express the shock of the modern in the early twentieth century, and of the contemporaneous emergence of avant-garde techniques in the visual and literary arts. Clearly, in historicizing the relation between emotion, affect, aesthetics, and politics, we must also acknowledge that the sensorial charge (and political potential) that specific aesthetic formulations and specific technologies call for(th) do not remain the same over time—what were once emergent structures of feeling become anchored into discursive formations with particular emotional valences. As noted by Paul Gormley, the edits and other formal devices that shocked spectators in the early years of the cinema no longer have that effect today.[17] Thus, any theorization of how film's formal mechanisms affect spectators must include an analysis of how they change over time.

The following sections identify and explicate two key tendencies in the NLAC's sensorial engagements: neorealist sentimentality and modernist disorientation. The first refers to the way films like Nelson Pereira dos Santos's *Rio 40 Graus* (Brazil, 1955) and *Rio Zona Norte* (Brazil, 1957) and Fernando Birri's *Los inundados* (Argentina, 1961), which otherwise shunned the formulaic devices characteristic of studio-made films, drew on an "archive of emotions" traceable to postwar Italian neorealism as well as to the foundational nationalist fictions of nineteenth-century Latin America. The second term describes the aesthetics of rupture that films such as *El chacal de Nahueltoro* and *La hora de los hornos*—as well as *El coraje del pueblo* (Bolivia, Grupo Ukumau/Jorge Sanjinés, 1971) and *El otro Francisco* (Cuba, Sergio Giral, 1974)—employed to jolt spectators into a new understanding of social injustice and economic inequalities. If at times utilizing stock figures (most notably, the innocent child), these later films also frequently disrupted existing emotional scripts to move spectators in ways that helped mediate the unsettling effects of modernization projects that had been taking place in many Latin American countries in their preceding decade. Deployed as part of a radical critique of those projects, the films' sensorial appeals at times exceeded the political framework to which they were attached.

### *Of Neorealist Sentimentality*

Although the NLAC shunned the emotional excess characteristic of 1940s and 1950s melodramas directed by "El Indio" Fernández, Ismael Rodríguez, Hugo del Carril, and others, the early works of some of the movement's most best directors clearly reveal a populist touch that encouraged spectators to form emotional attachments to the protagonists, even as the films experimented with new formal techniques to document the harsh socioeconomic conditions under which the majority of Latin Americans lived. In this regard, films like *Rio 40 Graus* and *Los inundados* drew inspiration from post–World War II Italian neorealism and nineteenth-century Latin American romances, both of which furnished an archive of emotions about what to feel and how to frame the story of those feelings.

While Italian neorealism has long been cited as an important influence on the NLAC, filmmakers and scholars alike have tended to focus exclusively on how that postwar cinema served as a model for an alternative mode of production or for a new realist aesthetic. Cuban filmmaker Tomás Gutiérrez Alea, who studied at the Centro Sperimentale (along with fellow Cuban Julio García Espinosa and Argentine Fernando Birri), contended that neorealism functioned more than anything else as an example of how to make films cheaply with the resources at hand.[18] Others have underscored thematic and formal concerns shared by both Italian neorealism and the NLAC: for example, the acute interest in national problems and, more specifically, in the socioeconomic inequalities experienced by common people, as well as the inclusion of documentary-like techniques in fiction films, including the use of on-location shooting and nonprofessional actors.[19]

Overlooked, however, is the way in which Italian neorealism also offered models for constructing emotional appeals as a means to strengthen a film's denunciation of socioeconomic ills and structural inequalities. This oversight might be attributed to the fact that even scholars of Italian cinema have given scant attention to the emotionalism of films like *Roma, Cittá Aperta* (Roberto Rossellini, 1945) and *Ladri de Biciclette* [Bicycle Thieves] (Vittorio De Sica, 1948). Patricia Keating is one of the few who has addressed the issue, arguing that "given the sentimentality of many neorealist films, it seems likely that the transfer of emotions is also a crucial neorealist function." She continues by noting that *"Bicycle Thieves* encourages us to develop an emotional connection to Ricci. We are not supposed to drop this emotional connection once we leave the theatre; rather, we are supposed to transfer our emotional connection to the external world."[20] Among Latin Americanist film scholars, John Hess is one of the only ones to discuss this aspect of Italian neorealism and its connection to the NLAC, and, like Keating, he situates this emotional appeal in relation to neorealism's oft-cited humanism.[21] However, for Hess, this sentimentality was a sign of the political limitations of the postwar cinema, as the films' emotional appeals allowed Italian filmmakers to avoid the type of radical critique that can be found in Latin American films like *Yawar Mallku / Blood of the Condor* (Bolivia, Grupo Ukumau, 1969). Following the conciliatory ideology of the Popular Front (rather than a more confrontational Marxist paradigm favored by Latin American filmmakers), Italian neorealist films "set good versus evil and freedom versus oppression (without further discussion)" and eschewed a more in-depth examination of class conflict: "Thus contradictions disappeared in the face of an intense sympathy for the poor and the wretched."[22] Hess characterizes neorealism's incitement of the spectator's emotional attachments as evidence of the films' limited commitment to social change and expresses much greater skepticism than Keating about the effect of the films' ability to "move" spectators toward action in the real world.

Putting aside for the moment the political efficacy of emotional engagements, it is important to note the way in which the films of Rossellini and De Sica formed part of the archive of emotions mined by Latin American filmmakers with similar humanist tendencies such as dos Santos and Birri.[23]

Playing on Brian Massumi's characterization of emotion as socially inscribed and narrativized,[24] I suggest that neorealism offered a narrative template for knitting together "proper" emotional responses and moral certitude according to the postulates of Catholic humanism. Films like *Roma, Città Aperta* and *Ladri di Biciclette* as well as *Rio, 40 Graus,* and *Los inundados* situate suffering, for example, as a morally redemptive feeling—for both characters and spectators.

As the exaltation of particular emotions was a key characteristic of the "old" studio-made films from Latin America, it is tempting to critique those early examples of the NLAC as exhibiting a residual aesthetic (and political) traditionalism. This interpretation can be supported in generational terms by noting that both Birri (b. 1925) and dos Santos (b. 1928)—who are sometimes characterized as the precursors or "fathers" of the NLAC—are slightly older than Fernando Solanas (b. 1936), Octavio Getino (b. 1935), Jorge Sanjinés (b. 1937), Glauber Rocha (b. 1939), and Patricio Guzmán and Humberto Solás (b. 1941).[25] And, as some of the first films to make substantive breaks with earlier filmmaking traditions, dos Santos's *Rio, 40 Graus,* and *Rio Zona Norte* (1957) and Birri's *Los inundados,* not surprisingly, shared certain characteristics with dominant film forms—namely, the moral hierarchies of "modernization melodramas" such as *Nosotros los pobres* (Mexico, Ismael Rodríguez, 1948) and *Mercado de Abasto* (Argentina, Lucas Demare, 1955), which opposed their good, honest, working-class protagonists against their corrupt, upwardly mobile antagonists.

As transitional filmmakers working in a volatile moment of industrial and aesthetic transformation, dos Santos and Birri learned from Italian neorealism how to deploy emotion in ways that differed from local studio productions. Much more invested in the critique of larger socioeconomic inequalities than *Nosotros los pobres* and *Mercado de Abasto* (for example), dos Santos's two films about favela dwellers and Birri's chronicle of a displaced, working-class family accomplish a scalar shift, moving our investment in the personal anguish of their individual characters toward a felt realization of structural inequalities experienced by particular social classes for whom the protagonists serve as representatives. Defined as personal (as attributes of particular characters *and* as evidence of the humanity of the spectators), the sensorial evocations of these films partake in existing scripts that endow those feelings with meaning.[26] Nonetheless, what is different is how the films "fix" that quality of experience into particular narrativized circuits. The "new realism" of dos Santos (like that of De Sica) oscillated between focalization tactics that encouraged spectators to identify with the plight of particular protagonists (a dominant device in the "old" melodramas) and other narrational techniques, including a roaming "observational" camera that pulled the spectator away from the perspective of the characters to make visible the scale of social inequities that were beyond their purview.[27]

Nineteenth-century Latin American sentimental novels served as another source in the archive of emotions upon which dos Santos and Birri relied. Unlike the works of Italian neorealism, novels like Argentine José Mármol's *Amalia* (1851), Brazilian Jose Alencar's *O Guaraní* (1857) and *Iracema* (1865), and Colombian Jorge Isaacs's *María* (1867) have not been previously noted as a source of inspiration for the NLAC. When discussing their literary interests, the NLAC filmmakers were more likely to cite postcolonial writers, such as Frantz Fanon and Aimé Cesaire, as well as homegrown revolutionaries like Ché Guevara. For their part, film scholars have been inclined to see the nineteenth-century novels in relation to the "old" Latin American cinema—as the source texts of specific filmic adaptations[28] or, more generally, as a precursor to the melodramas that would prove so popular in Argentina, Mexico, and elsewhere. With narratives revolving around the obstacles separating heterosexual lovers as well as a clearly delineated Manichean worldview, both nineteenth-century novels and early twentieth-century films constructed a good/evil divide through the repeated use of visual spectacles. Detailed descriptions or close-ups of the characters' facial expressions and bodily gestures showcased the protagonists' moral purity and encouraged readers or viewers to empathize with their suffering. Given these similarities with the "old" cinema and the tendency to see the NLAC as more rational, film scholars have ignored how the moralizing tone and sentimental appeals of the nineteenth-century novels were also present (albeit in a different way) in certain films of the NLAC.

Of equal interest is the way in which the novels mapped heterosexual passion onto love of country to stir up nationalist sentiments among readers. As analyzed by Doris Sommer in *Foundational Fictions: The National Romances of Latin America* (1991), the Latin American novels "marr[ied] national destiny to personal passion" in ways that demonstrated how cultural texts could catalyze an impassioned commitment to the national community.[29] Published in the aftermath of the nineteenth-century independence movements, the novels' tales about the struggles of star-crossed lovers from different social classes and/or races served as allegories about the diverse social and economic obstacles facing the unification of the young nations. Sommer underscores the literary texts' social significance, arguing that

> [the novels emerged] at mid-century, after independence had been won (everywhere but Cuba and Puerto Rico), civil wars had raged for a generation, and newspapers had become the medium for serialized European and American fiction. The local romances did more than entertain

readers with compensations for spotty national history. They developed a narrative formula for resolving continuing conflicts, a post[-]epic conciliatory genre that consolidated survivors by recognizing former enemies as allies.[30]

In this effort, the novels' emotional appeals were absolutely key. The romances encouraged the reader to sympathize with the protagonists and intensified those attachments by placing seemingly insurmountable obstacles between the lovers:

> As the story progresses, the pitch of sentiment rises along with the cry of commitment, so that the din makes it ever more difficult to distinguish between our erotic and political fantasies for an ideal ending… [E]very obstacle that the lovers encounter heightens more than their mutual desire to (be a) couple, more than our voyeuristic but keenly felt passion; it also heightens their/our love for the possible nation in which the affair could be consummated.[31]

Emerging in the wake of rapid modernization projects closely pegged to foreign ideals, the films of the NLAC were equally interested in (re)awakening a passionate commitment to the nation. Unlike the novels, however, the films did not place the romantic travails of a heterosexual couple at the center of their narratives. While their characters were situated as representative of particular social classes, the films demanded greater development of the protagonists as unique, more psychologically nuanced individuals. Nonetheless, the foundational fictions offered a narrative template for how to solicit the reader/viewer's emotional investment in and embodied commitment to the larger nation.

Dos Santos's *Rio, 40 Graus* is perhaps the work that best exemplifies the neorealist sentimentality just outlined. It shares with the Italian postwar films a concern for human relations (particularly, the affairs of poor, working-class characters) as well as an interest in revealing socioeconomic inequalities through the use of documentary-like techniques. Rather than a ruined postwar Europe, dos Santos's film trains its focus on the inequities of rapid urbanization experienced in Brazil starting in the 1940s.[32] Structured innovatively as a day in the life of Rio's residents, *Rio, 40 Graus* uses exterior shooting to track the characters' meanderings through the hillside favela of Cabaçú, Copacabana beach, the Maracaná stadium, the iconic Pão de Azucar, and Corcovado. This panorama of Rio's human landscape becomes the means to capture the mundane activities of a cross-section of the population. However, the film is most concerned with the experiences of the *favelados,* particularly the problems besetting two young women and five boys. Alicia and Rosa are trying to work out relationships with men, each of whom offers a way out of poverty. For their part, the boys spend their day running about Rio trying to sell roasted peanuts to passersby to earn a living for themselves and their families. As characters caught between the favela and the "outside," their struggles highlight the socioeconomic contrasts that riddle Brazilian society and, as vulnerable youth, their future prospects serve as measuring sticks of Brazil's development as a modern, capitalist nation.

The use of children as symbols of the precarious state of the nation to provoke an emotional reaction on the part of spectators was a key device of numerous films of the NLAC (as well as Italian neorealism)[33] and demonstrates important points of contact between films as starkly different as *Rio, 40 Graus* and *El coraje del pueblo.* Beginning and ending with the boys' stories, dos Santos film is dependent on the children for its emotional power. The narrative pays particular attention to the experiences of Jorge, who sells peanuts to support and buy medicine for his sick mother, and to the youngest boy of the group. In an early scene, the film follows the youngest lad as he slips into the city zoo after Catarina (his pet lizard) escapes from his hands, as the variations of the melodic score set the emotional tone of the events as they unfold. At one point, an accelerated musical passage signals the boy's dismay as Catarina runs into the cage of a hungry flamingo. Encouraging the spectator to sympathize with the boy's relief over her narrow escape and return to his care, the sequence then tightens our alignment with his point of view through a series of eye-line matches that allow us to share in his observations of the different animals and the sunlight dancing through the trees overhead.[34] The spectator's privileged access to the boy's wonder at his environment becomes a means of underscoring his humanity—an effect further heightened when a zoo guard yanking on the boy's arm causes Catarina to escape once again. Through such focalization tactics, the scene characterizes the guard's action as unjust and arbitrary—that is, as an unwarranted interruption of the lad's harmless foray into the zoo. The final long shot that depicts the saddened boy standing outside the gates of the zoo as a group of well-clad and well-shod young children pass through the entrance fully concretizes the film's critique of the socioeconomic differences that separate the privileged few from the impoverished many. The shot is a fine example of how *Rio, 40 Graus* combines focalization tactics with an "observational" camera to pull the spectator's emotional attachments from the individual to the social. This shift in the scale of the film's critique is also evident in the way in which Catarina's sad fate functions as a metaphor for the destiny of the boy who, in the sequences that follow, likewise falls victim to predators in situations that are beyond his control. Playing with Christian imagery, the scene situates the zoo as an edenic space for the young *favelado*—a site from which he is expelled by the snakelike guard—and in this revised version of the fall, innocence is lost at the hands of the brutal modern order.[35]

Throughout the narrative, *Rio, 40 Graus* fortifies its sympathetic chronicling of the experiences of the *favelados* by juxtaposing their travails with the hypocritical behavior of the characters from the ascendant middle class. In one particular sequence that takes place at Corcovado (the huge statue of Jesus Christ that overlooks the city), the film relies on references to Christian values as a moral framework in which to solicit and "fix" the viewer's emotional attachments, albeit in ways that differ from *Roma, Città Aperta*. It is there that an ambitious bureaucrat and his wife use their daughter as a seductive lure to ingratiate themselves with a rich landowner from the provinces who has just arrived in Rio (as the then-capital of Brazil) as a recently elected congressman. Called "um anjo de bondade" ["an angel of goodness"] by her father, the daughter proves even more calculating than her parents when, in a low-angle shot featuring the statue of Christ overhead, she makes a devil's bargain with the congressman. Rather than maneuvering to be his wife as her parents wish, she agrees to be his "secretary"—an agreement suggesting she will exchange sexual favors for access to money and greater personal freedom. The landowner-turned-politician demonstrates his own hypocrisy slightly earlier when, upon arriving at the site to fulfill a promise (presumably to pay homage to Christ), he sneeringly dismisses the attempts of one of the *favelados* to sell him peanuts and, brushing by him, says "to the devil with you and the peanuts." His words and actions reveal that his pilgrimage is a superficial nod toward Christian principles, as he displays none of the charity or love for his fellow human beings that characterize Christ's teachings. The film spectator's access to the perspective of these middle-class characters does not lead to a shared wonder at the world, but rather to the revelation of the characters' selfishness and avarice. The mise-en-scéne positions those moral failures within a Christian framework, contrasting the immorality of the middle classes to the selfless sacrifice of Christ, a figure aligned with the poor. In so doing, *Rio, 40 Graus* legitimizes the spectator's sympathetic alignment with the young *favelados* in moral terms.

Even as they work to encourage spectatorial sympathy for particular characters and their antipathy toward others, the film's emotional appeals extend beyond the personalistic to encourage viewers to invest themselves in the nation, particularly in the final nighttime sequence in Cabaçu. During this rehearsal of the favela's Carnival crew, the songs sung by the *favelados* (e.g., "A escravidáo em Brasil já se acabou" / "Slavery has ended in Brazil"; and "Reliquias do Rio Antigo" / "Relics of Old Rio") comment on the nation's past and present. The celebration brings together the residents of Cabaçu with those of Portela, another favela, promoting solidarity over competition as everyone participates in the performance. As Alicia (Cabaçu's Carnival queen) sings the final number, calling out, "Esta melodia para o Brasil feliz," even Alberto and Miro (her new fiancé and a jealous ex-lover, respectively) overcome their differences to pat each other on the back:

| | |
|---|---|
| Eu sou o samba, | I am the samba, |
| A voz do morro sou eu mesmo, sim senhor. | The voice of the *morro* am I, yes, sir. |
| Quero mostrar ao mundo que tenho valor | I want to show the world my worthiness |
| Eu sou o rei dos terreiros | I am the king of the public squares |
| Eu sou o samba | I am the samba |
| Sou natural aqui de Rio de Janeiro | I was born here in Rio de Janeiro |
| Sou eu quem levo a alegría | I'm the one who brings happiness |
| para milhões de corações brasilseiros.[36] | to millions of Brazilian hearts. |

The diegetic music and dance create an audiotopia (Josh Kun's term for music's utopic potential for bringing together races, classes, etc.) that helps provide narrative closure by defining Brazil as a united community of feeling.

In a recent essay on the film, Helidoro San Miguel argues that the film's humane and respectful treatment of its characters "avoid(s) excessive sentimentalism and unnecessary drama."[37] San Miguel is right in the sense that *Rio, 40 Graus* does not feature the spectacular emotional displays of a typical melodrama. Indeed, a scene in a cable car heading up to Pão de Azucar functions as a mise-en-abyme revealing the type of spectatorial response that the film wishes to avoid. The sequence features an encounter between another of the boys from Cabaçu and a middle-class family. While the couple's young son Antonito dashes frenetically from window to window, the woman converses with the more sedate peanut seller who, in response to her questions about what he is doing, where he lives, and where his parents are, tells her that he does not have either a mother or a father. Her outburst of compassion for the boy's hardships lasts until they arrive at their destination, where the family soon becomes caught up in taking photos of themselves and staving off Antonito's newest antics. The scene's inclusion in the film offers a clever indictment of pitiful middle-class glances that are little more than the facile expression of momentary sympathies.

This subtle denunciation of a certain type of emotional response does not cancel the film's deliberate invitations *to feel the need* for social change—a tactic employed in other works of the NLAC. In the case of *Rio, 40 Graus*, the interpretive framework for which I am advocating acknowledges the film's efforts to reorient the aesthetics and politics of the sentimental while recognizing the difficulty of accommodating sentimental appeals within a new type of realist framework. The awkwardness of this adjustment is most notable in the film's final sequence in the abrupt conclusion to the rivalry between Alicia's upwardly mobile suitor Alberto and the jealous, aggressive Miro that has built up throughout the narrative. Upon recognizing Alberto as a fellow participant in a recent strike, Miro quickly puts aside his personal animosity in favor of embracing working-class solidarity. Unlike earlier scalar shifts that move the spectator from the travails of individual characters to an embodied awareness of larger social inequalities (for example, through the long shot outside the zoo), the transfer that takes place in this final scene is unconvincing. It upsets the flow of the narrative that had included a substantive subplot setting up Miro's inclination toward violent bullying (in a scene at a market, at Maracaná, and through countless comments by tertiary characters) and encouraged the viewer to anticipate the coming showdown with Alberto and Alicia. In other words, rather than dismissing the awkwardness of this sequence as a minor deviation in a masterwork,[38] one can see the scene as symptomatic of the film's attempt to deploy sentimental appeals in new ways.

In contesting various aspects of San Miguel's reading of *Rio, 40 Graus,* I do not want to dismiss the essay's numerous merits. However, in its eagerness to minimize the role of emotion in *Rio, 40 Graus,* the piece exemplifies the scholarly tendency that continues to disassociate the NLAC from emotion.[39] As discussed more thoroughly in the next section, to speak of the NLAC's visceral impact has been to talk about the works' jolt to the cerebral process and their provocation to think (rationally) in new ways. After complicating that interpretive argument, I will problematize the patriarchal underpinnings of this critical paradigm in the chapter's conclusion.

## *Of Modernist Disorientation*

Neorealist sentimentality was not evident in works made after the early 1960s. As the films themselves became more formally experimental and proposed more radical political critiques, the "mature" works of the NLAC—including *La hora de los hornos* (Argentina, Grupo Liberación, 1966–68), *Memorias del subdesarrollo* (Cuba, Tomás Gutiérrez Alea, 1968), *El chacal de Nahueltoro* (Chile, Miguel Littín, 1969), *El coraje del pueblo* (Bolivia, Grupo Ukumau, 1971), *El otro Francisco* (Cuba, Sergio Giral, 1974), and *La batalla de Chile* (1975—79)—incited spectators to feel in other ways. This section will first explore how some of the filmmakers theorized the role of sensorial appeals in radical filmmaking by reviewing Fernando Solanas and Octavio Getino's 1969 manifesto "Hacia un tercer cine" (as well as some of their lesser-known writings) and Tomás Gutiérrez Alea's 1982 "Dialéctica del espectador" / "Viewer's Dialectic." While finding these essays illuminating, I will also discuss some of their limitations as theoretical templates, in part through close readings of Littín's *El chacal* and Solanas and Getino's *La hora*. These analyses will suggest that the works' affective engagements exceed the politicizing functionality ascribed to them by Solanas, Getino, and Alea and register the disorienting effects of second-wave modernization.

In "Hacia un tercer cine," Solanas and Getino characterize cinema as a medium uniquely suited to engaging spectators on the level of sensation as a means to radicalize and mobilize them. In their essay "El cine como hecho político" / "The cinema as a political fact," they argued that while cinema could not replace either street demonstrations or the informative reflections of a written article, it was capable of greater emotional penetration and was more persuasive than other means of communication.[40] Although they clearly privileged literature as a more deliberative and intellectually demanding medium, they praised film's ability to synthesize information, promote solidarity among viewers, and stimulate their potential interaction.[41] As noted in their 1969 manifesto "Hacia un tercer cine," it was essential to "movilizar, agitar, politizar de una u otra manera a capas del pueblo, armarlo *racional* y *sensiblemente* para la lucha..." ["mobilize, agitate, [and] politicize the people ("sectors of the population") in one way or another, to arm them *rationally* and *sensorially* for the [revolutionary] fight..."] (author's emphasis).[42]

While acknowledging the importance of reaching audience members on the level of sensation, Solanas and Getino nonetheless situated this type of appeal as a preliminary stage in a more complex process of radicalization. In so doing, they were following Mao Tse-tung's three-step model for acquiring knowledge. The first step involved coming into contact with the world "through sensation"; the second, synthesizing the data gathered by sensation to create "concepts, judgments, and deductions"; and the third stage, "activating" this knowledge and making a jump forward toward revolutionary praxis.[43] In adapting this model to theorize the radicalizing potential of the "film-act," Solanas and Getino suggested that the first two steps take place simultaneously through different aspects of film form. Image and sound engage audience members on a sensorial level while "in the film, the announcer, the reportings, the didactics or the narrator who leads the projection" help synthesize what they see and hear and to make abstractions.[44] The final stage takes place outside the text, in the participatory responses of the audience members, in their proposals about how to take action, and in the actions themselves that take place at a later point. This hierarchical model subordinating the sensorial to the rational is revealing and suggests that in order to reach a "higher plane" of understanding, audience members need a guide or a mediator to help them synthesize their sensorial impressions into more abstract frameworks that serve as a gateway to revolutionary action.

Emerging from Solanas and Getino's own work on *La hora de los hornos,* their template succinctly outlines the audiovisual counterpoint of the film's first part wherein rapid montage sequences overlaid with jarring music alternate with other sequences featuring didactic imagery illustrating the words of authoritative voice-overs.[45] Nonetheless, the model has severe limitations in terms of its explanatory usefulness. Other works of the NLAC, such as Santiago Alvarez's documentaries from the 1960s, which had a similar penchant for utilizing baroque montage and sensorial overload as demystifying tactics, eschewed the synthesizing narrator called for by Solanas and Getino. As detailed later in this section, the affective charge of even *La hora* was less tightly controlled than the filmmakers suggested.

While sharing Solanas and Getino's understanding of sensation/feeling and rationality as separate orders of experience, Alea offered a more complex account of their relationship in "Dialéctica del espectador." In that extended essay, he carefully mined the work of both Bertolt Brecht and Sergei Eisenstein to argue for the importance of engaging both the spectator's emotions and thought processes to promote revolutionary action. Alea agreed with Brecht's critique of Aristotle's notion of catharsis: a work of art should not function as an escape from social tensions, allowing the public to purify themselves of "unproductive" emotions. At the same time, rather than reject the role of emotion in art entirely, the filmmaker argued that it must be employed in tactical ways to unsettle the spectator—a position that he derives from pulling together Brecht and Eisenstein's theories about politicizing art.[46]

Alea's proposition responded to what he saw as the particularity of film. He argued that as a primarily visual (vs. verbal) medium, the cinema "particularized" meaning-production in terms of the represented object and that this indexicality did not allow for the same expression of "ideas, concepts, [or] abstractions" as was possible in the theater, where words dominated. According to Alea, the immediacy of the cinematic image "appeals directly to the senses and situates itself more comfortably on the emotional plane."[47] The trick was to use film's sensorial appeal in ways that would instantiate a new understanding of "reality" and lead the spectator to engage with the world in revolutionary ways.

Seeing the cinema's emotional appeal in its most simple form as a matter of identification with particular characters, Alea crafted his notion of the "viewer's dialectic," wherein a film simultaneously encourages and problematizes this alignment. Following Eisenstein, Alea argued that this form of "entrega emocional," or identification with particular characters, effects a paradoxical "separation [of the spectator] from [him/her]self," a breach that opens up the possibility for change.[48] This shift is not sufficient to instantiate radical change, but rather a necessary part of a process that leads to greater "intellectual [rational] comprehension."[49] Here, Alea invokes Brecht's notion of distantiation as a necessary countermovement that prevents absolute identification and "de-alienates" the spectator. Whereas in the theater (according to Brecht), this occurs through the performative techniques employed by the actors, film offers other resources, including "framing, narration, music…in a word: [what Eisenstein called] audiovisual montage."[50] Such techniques could be used, for example, to set up contrasts between the visual image and the audio track (between what is seen and what is heard) in ways that force the spectator to question the visual (or aural) perspective of a character with whom the spectator had been identifying. Through the deliberate deployment of such devices, along with others that encourage the spectator to identify with particular characters, the viewer's dialectic, as theorized by Alea, moves the spectator toward a revolutionary consciousness and the desire to act on reality outside the confines of the theater.

If at certain points Alea seems to agree with Solanas and Getino's hierarchy of reason over emotion, his proposal insists (citing Brecht) "on the necessity of overcoming the 'reason-emotion' antinomy" and on promulgating a revolutionary cinematic praxis that concedes emotion's unique status as an essential aspect of both human nature and the nature of film as a medium.[51] As noted in the following passage, the Cuban filmmaker characterizes emotion and reason as twin processes that (can) work together in fruitful ways:

Si por una parte Eisenstein va "de la imagen al sentimiento y del sentimiento a la idea," Brecht da un paso más y nos advierte que si bien el sentimiento puede estimular la razón, ésta, a su vez, purifica nuestros sentimientos.

[Whereas Eisenstein goes "from the image to the emotion and from the emotion to the idea," Brecht goes one step farther to advise us that while emotion can stimulate reason, reason purifies our emotions.]

For Alea, the productivity of this dyad in a work of art is made possible only when the techniques outlined by Eisenstein ("ecstatic" emotional engagement) and Brecht (distantiation) are placed in dialectical relationship to each other to force spectators to synthesize what they experience in the movie theater in ways that move them beyond those confines and influence their engagement with "reality."

"The Viewer's Dialectic" can be seen as a retrospective theorization of Alea's 1968 masterpiece *Memorias del subdesarrollo / Memories of Underdevelopment*, a film that exemplified the tension between techniques of identification and distantiation in the relationship it establishes between the spectator and Sergio, the main protagonist.[52] Published in book form in 1982, "The Viewer's Dialectic" can also be understood as a rumination on Alea's *Hasta cierto punto / Up to a Certain Point* (1983), the film he was working on while writing his essay, as well as on earlier Cuban films like Sara Gómez's *De cierta manera* (1974), which Alea helped to complete, and even Sergio Giral's *El otro Francisco* (1974).[53] Indeed, Alea's essay offers a fecund point of departure for analyzing the emotional appeals of several works made outside of Cuba. In characterizing emotion as a universal human experience that is always already named and categorized (e.g., anger, pity, sadness, joy), Alea's proposal captures the humanism underlying many films from the NLAC. One of the most visible signs of this humanism is the recurrent deployment of the figure of the suffering child and/or other "defenseless" beings (particularly animals) as a means to concretize the denunciation of socioeconomic ills. In contrast to Solanas and Getino, whose writings cast films' emotional appeals as a preliminary stage toward revolutionary thought and praxis, in Alea's dialectic emotion plays a more prominent role, in that only through significant emotional engagement does a subject undergo sustainable cognitive transformation.

Nonetheless, Alea's manifesto has a number of shortcomings and, ultimately, is not supple enough to account for all of the sensorial dynamics of the NLAC. By tying the role of emotion to the process of identification, "The Viewer's Dialectic" does not offer a suitable framework for examining documentaries like *La hora de los hornos* and *La batalla de Chile* that are not character-centered. Films such as *El coraje del pueblo* that feature a collective protagonist (the miners of Siglo XX and their families) similarly fall outside the parameters of Alea's model. Like cognitivist film scholars Murray Smith and Noel Carroll, Alea's account does not acknowledge the other means by which films invite their viewers to feel, including the use of audiovisual montage to create rhythms that are not connected to particular characters.

Moreover, even as it echoes the shared humanism of films as diverse as *Tire dié, Rio 40 Graus, Vidas secas, El chacal de Nahueltoro, La hora de los hornos*, and *El coraje del pueblo*, Alea's theoretical framework fails to capture the complexity and radical promise of these films' affective address.

As I hope to substantiate in the following pages, *El chacal de Nahueltoro, La hora de los hornos* (Part I), and other films work between emotional appeals and visceral jolts. They situate otherwise "recognizable" feelings in dislocating ways and, in so doing, move audience members from what is knowable to what is uncertain. Returning to the Deleuzian model of affective flows outlined by Massumi, we could say that the modernist jolt of the NLAC emerges when certain films work on the cusp between what is narrativizable and what remains unmoored from the continuities of established epistemologies. The films' carefully crafted sensorial appeals serve to dislodge calcified worldviews (e.g., modernization as a universally beneficial process that advances in a linear fashion) and invite participatory commitment to radical social change.

## A Child Is Crying

Littín's *El chacal de Nahueltoro* (1967) perhaps represents the most complex engagement with the sensorial in the entire NLAC. The film chronicles the life and death of José del Carmen Valenzuela Torres, a rural migrant who murdered a woman (Rosa Rivas Acuña) and her five young children in 1960, and was dubbed "the Jackal" by the contemporary media in their voracious appetite for scandal. In its retelling of this real-life crime story that had gripped Chilean society seven years earlier, *El chacal* harshly denounced both the sensationalist press and the dry rationalism of the law. Despite its critique of the media-inspired hysteria surrounding the crime, the film does not itself eschew affective appeals. Indeed, Littín's film is skeptical of the illuminating possibilities of cool rationality, as evident in its depiction of the mechanical rituals of the judicial process. The affectless voice-over reciting passages from the legal testimony, the detached demeanor of the trial judge who offhandedly characterizes José as a man "de tercera categoría," and the matter-of-fact tone of the firing squad commander who responds to a reporter's question about the potential difficulty of his job by saying that he has a "lot of practice executing people," all subvert our confidence that rational(ized) systems of justice can recognize and resolve larger socioeconomic ills.[54] While *El chacal* does not reject the role of feeling in public life, it does re-examine it. The film carries this out both within the narrative (by interrogating the role of emotional ties in José's social integration) and through spectatorial address (by priming the spectator to feel differently).

A critical moment in the film's exploration of affective social attachments occurs at the midpoint of the narrative after José has been imprisoned, in a section titled "Educación y Amansamiento" / "Education and Domestication." The sequence begins with numerous long shots and extreme long shots of jailed men walking back and forth in the prison yard, several of which isolate José standing by himself. This lengthy series of shots (lasting approximately two minutes) detailing the monotony and relative aimlessness of prison life is ruptured when a group of men playing soccer call on José to kick back the ball that has landed at his feet. After returning the ball and hearing the men's cheers, José's face explodes in a joyous grin that is held in a freeze-frame to signal the initiation of what turns out to be his successful socialization. This "interruption" in the flow of images reminds us that, until that moment, the main character had been notably affectless.[55] Subsequent shots show his hair being cut, his attempts to learn how to read, his participation in a soccer match, his presence in a class on Chilean history and at mass, and his efforts to learn a manual trade. In these scenes, the film situates José's integration into society in terms of solidifying affective ties with his fellow prisoners (who hearten him with praise about his new reading skills), the local priest (who pats him on the back after a successful soccer match), and even the prison personnel (with whom he jokes on the eve of his execution). *El chacal* celebrates the solidarity of the prisoners as men marginalized by society who nonetheless have forged a community and demonstrate an emotional commitment to each other and their families. This is poignantly portrayed in the scenes leading up to José's execution as, one after another, his cellmates call out their goodbyes and encouragement and José promises to die "sin chillar, porque sería feo" / "without a sound, because [screaming] would be bad."

Yet, the film's recognition of the binding power of emotion is not entirely acritical. *El chacal* exhibits skepticism about the state's role in encouraging the prisoners' sentimental ties to the nation and, in casting doubt upon the purposes of nationalist fervor, differs from *Rio 40 Graus*. In the classroom sequence, the film rapidly cuts back and forth between the professor, who narrates the famous battle of Iquique in the War of the Pacific (1879–80) between Chile and Perú; the listening prisoners sitting at individual desks; and a painting of Admiral Arturo Prat, Chile's greatest hero, who lost his life in the battle. The professor's words portray Prat as a patriot who sacrificed himself for the nation, while the rapid cuts suggest how the prisoners are encouraged to get caught up in the tale and imagine themselves as the heroic Prat of the painting—that is, as flag-draped partisans willing to surrender their lives for the nation. Whether or not this interpellation of the prisoners as citizens succeeds is questioned by the medium close-ups of the men, whose facial expressions vary from boredom to interest. José is one of the few whose attentive posture betrays his involvement in the story. In the end, when he agrees at the behest of a prison official and against his own inclination, to wear a blindfold over his entire face to avoid traumatizing his executioners, the film offers a final, subtle jab at the state's rehabilitation of José. In covering over the sign of his own unique humanity for the "greater good," José submits to an institutional authority that has been entirely indifferent to his suffering. In so doing, Littín's film demonstrates how nationalist sentimentality functions as the counterpart of the dry rationalism of the law and how both help to support dominant socio-economic structures.

*El chacal*'s critique, at the level of narrative, of how emotional ties binding the subject to the social legitimize existing power relations is coupled, at the level of spectatorial address, with an effort to rewire the viewer's sensorial circuitry. This takes place, in part, through the type of dialectical shifts outlined by Alea. Throughout the film, *El chacal* oscillates between aligning audience members with José's perspective and impeding any facile sympathizing with his plight. On the one hand, Littín's film struggles to recover the humanity of a man who had been thoroughly marginalized by society by reworking the conventions of the "crime film." Dispensing with the traditional detective-hero, the film investigates what happened by privileging the testimony of José, whose crime is seen in flashback after his arrest and only after other flashbacks detailing his impoverished childhood and adolescence spent wandering from farm to farm as an exploited worker. In these scenes of recollection, José's halting voice-over is matched with discontinuous images that alternately situate audience members as "external" witnesses to moments in his life or, through the use of a subjective camera, as participant-observers who "partake," for example, in José's drunken reveries.[56] At the same time, *El chacal de Nahueltoro* shows little interest in forging a simple or unfettered identification between the spectator and the main character, whose frequently incoherent words, affectless demeanor, and seemingly unmotivated actions provoke our discomfort even as his voice-over and the visual flashbacks lead us to a greater understanding about the miserable conditions in which he (and others) live. In sum, in its fluctuation between identification and distantiation, Littín's film features the type of dialectical tension hailed by Alea as a means to propel the spectator toward a new understanding of the underlying structures of inequality that are frequently masked or covered over in tales of individual crimes and individual heroes.

Yet, this tension does not entirely account for *El chacal*'s deployment of emotion and affect as tools for critical reevaluation. Many of the film's sensorial appeals exceed the alignment of audience members with a particular character. In two key sequences, the film ingeniously uses a baby's cry to shift the scale of its critique from the individual to the social. The cry first appears when José stumbles upon Rosa working outside a miserable hovel as her children listlessly play in the dirt-covered yard. Cutting from a shot of José staggering around in the early hours after a night of carousing, the sequence opens with a tight medium shot of Rosa swinging an ax downward to cut firewood as a baby's scream sounds from off-screen. The shot is jarring as it plays with the audiovisual mismatch that ties the baby's cry to the violent swing of the ax. In so doing, it foreshadows the brutality that will destroy the family. However, it also serves a another function. On the most immediate level, the mismatch quickly and economically signals that this family does not function as an emotional safe haven for its members. The subsequent handheld, four-minute sequence shot that follows Rosa around the yard as she stacks the firewood, takes down the laundry, and snaps at her children to corral the chickens, all the while talking to the off-screen José, reveals that there is little time to comfort a child. On a more abstract level, the baby's almost unremitting yowls—which are only somewhat less articulate than José's murmured half-phrases—function as an effective metaphor for the relentless suffering of those who, like Rosa, her children, and José, live in extreme poverty. This scene examplifies how *El chacal* employs emotion in dislocating ways as it invokes the baby's cry as a seemingly universal sign of distress only to dislodge it from its referent and resemanticize it as a call for help that moves beyond individual need.[57]

When the baby's cries resurface in the pivotal flashback wherein a drunken José murders Rosa and her children, the film calls for(th) a similarly unsettling response. As noted by Stephen Hart, the sequence of the murders is highly disruptive.[58] The film moves audience members back and forth between the present and the past as it cross-cuts between José's testimony in front of the judge and a visual flashback of the murders. At the same time, the murders themselves are depicted in a markedly discontinuous manner. The shots shift visual perspectives—from "external" tracking shots documenting José's actions to handheld subjective shots allowing us to see his victims' terror from his perspective[59]—and the soundtrack replaces the characters' words with a dissonant musical composition alternated with notable silences. The baby's wail returns only at the very end of the sequence, after José has murdered Rosa and the other four children, as he gathers together his things. The cry pierces the surrounding silence and is quickly overlaid by the dissonant music. This excruciating sonic discord continues unabated until José, depicted from waist down in a low-level shot, crushes the baby with his foot (figure 1.4). The film then cuts to the present and the hysteric cries of the public as the judge asks José with soft disbelief: "Pero, ¿por qué mataste a los niños, hombre? / "But, why did you kill the children, man?"

This sequence would seem to confirm Hart's contention that Littín's film establishes a parallel between the public reaction within the diegesis

**Figure 1.4** José crushes the baby in *El chacal de Nahueltoro*

and the viewer's reaction.[60] The low-level shot focuses our attention on the inhumane act of deliberately crushing a baby to death as the discordant soundtrack works to accentuate our deep unease. Like the hysteric crowd, we are horrified by the brutality of the murders as the visual flashback has done nothing to explain José's motivations or attenuate the horrendous nature of his actions. However, as I hope I've suggested in previous paragraphs, Hart's suggestion does not sufficiently acknowledge the complexities of the film's affective engagements. If the judge's question gives voice to the viewer's own perplexity, José's response ("Para que no sufrieran" / "So that they wouldn't suffer") resonates, at least to some degree, with the film's depiction of the far-from-idyllic childhoods of the impoverished. Placed within the larger narrative, the cross-cut sequence moves us in a number of ways. Despite invoking the baby's cry to underscore the atrocious nature of his crime, the film also calls into question the media's exaggerated depiction of José as a heinous "jackal" that preys indiscriminately on whoever crosses his path. Aligning us momentarily with the crowd, the film nonetheless dissuades us from following their blanket condemnation of José as a depraved monster. Most importantly, in departicularizing emotion, the film underscores how the real crime or injustice is not the murders (as suggested by both the sensationalistic press and the legal system), but rather the socioeconomic inequalities that determine the squalid living conditions of large sectors of the Chilean population. A child is crying, and its meaning lies elsewhere.

## A Child Is Being Bombed, Starved, Killed

Strangely enough, in its raw emotional power, Part I of Solanas and Getino's triptych *La hora de los hornos* is more akin to Littín's fictional reconstruction than to *La batalla de Chile,* the other three-part documentary with which it is often compared.[61] Unlike the frequently dry chronicling of Guzmán's epic work, Part I of *La hora* is an unremitting assault on the senses; from its rhythmic montage sequences to its zooming intertitles, *La hora* tries to hammer its denunciation of neocolonial exploitation into the body of the audience. The intensity of these sensorial demands has been discussed by numerous critics. In a 1970 review published in *Film Quarterly,* James Roy MacBean described the first part as "a rather flamboyant but impressive exercise in montage, in which the viewer's emotions are manipulated quite sophisticatedly by the rhythmic cutting."[62] Thirty-odd years later, in his essay "Politics and the Documentary Film in Argentina," Emilio Bernini similarly underscored the film's visceral charge. While arguing that Part I was not Eisensteinian in terms of "programming" a reflex response on the part of the spectator, the Argentine critic noted that the enigmatic opening montage that overlays images of flames, white light, and police repression with a reiterative drum beat "suspend[s] reason and...capture[s] the audience emotionally, precisely to the extent that they cannot come to a decision about the meaning of the images."[63] These and other studies have understood Part I's sensorial shock value in terms of Solanas and Getinos' interest in attacking the spectator's passivity.[64] While correct, we need to go further to appreciate how Part I's sensorial engagements function as an essential part of the segment's architecture. Solanas and Getino's theoretical discussion about the appropriate deployment of such appeals in militant films is useful as a point of departure for understanding how *La hora* attempted to channel sensation to foster revolutionary sensibilities.

According to Solanas and Getino's manifesto, *La hora de los hornos* weaves together a complex, evocative audiovisual montage (combining startling images and compelling musical rhythms) with two highly authoritative voice-overs to appeal to both body and mind. The visual tapestry features a wide variety of shots—some taken on the streets of Buenos Aires and in the outlying provinces, and others pulled from magazines, movies, and newsreels. These images are often juxtaposed in startling ways and overlaid with music, isolated phrases, and ambient sounds that "clash" with the shots' visual content to put the viewer in contact with the world "through sensation."

One excellent example comes from the oft-cited twelfth section of the film entitled "Guerra ideológica" / "Ideological Warfare," which ties the invasive power of U.S.-backed consumerism to that country's neocolonial efforts in Vietnam. The sequence demonstrates both an immense affective potential (i.e., the ability to solicit strong feelings as yet unclaimed by meaning) and a reliance on the conventional figure of the suffering child. A rapid-fire montage overlays advertising images, movie stills, high art (da Vinci, Manet), and comics with Ray Charles's "I Don't Need No Doctor" and the inane chatter of the bourgeoisie (some repeated from earlier in the film). Interspersed are occasional images of starving children, a bedraggled man, a lynching, and scenes of state repression that slowly gain in frequency. Detached from their original contexts and placed in juxtaposition, these heterogeneous images and sounds force viewers to reassess their meaning through a process of modernist defamiliarization and suggest a connection between First World consumption (on the one hand) and Third World poverty and violence (on the other). The clash between the confident, happy (white) faces in the ads and the anguished faces and impoverished bodies of "real" (darker-skinned or "peripheral") peoples is evident and disturbing—an effect accentuated by the equally disjunctive soundtrack. Interrupting this audiovisual barrage, a newsreel sequence shows a Vietnamese boy with his arms in the air crossing a street where armed U.S. soldiers crouch with machine guns. As the boy retrieves an even younger child (his brother?) from the sidewalk on the other side of the street, a woman's riotous laughter erupts on the soundtrack. The incongruency between audio and visual tracks is jarring. Yet, the disruptive force of this extended shot nonetheless anchors the suggestive potency of the previous juxtapositions through the inclusion of the figure of the children, who stand in for the innocence and vulnerability of the entire Vietnamese population (and, indeed, of all oppressed peoples). Their presence heightens the emotional charge of the sequence while hardening the previous associations into a specific, anticolonial critique. Overlaid with the raucous laughter, their perilous journey encourages the viewer to feel the horrifying nature of colonialist aggression.

The recourse to the figure of the child (with its attendant sentimental force field) is one of the means by which *La hora* harnesses its dense, unsettling audiovisual interplay in purposeful ways (indeed shots of suffering children are deployed throughout the film). Another formal mechanism, the use of recurrent voice-overs, provides the audience with specific cues on how to synthesize Part I's brilliantly disjunctive montage sequences in ways that support the film's dualistic perspective about the centuries-old struggle between the evil forces of (neo)colonialism and the innocent masses who suffer unwittingly under its yoke.[65] As noted by Robert Stam, for all of its formal openness, *La hora de los hornos* is also highly authoritarian. The controlling discourse of the voice-overs is supported by the film's relentless citation of statistics (that are, at times, given double "exposure" through their graphic representation and their oral recitation) and by the inclusion of long citations of well-known national and international scholars and political figures (from Argentines Hernández Arregui, Scalabrini Ortiz, Perón, and Guevara, to Castro, Fanon, and Cesaire). Whereas the statistics seemingly offer objective evidence of Argentina's and Latin America's successive exploitation by colonial and neocolonial powers (specifically, Spain, England, and the United States), the quotes further develop the film's ideological perspective. Cumulatively, the citations and statistics serve to further substantiate the contentions of the film's narrators and help place the Argentine situation within a global context of revolutionary struggle. In conjunction with the voice-overs, these commanding quotes effectively provide direction to audience members for synthesizing the otherwise disparate audiovisual material in "appropriate" and adequate ways—that is, to understand that neocolonial violence reaches beyond military battlefields (Algeria, Cuba, and Vietnam) and infiltrates civilian spaces. In the Argentine case, according to the film, neo-colonial violence mows down national(ist) traditions by cultivating the worldly pretensions of upper-class Argentines, the Europeanized sensibilities of artists and intelligentsia, and the everyday consumer practices of "rebellious" youth.

Midway through Part I, this ideological framework has solidified to the point that additional audio-visual information can be introduced without the use of directive markers (narrators, citations, statistics). Like a rodeo chute, it channels the viewers' disconcerted responses, maneuvering him or her through the defamiliarization process toward a particular understanding of neo-colonialism and its consequences. In the aforementioned "Ideological Warfare" section situated near the vend of Part I, after almost an hour and fifteen minutes of running time, most viewers overcome their initial disorientation and can readily recognize the woman's laugh as a metonym for U.S. imperialism's careless brutality.[66]

As much as the voice-overs function to discipline the sensations that the film aims to evoke, the audiovisual tempo also mobilizes *La hora*'s decolonizing critique. To be more specific, the film's "pulse" allows audience members to feel the dehumanizing nature of (neo)colonialism. In so doing, these sensorial appeals help to naturalize *La hora*'s critique. This comes through with particular cogency in the many scenes of urban life in downtown Buenos Aires that are framed in low-angle traveling shots highlighting the city's functionalist high-rises and marginalizing pedestrians in the lower portion of the frame. In such sequences, the speed of the dolly shots and their short duration effectively capture how the quick pace of modern life in the city limits human interactions. The dehumanizing feel of urban life becomes a central theme of the third section entitled "Violencia cotidiana" / "Daily Violence" in which traveling shots of high-rises give way to others that feature workers walking inside a factory. Trailing behind different workers, the camera shots mask the laborers' individuality and, linked by jump-cuts, suggest how one worker often substitutes for another. This effect is enhanced by the complex orchestration of the sound and image tracks as the visuals are overlayed with asynchronous voice-overs and the repetitive clank of machinery. As various workers attest to the poor working conditions and repressive measures enacted by their bosses, their words are almost overpowered by the insistent beat of the machines and the tick of the time clock that measures the monetary value of their labor. Mariano Mestman argues that this sequence points to the dehumanizing nature of factory work where workers are not treated as individuals, but rather as cogs in a larger mechanism, their voices subsumed by the clatter of production.[67] This critique also takes place at the level of spectatorial address, as the jump-cuts and asynchronous sound encourage audiences to experience the disorienting effects of capitalism's disciplining of time-space.

In a similar fashion, the slaughterhouse sequence engages the spectator's sensorium to make the alienation of the common worker palpable—particularly to those who are not workers.[68] Placed quite a bit later in the ninth section entitled "La Dependencia" / "Dependence", the slaughterhouse sequence helps to materialize the deadening effect of the First World's dominant role in the world economy through its aggressive montage likening the people of the Third World to cattle being led to slaughter. The graphic images of cattle being stunned by a mallet, hung on a hook to bleed out, and flayed of their skin become all the more horrific through the interspersion of shots of innocuous ads of smiling white people drinking Coca-Cola under a soundtrack of frivolous Muzak. One particular shot—a zoom-in on the quivering eye of a stunned cow about to be butchered—is particularly effective in solidifying the analogy being drawn between the cattle (Argentina's top export item to the First World) and the Third World laborers whose blood-work sustains the global flow of goods aimed not at themselves, but rather at lighter-skin folk living (and consuming) elsewhere. By isolating the eye and, thus, humanizing the animal, the zoom-in invites the spectator to empathize with the creature's final trembles and, by extension, with the vulnerability of the workers. In my experience with university audiences over the years, the sequence has never failed to draw an immediate visceral response (groans, horrified gasps, eyes turning away from the screen, and chairs being pushed backwards). It is precisely this ability to provoke a tangible reaction on the part of viewers that gives the film's critique of the dehumanizing power of structural socioeconomic inequalities its force and persuasiveness. In encouraging/forcing audience members to recognize the violence of neocolonialism in ways that are deeply felt, the film naturalizes its critique; viewers understand their own response as authentic, true, and profound.

While many of the urban scenes in *La hora* stress the mechanization and animalization of the working classes who have been directly victimized by the neocolonial system, those that take place in rural areas (or in the outskirts of the capital) aim to humanize those who are peripheral to that system by establishing a more contemplative rhythm that encourages the spectator to take the time to ponder what is often ignored. Instead of rapid dolly shots and dizzying montage sequences, there are slow-moving, high-angle tracks past barefoot children sitting in a row on the ground and eating bowls of stew handed out at a communal kitchen. The high-angle shots effectively accentuate the children's vulnerability. In another sequence, leisurely traveling shots tour the unfinished house of a young prostitute in Villa Sapito in the southern working-class district of Avellaneda; the shots meander past school-age boys who stand in line in the living room waiting for her "services" as the young girl eats her lunch on the bed in the adjoining room. In pausing over the image of impoverished youth, both of these scenes solicit the viewer's sympathies by playing to common humanist beliefs about the innocence of childhood—a tactic that Solanas would use again thirty years later in *Memoria del saqueo* and *La dignidad de los pobres*.

The effort to underscore the dignity of the poor becomes explicit in the eighth section entitled "El neoracisimo" / "Neoracism." As the narrators comment on the phrases (like "chusma" and "cabecita negra") frequently invoked to name the marginalized, the image track presents numerous shots of common folk, often in close-ups that stress their individuality. A short while later, the camera slowly tracks past members of an indigenous family at work and with their children as the voice of the elder Don Ambrosio speaks about their poor treatment at the hands of *criollos* (i.e., lighter-skinned Argentines of European descent). In the next image, a medium shot fixes on Don Ambrosio, his wife, son, and grandchildren as he criticizes the *criollos* for devaluing indigenous people, asking "Are we [not] of the same blood?" While these sequences may not have the visceral charge of the earlier scenes, they perform a necessary function, encouraging the spectator to acknowledge the common humanity shared with those depicted, whose faces may look different, but whose direct gazes demand recognition.

Such scenes, which bring into relief the lived experiences of suffering people and draw out the particularities of human existence under extreme conditions, serve as a necessary compliment to the voice-over narration that comments on overarching, structural issues in quite abstract terms. In sum, the emotional power of the sequences enumerated "enables" the analytical argument of the voice-overs to seem not only reasonable, but also to be persuasive. In attacking the passivity of the spectator and making him or her think in new ways, Part I of *La hora de los hornos* encourages the viewer to feel differently, to recognize the "experience" of poverty and suffering in ways that exceed conscious knowledge about an oppressive system.

## Passionate Politics

Rather than eschewing sensorial appeals, the NLAC utilized them tactically in ways that encouraged audiences to feel the urgent need for social, economic, and political change. Earlier works like *Rio 40 Graus* moved the spectator by drawing on an archive of tropes and cultural traditions that associated particular emotional states with moral positions and by aligning him or her with morally superior protagonist(s). At the same time, the films "socialized" emotion; they rechanneled established traditions of sensorial appeal through scalar shifts, moving the spectator's alignment with the individual toward a wider engagement with the social. Later works engaged the sensorial in more radical ways. In the case of *El chacal de Nahueltoro*, the filmmakers carefully deployed emotional appeals in ways that ultimately unsettled their mooring to particular meanings and, in the process, encouraged spectators to make sense of Chilean society in new ways. For its part, *La hora de los hornos* (Part 1)'s audiovisual assault on neocolonialist structures via relentless rhythmic modulations called for(th) a rawer visceral response on the part of the spectator. While relying on authoritative voice-overs and the stock figure of the suffering child to rein in and direct the revolutionary sensibilities it sought to provoke, the film's sensorial charge often exceeds its intention to move spectators toward a particular form of political praxis. By stirring up feelings that were not entirely containable, films like *El chacal* and *La hora* registered the jolt of the modern as experienced in the aftermath of mid-twentieth-century modernization efforts. It was not the shock of the early 1900s as described by Benjamin: the clashes between older social forms and new life rhythms were not as stark. Instead, the films convey the disturbances of a national(ist) imaginary under pressure from an ever-more urbanized, media-ted consumer culture.

Hopefully, this discussion of the sensorial aspects of the NLAC and its relation to larger sociohistorical dynamics invites us to rethink standard film histories. Instead of breaking down the history of Latin American cinema into successive historical periods separated by watershed moments of aesthetic and/or industrial rupture, we might trace multilayered genealogies in which aesthetic and/or industrial tendencies branch out and converge. Such a paradigm would better account for the ways in which the NLAC broke with many of the formal tendencies of the "old" Latin American (and classic Hollywood cinema) while retaining others (e.g., the sentimental appeal) to re-use in new ways. This historiographical model also would allow us to acknowledge how the aesthetics of the militant films from the 1960s and 1970s anticipated the visceral aesthetics of more recent films from the 1990s and 2000s.[69]

Of course, there are dangers with establishing facile equivalencies—for example, suggesting that contemporary films are "just as" political as those of the NLAC. Yet, a shift toward a more genealogical paradigm of film history might help us break old habits of analysis. Among other things, we might heed literary critic Isobel Armstrong who has warned against established critical practices that worry about "giving in" to the text's emotional appeals or that bracket off the "constitutive nature of affect" in aesthetic practices by characterizing them as resistant to analysis.[70] As she notes in her book *The Radical Aesthetic* (2000) and I will be arguing throughout this book, we want "to reconnect emotion and reason, and to affirm the epistemic status of emotion and knowledge; [and] reclaim the social function of emotion."[71] By holding steadfastly to an established historiography that separates out the NLAC as an entirely new type of cinema, we run the risk of overlooking the patriarchal underpinnings of this critical paradigm and diagnosing contemporary Latin American cinema's emotional appeals and affective dynamics as symptoms of a dominant filmic conservativism tout court. As discussed in subsequent chapters, the sensorial charge of recent films serves a variety of functions, from addressing unresolved traumas of military dictatorships to articulating anxieties about the present. Any analysis of their political/politicizing potential must first examine the degree to which certain films invite audiences to feel and experience a different way of knowing.

# CHAPTER 2

# Thrilling Histories: Replaying the Past in Genre Films

As detailed in the introduction, Beatriz Sarlo, Nelly Richard, and other scholars have underscored the connection between contemporary media's unheralded penetration of daily life, the invidious growth of consumer culture, and the waning of historical sensibilities. In countries like Argentina and Chile where the dominant neoliberal politics have consecrated the work of truth commissions as the sole, official means to deal with the dictatorial past, these intellectuals (along with activists and artists) have worried publicly about transmitting the lessons of recent history to a younger generation more concerned about watching old 1970s reruns on retro cable channels or downloading the latest video games. In Brazil, efforts to recall the repressive actions of the military regime (1964–85) have been even more difficult. As noted by Leslie A. Payne, until the 1990s there was an "absence of institutional mechanisms for addressing past human rights violations" and human-rights activists have found it difficult to "devise creative methods of overcoming security-force and societal silence."[1] While Payne argues that the Brazilian media has not sensationalized the past, film scholar Luiz Zanin Oricchio suggests that the rise of an individualistic (vs. collective) and generally depoliticized ethos in the 1990s made it difficult to make films about power dynamics and to discuss the years of dictatorship in substantive ways.[2] The critique offered by Oricchio (and others like Sarlo and Richard) clearly resonate with the concerns expressed by scholars like Frederic Jameson about the loss of an in-depth understanding of the past in a postmodern era plagued by an unceasing barrage of new visual images.

What then are we to make of the proliferation of fiction films since the early 1990s from many different Latin American countries dealing with the troubling years between the late 1950s and the 1980s? Many are historical films set in the immediate past—for example, *Rojo amanecer / Red Dawn* (Mexico, Jorge Fons, 1989), *Un año perdido / A Lost Year* (Mexico, Gerardo Lara, 1992), *Fresa y chocolate / Strawberry and Chocolate* (Cuba-Mexico-Spain, Tomás Gutiérrez Alea and Juan Carlos Tabío, 1993), *Tango feroz: la leyenda de Tanguito / Tanguito* (Argentina-Spain, Marcelo Piñeyro, 1993), *Lamarca* (Brazil, Sergio Rezende, 1994), *O Que É Isso, Companheiro? / Four Days in September* (Brazil-United States, Bruno Barreto, 1997), *Garage Olimpo* (Italy-Argentina-France, Marco Bechis, 1999), *¿De qué lado estás? / Francisca* (Germany-Spain-México, 2002, Eva López Sánchez), *Kamchatka* (Argentina-Spain, Marcelo Piñeyro, 2002), *Cidade de Deus / City of God* (Brazil-France-United States, Fernando Mereilles, 2003), *Diarios de motocicleta Motorcycle Diaries* (United States-Germany-UK-Argentina-Chile-Perú-France, Walter Salles, 2004), *Machuca* (Chile-Spain-UK-France, Andrés Wood, 2004), *Crónica de una fuga / Chronicle of an Escape* (Argentina, Adrián Caetano, 2006), and *O Ano em Que Meus Pais Saíram de Férias / The Year My Parents Went on Vacation* (Brazil, Cáo Hamburger, 2006). Other films take place in the present and invoke the past through flashbacks or narrative references. These include *El Bulto / Excess Baggage* (Mexico, Gabriel Retes, 1990), *Alma Corsaria / Buccaneer Soul* (Brazil, Carlos Reichenbach, 1993), *Johnny Cien Pesos* (Chile-Mexico-United States, Gustavo Graef Marino, 1993), *Madagascar* (Cuba, Fernando Pérez, 1994), *En el aire / On the Air* (Mexico, Juan Carlos de Llaca, 1994), *Buenos Aires vice versa* (Argentina-Netherlands, Alejandro Agresti, 1996), *Ação Entre Amigos / Friendly Fire* (Brazil, Beto Brant, 1998), *Dois Córregos* (Brazil, Carlos Reichenbach, 1999), *Amores perros* (Mexico, Alejandro González Iñárruti, 2000), *Cautiva / The Captive* (Argentina, Gaston Biraben, 2003), and *Paisito / Small Country* (Uruguay, Spain-Argentina, Ana Díez, 2008). Despite their many differences, these films address similar issues, including the nature of state-sponsored violence, the personal costs of political militancy, the importance of personal tranformation or self-realization, and the historical roots of contemporary poverty and crime.

The commercial success of many of these films suggests that they somehow resonate with present-day concerns about the lingering effects of the troubling past.[3] At the same time, in order to appeal to the widest possible audience, many of these films gloss over the complexities of prior decades. This is particularly true of coproductions directed at multiple national markets, which often minimize specific referential markers that might confuse audiences located "elsewhere." For example, Brazilian director Walter

Salles's film *Diarios de motocicleta* (United States-Germany-UK-Argentina-Chile-Perú-France, 2004) about Ché Guevara (starring Mexican heartthrob Gael García Bernal) fails to identify the presidency of Juan Perón in the initial sequences set in 1952 when Ernesto and Alberto decide to leave Buenos Aires and, later on, makes no mention of the alliance between the tin oligarchy and the government in Bolivia that led to the state's repression of the miners, whose situation so impressed the cinematic Ernesto. In a similar way, the political and economic frameworks that became the basis of Ché Guevara's rejection of capitalism are largely ignored in favor of his personal maturation.

The lack of specificity of these films is due, in part, to the fact that many are genre films and thus follow particular formal conventions.[4] Whereas *Diarios de motocicleta* utilizes the trappings of the road film to tell the tale of Ernesto (Ché) Guevara's "early years,"[5] Jorge Fons's *Rojo amanecer* and Eva López Sánchez's *¿De qué lado estás?* deploy the conventions of the melodrama. Marcelo Piñeyro's *Kamchatka,* Andrés Wood's *Machuca,* Cao Hamburger's *O Ano em Que Meus Pais Saíram de Férias,* and Ana Díez's *Paisito* are all bildungsroman, chronicling the conflicts of the 1960s and 1970s through the eyes of a child. Meanwhile, Gustavo Graef Marino's *Johnny Cien Peso,* Beto Brant's *Acão Entre Amigos,* and Bruno Barreto's *O Que É Isso, Companheiro?* are thrillers.[6] In their deployment of generic conventions, these films might be accused of presenting the past as a twice-told tale, an already understandable object, in a gesture that wipes away historical specificities in favor of plot and character development. As genre films playing with the expectations of their audience, such films cast the past into the narrative dye-work of the already knowable. Set within the parameters of the road film, Ernesto's journey in *Diarios de motocicleta* becomes a story of the protagonist's personal evolution through his encounter with a series of Others. In *Kamchatka*'s coming-of-age tale, Harry will lose his innocence but gain an understanding that life is unfair.

The formulaic structure of such genre films as well as their conventional realism invite comparisons with the disruptive aesthetics of the New Latin American Cinema (NLAC) that engaged the past in highly reflexive ways in films such as *Ganga Zumba* (Brazil, Carlos Diegues, 1963), *La primera carga al machete / The First Charge of the Machete* (Cuba, Manuel Octavio Gómez, 1968), and *El otro Francisco / The Other Francisco* (Cuba, Sergio Giral, 1974). Whether by exploring unexamined topics (e.g., the experience of enslaved Africans in the eighteenth and nineteenth centuries) or employing innovative formal devices (e.g., mixing documentary with fiction; disrupting chronological order), the NLAC challenged official histories as well as historiographical conventions. For example, *La primera carga*'s anachronistic inclusion of a documentary news crew filming the 1868 uprising led by General Máximo Gómez made the rebellion against the Spanish come alive for contemporary Cuban audiences. Accustomed to the innovative format of the documentaries dominating local production in the 1960s, postrevolutionary spectators were encouraged to see parallels between the nineteenth-century rebellion and the 1959 revolution. Films like *La primera carga* problematized the spectator's knowledge of history and encouraged a reconsideration of its relationship to the present.[7] In sum, they answered Walter Benjamin's call to "go forward looking back" or to shift through the shards of the past in order to find in those fragments, in those truncated possibilities, a means to uncover the potentialities of the present day.

As discussed in the previous chapter, this formal experimentation promising a cognitive jump forward in the spectator—in this case, toward a radical historical consciousness through the rupture of realist transparency—did not necessarily eschew the utilization of emotional appeals. In terms of the NLAC's historical films, one might point to the sensorial dynamics of Giral's *El otro Francisco,* a radical reworking of Anselmo Suárez y Romero's 1938 antislavery novel *Francisco.* As a film that thoroughly interrogates the novel's melodramatic underpinnings in an effort to discredit reformist (in this case, abolitionist) platforms and to bolster revolutionary projects, Giral's work nonetheless ends in a highly sensationalist manner with shots of slaves being dismembered and killed in the aftermath of a slave rebellion—including a slow track-in to a man hanging by a hook through his heart.[8]

There is a prevailing tendency among film scholars to draw a distinction between the politicizing potential of such shock tactics (designed to roust the spectator into political action) and the apolitical (if not depoliticizing) effects of genre films' emotional appeals. This is particularly true of the melodrama and the thriller, which are perhaps better understood as narrative modes given the primacy of their affective address and their relative lack of set semantic features (i.e., types of characters; specific settings) when compared to the Western or the horror film.[9] If the work of critics like Linda Williams, Christine Gledhill, Ana López, and numerous others have problematized traditional understandings of melodrama to underscore its potential for sociopolitical critique, studies of the thriller still tend to emphasize its function as mindless entertainment. In his 1999 book on this "metagenre," Martin Rubin argued that the thriller is defined by "visceral, gut-level feelings" that exceed the needs of the narrative and contrast sharply with the "more sensitive, cerebral or emotionally heavy feelings, such as tragedy, pathos, pity, love, nostalgia." In his words, "the thriller stresses *sensations* more than sensitivity."[10] Although he does not directly comment on the thriller's relationship to politics as does Guy Hennebelle, Rubin emphasizes its inability to transform the thoughts and feelings of spectators.[11] This critique of the thriller's lack of cognitive engagements is similar to the one offered by Frederic Jameson in his book *The Geopolitical Aesthetic* (1992). Underscoring the limitations of a subgroup of "guerrilla-war correspondent films" like *Under Fire* (United States, Roger Spottiswoode, 1983) and *Salvador* (United States, Oliver Stone, 1986), Jameson contends that such works use the "emotional securities of individualizing narrative paradigms" as a fall-back strategy given the "ideological incapacity of North Americans to imagine collective processes" and their "structural incapacity... to construct a narrative that can map totality."[12]

As valid as such critiques about the potential limitations of the genre film may be, they betray a nostalgia for alternative forms of political engagement and modernist aesthetics reminiscent of Latin Americanist film scholars who hold onto the NLAC as the gold standard. Likewise, Jameson, Rosenstone, and others also have a propensity to discover such practices in what was (is still?) understood as the Second and Third World. Whereas Jameson finds a "geopolitical unconscious" outside Hollywood in what he calls Soviet magic realism and Filipino "art naïf," film scholars and historians interested in the representation of the past limit their treatment of "non-Western" works to films like Ousmane Sembene's *Ceddo* (Senegal, 1977), Glauber Rocha's *Deus e o diabo na terra do sol / Black God/White Devil* (Brazil, 1964), and Carlos Diegues's *Quilombo* (Brazil, 1984) that conform to the dictates of Third Cinema and canonize this "other" cinema as uniquely situated to question Western historiographical practice.[13]

In an effort to problematize some of these critical tendencies, this essay will examine three mainstream political thrillers that, although they adhere in varying degrees to genre conventions, probe the Latin American past in fresh ways: Bruno Barreto's *O Que É Isso, Companheiro?* (1997), Beto Brant's *Ação Entre Amigos* (1998), and Roman Polanski's *Death and the Maiden* (United States-UK-France, 1994).[14] These thrillers function as affectively engaged interrogations that encourage us to reconsider our knowledge about the dictatorial past in Brazil (1964–85) and Chile (1973–90), and its relationship to the present. The films' deliberate evocation of unsettling emotions sharply contrasts with the soporific inducements held out by the civil administrations in both countries that were shepherding the transition from dictatorship to democracy. As argued by Nelly Richard in relation to post-dictatorial Chile, the rush to produce consensus after the so-called return to democracy has "rationalized" politics.[15] Addressing the crimes committed by the military government was reduced to a legal investigation, subject to the rules and regulations of court systems that had proved entirely bankrupt under the dictatorships that ruled the Southern Cone during the 1970s and 1980s. According to Payne, the Brazilian military's control over the transition and its ability to discipline its members to remain silent about prior human-rights violations had the effect of dampening public discussion of the recent past. Efforts to either account for the "excesses" of the past through the rationalistic methods of truth commissions and the circumscribed realm of jurisprudence (as in Chile) or to simply sweep them under the carpet (as in Brazil) had numerous consequences. Principle among them was truncating highly charged public debates about what constitutes a "satisfactory" understanding of that past. Such delimitations might have been understandable during the initial years of redemocratization given fears about the return of the military, and perhaps remain so to a certain degree, given the immense difficulty of addressing thorny questions like the nature of complicity, the limits of responsibility, and the place of public remembering. And, yet, well into the 1990s, there was an ongoing sense of incommensurability between past and present that the reigning logic of neoliberalism merely exacerbated.

In this postdictatorial context of "rationalized" politics and tightly constrained public discussion about the trauma of dictatorship, thrillers offered an alternative way to address the past's sensorially dense hold on the present. Indeed, the popularity of these films might be attributable, at least in part, to the way they provide an outlet for the affective charge of memory and reckoning. As with all thrillers, *O Que É Isso, Companheiro?*, *Ação Entre Amigos*, and *Death and the Maiden* are built around questions of knowledge and time in ways that involve both the characters and the spectators. In creating a sense of epistemic urgency and cultivating the desire to know in a timely fashion, the thriller offers a generic apparatus particularly suited for queries about a past that troubles the present. However, only some of the films within this genre generate a sufficient degree of epistemological uncertainty to allow for more radical interrogations of the past. As developed more fully in the next sections, it is this quality that distinguishes *Acão Entre Amigos* and *Death and the Maiden* from *O Que É Isso, Companheiro?* Although Barreto's film encourages viewers to reconsider the past and, in particular, to find out more about the kidnapping of U.S. Ambassador Charles Burke Elbrick in 1969 by a revolutionary cell of MR-8, the text stays within the bounds of historical revisionism. It offers new perspectives on this event, and thus questions what many know about guerrilla movements and military repression, but never disturbs our sense of how we know about the past or of what the past means for the present. *Death and the Maiden* and *Acão Entre Amigos*, on the other hand, work on a metaphorical level wherein the desire to find out what will happen to particular characters grafts easily into an inquiry into larger questions about society. As stories centered

around characters who were tortured during dictatorships (and their obsession with their former torturers), these two films attend to epistemic possibilities of the sensorium and acknowledge a sense for the past that exceeds
the merely rational. In the process, the films encourage us to consider what
it means to come to terms with the past and where to draw the line between
punishment and vengeance.

### Knowing Suspense

Of the three films under discussion, *O Que É Isso, Companheiro?* most
closely adheres to the mechanisms of filmic suspense. According to Noel
Carroll, one of the few scholars to theorize at any length on the subject, suspense films are "organized virtually in their entirety around resolving certain dominant, suspenseful questions" and are characterized by their focus
on probabilities. He argues that such films invest the spectator with the
desire for an improbable outcome through moral appeal—that is, through
the depiction of a morally differentiated world in which virtuous characters
are unlikely to achieve their goals.[16] Yet, equally important for the spectator's emotional involvement in the events depicted on screen are the films'
narrational strategies—specifically their distribution of story information in
such a way that the spectator's knowledge exceeds that of individual characters at key junctures. In other words, in suspense films, the spectator's
heightened preoccupation with what will happen is predicated on already
knowing more than the characters themselves. In sum, our emotional state
is keyed to the issue of knowledge—to who knows what and when.

It is this latter issue of the distribution of knowledge that is vital in order
to understand the workings of *O Que É Isso, Companheiro?* as a suspense
film, a narrative mode often defined by its evocation of "future-oriented
emotion" about what is unknown.[17] After all, Barreto's film is based on a
well-known episode of recent Brazilian history and, more specifically, upon
the testimonial account of one of the participants in the guerrilla action:
Fernando Gabeira, a former political militant, journalist, and congressman whose 1979 book of the same name became a best seller in Brazil.[18]
The film's historical referents defy Carroll's description of suspense as a
"future-oriented emotion" or a "posture that we typically adopt [in relation]
to what will happen, not to what has happened." Yet, despite the fact that
many audience members would have *already known* the outcome (Elbrick's
release, the eventual capture of the MR-8 cell, the military's continued hold
over Brazil until 1985, and the defeat of leftist guerrilla movements in the
region), the film was a commercial success in Brazil and, to a certain degree,
in the United States. This familiarity was not an impediment to the film's

appeal, but rather useful to its historiographical project. The armature of the suspense film allowed even historically informed audience members to reckon with the past in a way that confirmed their knowledge of the present, as if to say, "If we had only known then what we do now..."[19]

Indeed, the issue of circumscribed knowledge is central to the film's setting in 1969, immediately after the 1968 "coup within a coup" wherein a hard-right faction of the military took over the junta that had ruled Brazil since 1964 and declared Institutional Act #5 allowing for the circumscription of political activities and censorship of the media. In the film, this suppression of Brazilians' rights becomes the impetus behind Fernando's decision to leave behind the student opposition movement and join a clandestine guerrilla group like MR-8 under the pseudonym of Paulo. As he tells two of his friends, by preventing any news about the opposition from reaching the wider Brazilian public, the censorship laws have effectively blocked nonviolent means to protest the dictatorship and this warranted more radical social change.[20] The guerrillas' secretive tactics (e.g., their use of nom de guerre and cellular organization) offer an ironic corollary to state censorship by restricting the government's knowledge of their movement. As one of the military intelligence officers tells his wife in an attempt to justify his torture of captured militants, such brutality is the only means to overcome the militants' tactics and extract needed information. Thus, rather than highlighting the different socioeconomic philosophies and political projects that separated the guerrillas and the state, *O Que É Isso, Companheiro?* portrays the conflict that ripped apart Brazilian society as a struggle over knowledge.

Through its juxtaposition of the perspectives of different groups (the guerrillas, the ambassador, and the military), the film situates itself as an attempt to redress the earlier acts of epistemic repression and to present a fuller, "balanced" account of the period. Although it includes the perspectives of two members of military intelligence, Barreto's film anchors the plot to the words and actions of Fernando/Paulo and the other members of MR-8 (particularly Rene, Maria, and Oswaldo). Their depiction as well-meaning youth, whose commitment to protesting the repressive military government demands personal sacrifice, encourages the spectator to sympathize with their efforts.[21] Equally compelling, particularly in the second half of the film, are the words and actions of Ambassador Elbrick (Alan Arkin), who is portrayed as a dignified and deeply intelligent man. Yet, despite its oscillation between the different perspectives of these characters, the film's narrational strategies ultimately privilege Elbrick's point of view as uniquely situated, like that of the spectator, to comprehend what is happening and what is to come.

The plot splits the central interrogative (will the plan to kidnap Elbrick be successful?) into a series of smaller uncertainties:

- Before the kidnapping, will Rene gain the confidence of the security guard and acquire the necessary information about the ambassador's habits?
- On the day of the kidnapping, will they be able to get away before a neighbor convinces the police that something is wrong?
- After the kidnapping, will the government concede to their demands for the release of political prisoners within four days, or will the police find their whereabouts in a timely fashion and stop them before the deadline?

In some of these plot segments, the spectator's knowledge is limited. For example, our knowledge of the security guard and his duties are limited to what he tells Rene, whom he believes to be a young woman from the countryside looking for work. Much later, as the guerrillas get ready to release Elbrick, we don't know if the pursuing officers will apprehend them or not; indeed, we are as surprised as the characters themselves when the officers' superior cuts off their car to prevent their pursuit from injuring Elbrick. These scenes produce a relatively contained sense of anxiety that encourages the spectator to identify with the tensions experienced by the guerrillas.

Other sequences generate a greater level of suspense by providing the spectator with a more privileged vantage. For example, the scene of the kidnapping crosscuts between shots of the guerrillas on the street waiting for Elbrick's limousine, and others of a neighbor woman calling the police about their suspicious behavior. This unrestricted narration invests the spectator with a heightened sense of urgency about whether or not Rene, Maria, and the others will be able to pull off the kidnapping before the woman convinces the police to check out what is happening.[22] The spectator's superior understanding of the unfolding events becomes even greater after the kidnapping as the film begins to juxtapose sequences at the guerrilla's hideout with those of the military intelligence officers who are searching for them. Will the torture of Oswaldo, an MR-8 member caught in an earlier action who knows Fernando's true identity, help the police in their search? Will a grocer and his deliveryman who sold food to the guerrillas lead the police to the hideout? And, after the release of Elbrick, will the newspapers that Maria left behind in the old hideout allow the police to locate their new ones?

This alternation between restricted and unrestricted narration has an interesting effect on the spectator's understanding of history. In many ways, the film's narration cultivates the spectator's sympathies for Fernando and his fellow militants. We want them to pull off the kidnapping and we hope the police will not capture them "in time." In this way, Barreto's revisionist history crafts an affective reckoning by encouraging viewers to sympathize with the guerrillas whose perspective had been repressed during the dictatorship and afterward. At the same time, the unrestricted narration of particular scenes also truncates that sense of emotional identification by highlighting the guerrillas' limited understanding of unfolding events –in comparison to the uniquely transhistorical perspective of Ambassador Elbrick.

The film turns to the motif of blindness to draw out this difference. Unlike his kidnappers, Elbrick's sight is severely limited after his capture. He is taken to a single room where he remains throughout the four days of his abduction. In order to hide their identities, the members of MR-8 either wear hoods in his presence or force him to put on reinforced sunglasses that block his sight. Despite these visual limitations, the ambassador proves to be uncannily perceptive, able to see what others cannot about the present and the future.

On the second day of his kidnapping, Elbrick is told to write a letter to his wife to prove that he is alive. The exercise becomes a means for a series of imagined communications in which he tells her about his experiences during captivity in voice-over. His observations about each of his hooded captors, whose character he divines solely based on the hands that they place before him, reveal his capacity for insight. Elbrick easily distinguishes between the skinny hands of the youthful Julio whose childlike political sensibilities lead him to give Elbrick a copy of Ho Chi Minh while Julio himself reads dime-store fiction about rough-and-tumble outlaws; the "farmer's hands" of the murderous and authoritarian Jonas who has threatened to kill Elbrick and who the ambassador sees as "the product of a Cold War" that the guerrilla doesn't understand; and the "delicate hands" of René, a middle-class youth interested in fashion and music who treats Elbrick kindly despite what the ambassador sees as her misguided commitment to revolutionary ideals. Verified by what the spectator has witnessed in earlier scenes, the accuracy of Elbrick's depictions is startling and helps portray him as uniquely able to detangle the contemporary contradictions that others cannot.[23]

In other scenes, the film goes further to suggest Elbrick's prescient capacity to place current events in their "proper" historical perspective. When asked about U.S. support for the Brazilian dictatorship during an interrogation by his kidnappers, Elbrick tells them that, in his personal opinion, the United States should only support democratically elected governments, as military administrations "only create short-term stability and then generate hatred." His comments demonstrate his ability to foresee the eventual downfall of the military government in the mid-1980s from the perspective of 1969, a time at which the dictatorship appeared particularly powerful. This transhistorical sensibility encourages the spectator to identify with Elbrick. This is true even in the case of U.S. spectators with limited knowledge of modern Brazilian history as the film establishes clear parallels between what was happening in that country and what was happening in the United States in the late 1960s. Elbrick's comments about the ill-conceived nature of U.S. military involvement in Vietnam, coming as they do a day after his captors hear a radio broadcast about President Nixon sending more troops into the conflict, are further proof of his foresight. Even Fernando, who is depicted as a particularly bright and articulate young man, fails to see the present or envision the future any more clearly than his fellow militants (until the very end of the film). Caught up in the rhetoric of radical socioeconomic change, Fernando tells Elbrick that the Black Panthers are harbingers of revolution on U.S. soil—a declaration that the ambassador strongly, if kindly, dismisses as a gross misunderstanding of U.S. culture. It is Elbrick's ability to see beyond the immediate historical moment (and beyond national borders) that defines his privileged viewpoint and aligns it with the perspective of contemporary spectators sitting in theaters in the mid-1990s.

In its tendency to re-present the past in light of contemporary perspectives, Barreto's *O Que É Isso, Companheiro?* functions as a work of historical revisionism. Its underlying humanism and its interest in giving voice to a variety of perspectives (the guerrillas, the ambassador, and even the military intelligence officers who torture prisoners) allow for a liberal reconsideration of the past in a way that is particularly inviting even for U.S. audiences entrenched (even before 9/11) in facile moralizing about armed revolutionary militancy and the benevolent nature of U.S. foreign policy. Appealing to the larger U.S. market would have been a central concern for the Brazilian-U.S. coproduction and clearly influenced its reworking of Gabeira's testimonial. As noted by Ellen Spielmann, the film circulated quite widely in the United States, despite the government's insistence that Fernando Gabeira himself never set foot in the country. Without ignoring the film's problematic portrayal of the events (particularly its celebration of Ambassador Elbrick and its minimizing of U.S. involvement in human-rights violations), Spielmann argues that Barreto's work has served an important politicizing function by opening up a discussion about an era otherwise forgotten by the U.S. public.[24] Moreover, as it encourages spectators to sympathize with the members of MR-8, the film also disturbs simplistic characterizations of such militant groups, in a post-9/11 era, as the crazed Other.

Yet, the film's affective work does very little to problematize traditional historiographical certainties. In offering the audience a greater knowledge of unfolding events, the film ultimately channels his or her responses to the traumatic years of the dictatorship into recognizable emotions that affectively manage that past. The short-sightedness of the MR-8 becomes a matter of pity as in the film's final scenes. Now in hiding after Elbrick's release, an isolated and exhausted Maria tells the visiting Fernando about Gilberto Gil's new album, which, apparently, if played backward, shouts out the name "Marighella" (the name of a revolutionary leader), something she interprets as a sign of defiance and solidarity. Having just shown us that military intelligence has picked up their trail, the film casts her words as a desperate attempt to continue believing that resistance to the dictatorship is possible in the face of certain entrapment. The spectator's wider knowledge of what is to come (for the characters in the film and/or the resistance movement in Brazil) casts Maria's current hopes and previous actions as pointless and futile exercises. The very last sequence in which her wheelchair is pushed onto the tarmac where other liberated political prisoners, including Fernando, await deportation is moving, but its affective charge is not transformative. The pity evoked for the crippled Maria, the similarly tortured Fernando, and the sufferings of the other political prisoners does not disturb our certainty about what occurred or our understanding of what those past events mean for the present. The subsequent kidnappings of other diplomats did not lead to a true, more wide-ranging liberation of "the people." As the explanatory intertitles note at the end of the film, the reestablishment of democracy was a gradual process and direct elections did not take place until 1989, twenty years after Elbrick's kidnapping. For all its shortcomings, the contemporary moment is characterized as a more enlightened time when the cycle of violent combat between the military and guerrilla groups has ended.

## Making Sense of the Past

Unlike *O Que É Isso, Companheiro?*, *Death and the Maiden* (1994) and *Ação Entre Amigos* (1998) are interested less in what we know and when we know it, than in how we know what we know and what should be done with that knowledge. Both films elaborate linkages between thought and feeling in ways that problematize standard epistemologies and question the nature of evidence in historical inquiry. Instead of channeling the spectator's affective responses into identifiable emotions like sympathy and pity, the two films open up the disruptive possibilities of errant affects.

As a Brazilian thriller dealing with the legacies of the dictatorship, Beto Brant's *Ação Entre Amigos* (1998) offers a useful counterpoint to Barreto's *O Que É Isso, Companheiro?*, released one year earlier. Full of edgy camerawork, flashy edits, and a hip soundtrack, *Ação* employs music video aesthetics common to Brant's generation of filmmakers. While apparently a more trendy engagement with the past than Barreto's film, *Ação*'s formal manuevers render the affectively charged nature of interrogations into the traumatic past.

The plot is set in 1996 and is structured around a fishing trip taken by 40-something friends Miguel, Oswaldo, Paulo, and Eloi, who twenty-five years earlier had been political militants during the dictatorship. Unbeknownst to the other three, Miguel is using the trip to go after Atilio Correia, the man who had tortured them in prison after a failed attempt to rob a bank in 1971 and who Miguel believes he spotted in a small town when working as a consultant on a political campaign. Although Miguel's friends initially resist his proposal to find and confront Correia, the film highlights the difficulty of suturing the wounds of the past. From the opening frames, the film underscores the way in which the past remains present by repeatedly crosscutting between scenes of the present and scenes of the past. Brant's frequent recourse to black-and-white negative images, rotating overhead shots, and other distorting visuals to represent the bank robbery and torture of Oswaldo and Miguel register the nightmarish quality of their unsettling memories and the way in which such memories continue to inform the characters' subjectivity.

Like *Death and the Maiden*, *Ação* aims to make sense of that which exceeds the merely rational and, in so doing, questions the nature of evidence as well as the difference between justice and vengeance. The first part of the film deals with the former as Miguel tries to convince the others that he has indeed found Correia. His three friends initially discount the photographs he shows them, as they do not recognize Correia in the fuzzy enlargements. They also remain highly skeptical of the fact that the body of Correia's widow was recently disinterred from a cemetery in São Paulo and moved to one in the small town that they are visiting. They scoff at the insufficiency of Miguel's "evidence" and remind him of the widely circulated, published reports of Correia's death. In response, Miguel questions their belief in the reliability of press reports, given the military's control over the media during the dictatorship and the possibility that they could easily have planted such a story. In these and other scenes, *Ação*'s narration remains tightly restricted to the perspectives of its protagonists and, unlike *O Que É Isso, Companheiro?*, fails to provide the spectator with superior knowledge. Thus, the film unsettles epistemic certainty about the past by calling into question the nature of historical evidence.

Despite Manuel's lack of objectivity and his obvious obsession with the death of Lucia, a fellow militant, who was carrying Miguel's child at the time she was captured by Correia and his men, the film initially validates Miguel's investigatory method. When the four men eventually identify Correia at a cockfight they attend, the film never questions the legitimacy of their recognition. Instead of providing some other, more "objective" means of proof, the film strengthens the validity of their visual and visceral identification by demonstrating, through a series of tightly framed reaction shots and eyeline matches, how the shocked response of each mirrors and, thus corroborates, that of the others. This exchange between the three more skeptical friends functions as an unwitting parody of the historiographic imperative to triangulate—that is, to use at least three different sources to verify the validity of any interpretation and to demonstrate the historian's "proper" distance from his or her object of study. In *Ação,* there is little recourse to a more objective, disinterested, or omniscient position from which to evaluate the merit of the evidence. Indeed, the sequence highlights the highly subjective response of Oswaldo, the one most plagued by memories of his own torture at the hands of the military. Crosscutting between close-up, fish-eye shots of Oswaldo walking away from the cockfight, out-of-focus eyeline matches of the bar, and flashbacks of his torture using negative stock, the sequence underscores the sensorial impact of Oswaldo's recognition of Correia. In its very lack of thoughtfulness and calculation, Oswaldo's visceral response serves as "proof" of the accuracy of their identification of Correia—a "fact" that is further corroborated near the end of the film by his confession.

This exploration of the epistemic possibilities of emotionally charged interrogations of the past and the role of personal witnessing eventually leads to questions of accountability and the difference between justice and vengeance. By encouraging the spectator to identify with the four friends, *Ação* underscores the inadequacy of political and institutional remedies to collective social trauma. When Oswaldo reminds Miguel that the government had pardoned Correia as well as former militants like themselves, Miguel cries, "I didn't pardon him." This call for personal vengence "makes sense" to the spectator as a result of the motivated flashbacks that had peppered the film up until that point. Like the four protagonists, the spectator "relives" Miguel's last discussion with Lucia on the night before the robbery (in which she tells him of her pregnancy and her desire to leave the movement); Correia's subsequent torture of Miguel, during which he mocks Lucia's bravery during her torture; and the aftermath of Oswaldo's torture as his naked body is dropped into a filthy cell alongside Paulo. By generating a series of urgent questions and aligning the spectator with the "lived past" of the four men, the film encourages our desire to catch and confront the former torturer and establishes the moral legitimacy of such actions. In sum, *Ação*'s affective work destabilizes attempts to dismiss the "past as past," while the apparatus of the thriller stresses the urgency to redress past wrongs in a timely fashion.

Roman Polanski's *Death and the Maiden* distills many of the concerns of Brant's film into a tighter and more radical challenge to standard historiographical method. It is based on a play by Chilean writer and critic Ariel Dorfman who became an exile after a coup led by General Augusto Pinochet ousted democratically elected President Salvador Allende in 1973. Set in an unnamed country in 1982, two years after the end of a five-year dictatorship, the film abstracts itself from the specifics of Chilean history (where the military remained in power for nearly twenty years) to speak more generally about the legacies of dictatorship in the region.[25]

The attempt to reach beyond the confines of Chile is apparent from the film's opening intertitles ("A country in South America after the fall of the dictatorship...") and the delimitation of its mise-en-scéne to a single, symbolic location: the isolated beach house of Gerardo Escobar and his volatile wife Paulina, two characters whose marriage symbolizes the uneasy alliance between two radically different approaches to the traumatic past. A lawyer who has just been appointed to head the president's committee to investigate human-rights abuses by the dictatorship, Gerardo believes in the rule of law as a bulwark against the excesses of the former regime. As a former political prisoner and torture victim, Paulina is enraged by the limitations placed on the commission (which will investigate only those cases that ended in death) and its lack of prosecutorial power. In the film, their home serves as a site of struggle between personal knowledge and public recognition.

There, on a dark and stormy night, the couple confronts the presence of the past in their lives when Gerardo invites into their home Dr. Roberto Miranda, a gentleman who had stopped to help Gerardo when his car broke down on the side of the road. Upon hearing Miranda talk to her husband from the confines of the bedroom, Paulina believes that she recognizes the doctor as the man who had tortured and raped her during the dictatorship. The plot chronicles her struggle with both Miranda and her husband over what "really" happened back then.

From its opening, *Death and the Maiden* lays the groundwork for an epistemological conundrum (about what is recoverable from the past) that unsettles standard historiographical practice. Central to this effort is an extended interrogation of the efficacy and value of witnessing and the nature of evidence. Like *Ação Entre Amigos*, Polanski's film appropriates the apparatus of the thriller (a genre with which the Polish filmmaker is intimately familiar) not only to foment the spectator's desire for knowledge about the past, but also to acknowledge that making sense of what happened goes beyond the rationalist confines of political rhetoric and judicial logic.[26]

From the opening scenes, the film presents Paulina as a highly unstable and emotionally volatile woman plagued by insomnia and obsessed by the memories of what happened to her at the hands of the military. Her constant agitation and irritability contrast sharply with the calm and measured reasonability of her husband. Although the film privileges Paulina's perspective (particularly in the opening sequences), it never employs the type of subjective camerawork favored by Brant's film to validate her actions. Indeed, her decisions often appear rash and imprudent. Upon hearing Miranda's voice, Paulina shoves some clothes into a suitcase, grabs the gun she has with her, and flees the houses by stealing the doctor's car without ever speaking to her husband or confronting Miranda face to face. Stopping abruptly in the road after her escape, she rifles through the car, where she finds, among other tapes, a cassette of composer Franz Schubert's "Death and the Maiden," the string quartet played again and again by her torturer as he raped her. Believing this to be further proof of Miranda's identity, Paulina pushes his car off a cliff and hikes back to the house to confront him. Finding the doctor asleep on the couch, she ties him up, gags him with her underpants, and begins to interrogate him about what happened to her with a gun pointed at his head until Gerardo awakens and demands that she release Miranda.

Given the film's restricted narration, the spectator remains as skeptical as Gerardo of the validity of Paulina's accusations and, more particularly, the nature of the evidence that she provides: the presence of the Schubert recording in Miranda's car and, more generally, her auditory and olfactory memories of her torturer. The film initially encourages us to dismiss the presence of the tape as circumstantial, as does Gerard. And, in a medium limited to audio and visual registers, her assertion that Miranda smells like her torturer appears similarly unconvincing—highly subjective and unverifiable, either by other characters or by the spectator. The possibility of visual identification is foreclosed. As Gerardo reminds her, she was blindfolded during the torture sessions and never saw the man who tortured her, so how could she possibly identify him? Only her argument about Miranda's use of particular catchphrases favored by her tormentor appears worthy of consideration, but even this possibility lacks probative value.

The film stokes this skepticism about the trustworthiness of Paulina's account of past events through the impromptu trial that she sets up for Miranda. In response to Gerardo's insistent pleas that what happened must be dealt with through the rule of law, Paulina sets up a kangaroo court in which she acts as both chief prosecutor and judge-arbiter. She tells her husband that in order to live Miranda must confess to his crimes against her with sufficient specificity to prove that he is telling the truth. Although Paulina allows Miranda to consult with Gerardo, as his counsel, she dismisses the admissibility of external evidence—most specifically, the doctor's suggestion that they call a hospital in Barcelona, Spain, to corroborate that he had been serving his residency there between 1975 and 1977, the time during which she had been imprisoned.

As noted by Ariel Dorfman and aptly analyzed by critic Francisco Javier Millán, *Death and the Maiden* is taking pointed aim at the limitations of truth commissions and other legalistic investigations of military repression that took place after the dictatorship in Chile and elsewhere.[27] Even as the film highlights Paulina's inability to act as an impartial witness or disinterested judge of past events, the film picks away at the obfuscating possibilities of official investigations of past traumas. From the beginning of the film, Paulina rails at Gerardo for agreeing with the president that the truth commission will only investigate cases that ended in death as such efforts fail to account for the trauma experienced by Paulina and others like her who survived. She also criticizes the commission's strictly informational charge which lacks the prosecutorial capacity to bring charges for the abuses they expect to document. When Paulina reminds Gerardo of what he had once told her, that the military had prepared for the postdictatorial years (presumably by destroying documents and preparing alibis), she calls into question the adequacy of his historiographical method—the careful review of an already tainted evidentiary trail.

The structure of the thriller makes the need to resolve this conundrum urgent, rather than esoteric. Precipitating the rush to put Miranda on trial is a telephone call from the president of the republic who tells Gerardo that there have been death threats against him as head of the commission and that guards have been dispatched to his beach house for security. Suddenly, determining whether or not Miranda is truly the man who tortured Paulina becomes vital for Gerardo as well, who must put an end to the issue within four hours, before the guards reach the beach house. Such narrative conceits become particularly useful in exacerbating the spectator's own desire for resolution without providing a clear means/method to do so. In sum, *Death and the Maiden* utilizes the format of the thriller to whip up both the spectator's epistemic desire and epistemological uncertainty.

This contrary movement facilitates the film's eventual support for the epistemic possibilities of nonvisual senses that are less privileged by standard Western epistemologies. At the end of the film, when Paulina takes Miranda outside to kill him, she proves that her knowledge (based as it is on her auditory and olfactory recall) is superior to Gerardo's (who favors "objective" documentation by third-party sources and visual identification). Disregarding the desperate words of her husband who has called the Barcelona hospital and talked to a woman who confirms Miranda's presence there during the key months under dispute, Paulina pushes the doctor toward the very edge of the cliff. It is there, facing his imminent death, that Miranda finally confesses; not only had he been Paulina's torturer, but he had enjoyed wielding unchecked power over other human beings. The lavish details he includes mark the confession as true, rather than as a perfunctory exercise to save his own life.

This ending distinguishes the radical historiographical critique of *Death and the Maiden* from that of *Ação Entre Amigos*. In Brant's film, Miguel's affectively charged hunt for his tormentor leads him to the right man, but unleashes a level of repressed violence that cannot be controlled and quickly leads to tragedy. In an ambush staged with the help of Paulo and Eloi, he kidnaps Correia and takes him to a wooded hill where Miguel extracts a confession by shooting him in the leg. Taunting the three friends ("It was a war. We won; you lost"), Correia reveals that he was able to capture them on the day of the bank robbery because one of them had betrayed the others. Quickly coming to the conclusion that it must have been Oswaldo (who had arrived late to the bank heist twenty-five years ago), Miguel rushes back to the bus stop where they had left Oswaldo, who had refused to participate in the kidnapping. Despite the frantic efforts of Paulo and Eloi to catch up and stop him, Miguel arrives before them and shoots Oswaldo.

In this final move, the film undermines the possibility that reckoning with the affective legacies of dictatorship can be productive. Rather than leading to the punishment of the guilty, Miguel's obsession has perpetuated a cycle of violence that culminates in the slaughter of those who are innocent. As we find out as Paulo and Eloi rush to stop Miguel, it was Eloi who had betrayed his friends in order to protect his own father, who had been kidnapped by Correia and used to blackmail the son. The final close-up on Eloi's anguished face as he watches the police lead Miguel away from the bloody body of Oswaldo lying on the floor of the bus stop suggests that nothing has been resolved and that the errors of the past can never be redressed.

The voices that play over the final credits echo the words of the protagonists and force us to reconsider what we have previously witnessed in light of what has happened. This ghostly reminder of the past is cut short by the words of Oswaldo, who had responded to Miguel's insistence on finding Correia in this way: "For me, it's over, Miguel. It's over. You got me?" / "Para mim, acabou, Miguel. Acabou. Esta me entendendo?" As the character whose nightmares about his torture are the most vividly portrayed and as the one who most rejected dredging up the past, Oswaldo's unjustified assassination by his friend appears particularly cruel. His final words assume particular weight, underscoring the film's assertion that it is vital to let go of the past and move on, even as the driving rhythm of the final chase sequence and the abrupt ending carry an affective charge that gestures toward the difficulty of doing so.

Unlike *Ação Entre Amigos, Death and the Maiden* insists on the productive possibilities of recognizing the continuities between the past and the present even as the ending of the film makes clear that the traumas of dictatorship will never completely be resolved. In the final scene, a long take tracks back from Paulina and Gerardo as they sit in a theater listening to Schubert's "Death and the Maiden" to follow her gaze as she peers upward toward Dr. Miranda, sitting in the balcony with his wife and two sons. The position of the characters suggests Miranda's continuing power over Paulina and, by extension, the military's continued position of authority during the democratic period.[28] Yet, the sequence shot emphasizes an exchange of glances, a type of mutual recognition that belies a relationship of mere dominance and submission. On the cliff, Miranda had acknowledged his role as a torturer and, in so doing, had ripped away his veneer as a compassionate doctor. As Paulina had told Gerardo, from that point on, the doctor would have to live with the recognition of his own moral failings and sadistic urges. Her gaze at the theater functions as a reminder of his past complicity and threatens his role in the present as a civilized family man. The ending also acknowledges Paulina's ability to "reclaim [her] Schubert" in a contemporary public sphere that has denied her claim to the past. Although she must live an "(en)forced coexistence" with Miranda, Paulina's presence at the concert has denied the dictatorship's continuing powers of repression.[29] As a thriller about personal trauma and the difficulties of social reckoning, *Death and the Maiden* leaves us with a disturbing lack of closure that contests the call for forgetful reconciliation.[30]

## Thrilling Histories

In this examination of the potential of mainstream thrillers to productively interrogate the traumatic past, I have argued that such films' invitations "to feel" facilitate a way of accounting for the past that has been disavowed by other, more rational modes of historical inquiry. Despite this shared concern for the affective weight of history, what these films have to say about the past and its relationship to the present varies and depends, to a great degree, on their willingness to employ the armature of the thriller to question the nature of historical knowledge. The level of their interest in destabilizing how we know what we know about the past can be gleaned from the way each work engages the issue of sight. In *O Que É Isso, Companheiro?*, sight functions as a metaphor for historical understanding. In contrasting the blindness of both the military and the guerrillas with the insights of Ambassador Elbrick, the film relies on the privileged status of vision in Western epistemologies and its association with measured distance and objectivity. In so doing, the film never questions what happened "back then" or its place as a discrete temporal horizon distinct from the present. Moreover, by endowing Elbrick with a transhistorical perspective akin to that of the spectator, Barreto's film secures the present's progressive potential as a place of increased understanding.

Like *O Que É Isso, Companheiro?*, *Ação Entre Amigos* upholds the epistemic primacy of vision, but takes it out of the realm of the metaphor and questions its association with objectivity. The film's recurrent flashbacks encourage us to envision the past in highly subjective ways through the dreams of its protagonists. In the scene at the cockfight, the film underscores the visceral impact of the men's visual recognition of Correia. In sum, even as it points to the importance of letting go of what happened, *Ação* does not imagine the present as a more distanced position from which to comprehend the past as a series of causally linked events. In Brant's film, our understanding of the past is necessarily fragmentary, highly charged, and incomplete.

*Death and the Maiden* offers the most striking challenge to the epistemological tendencies subtending traditional historiography. Of the three films, this is the only one that turns away from sight as a privileged means of knowledge and disturbs our understanding of how we acquire knowledge about the past and what we know about the present. As discussed earlier, Polanski's film ultimately validates the role of other senses in recalling past experiences and makes evident the obfuscating possibilities of other "well-reasoned" inquiries into/about the past. Moreover, by aligning the spectator with the reasonable position of Gerardo throughout the bulk of the narrative, the film implicates the spectator in the unfolding events. Like Gerardo, we are an uneasy participant, rather than an outside observer in the struggle over what happened in the past.[31] The film encourages us to contemplate the continuities between the past and the present and to understand the issue of complicity as something not limited to the years of the dictatorship, but rather imbricated in the way we process the past in the present.

Films like *Ação Entre Amigos* and *Death and the Maiden* do not weaken historical sensibilities (despite the latter's pointed detachment from specific referents), but rather reveal an obsession with history. Speaking of a similar tendency in Germany and the United States, cultural critic Andreas Huyssen and film scholar Vivian Sobchack characterize this insistent attention to the past as a response to the emergence of new technologies that have accelerated life-rhythms and transformed our perception of time. Increased representational immediacy, communicative possibilities, and mobility around the globe have led, they argue, to a desire for "temporal anchoring" as a means of attenuating the unsettling influence of such time-space compression on subjectivity and social life.[32] In ways that clearly differ from the historical films of the NLAC, the contemporary thrillers discussed in this chapter provide what Sobchack has called a "novel form of historical consciousness."[33] Their gripping histories encourage the spectator to experience the vital charge of the past and to question the limitations of what is knowable. To the degree that they implicate the spectator as historical actor of the "then" and the "now" (rather than as a distanced bystander to the spectacles of the past), such films help to fuel debates about the connections between dictatorship and democracy.

This is not to suggest that such films are ideologically or politically radical. Liberal films like *O Que É Isso, Companheiro?*, which position themselves as balanced, fair-minded depictions of the contentious past, contribute to a growing relativism that dismisses the years of dictatorship as the result of "excesses on both sides." As Oricchio notes, the inclusion of the villainous Jonas as a high-level member of MR-8 tempers the film's negative portrayal of the right-wing military government by encouraging audience members to consider what Brazil might have been like had such leftist tyrants taken power.[34] In recasting the collective struggles of the 1960s as tales of personal vengeance, films such as *Ação Entre Amigos* and, to a certain degree, *Death and the Maiden* participate in the contemporary preoccupation with the individual.[35]

And yet, a film's ideological stance (as measured through its narrative strategies and levels of formal experimentation) is not the sole determinant of the sociocultural work it may perform. Nor do a film's sensorial appeals always work to serve or uphold its political propositions. As feminist scholars of melodrama have long noted, the patriarchal moral principles upheld at the end of such films frequently fail to contain the unsettling yearnings whipped up throughout the narrative. In a similar way, the sensorial dynamics deployed in thrillers need to be recognized as semiautonomous from a particular film's conservative politics. If *O Que É Isso, Companheiro?* aims to put the past "to rest" and to bolster an understanding of the present as a more enlightened historical period by channeling the spectator's affective investments in particular characters, *Ação Entre Amigos* and *Death and the Maiden* leave us with no such certainty. Brant's film, in particular, cannot seal off the troubling emotions that its generic framework has unleashed and this affective excess drips over the abrupt ending.

While the thriller genre provided some filmmakers with the formulaic comfort and meditational space necessary for tackling the authoritarian past, other directors treat dictatorial legacies more obliquely, as subtexts in films set in the present. Chapter 3 will examine more aesthetically innovative films whose narratives invoke the 1960s and 1970s to map the influence of those decades on contemporary affective formations. Engaging Raymond Williams on "structures of feeling" and Thomas Elsaesser on filmic modes of address, the chapter attempts a more sustained effort at historically situating collective sensibilities and how the sensorial dynamics of films contribute to such constellations.

# CHAPTER 3

# Affecting Legacies and Contemporary Structures of Feeling

A esthetic innovation and visceral appeal have been considered two signature features of contemporary Latin American cinema—exemplified in the eye-catching color contrasts of *Amores perros / Love's a Bitch* (Mexico, Alejandro González Iñárruti, 2000), the stunning montage of *Cidade de Deus / City of God* (Brazil-France, Fernando Mereilles and Katia Lund, 2002), the riveting camerawork of *Tropa de Elite / Elite Squad* (Brazil-Netherlands-United States, José Padilha, 2007), the disorienting soundtrack of Lucretia Martel's *La ciénaga* (Argentina-France-Spain, 2000) and *Niña Santa* (Argentina-Italy-Netherlands-Spain, 2004), and the haunting mise-en-scéne of Fernando Pérez's *Madagascar* (Cuba, 1994) and *Suite Habana* (Cuba-Spain, 2003). Seemingly designed to absorb the spectator in the profilmic events (and perhaps to encourage him or her to marvel over the filmmakers' artistry), this formal virtuosity has often been seen as the source of the films' commercial success as well as a sign of their depoliticizing effect. The works' thematic preoccupations with intimate relationships and family dynamics appear to serve similar functions, appealing to diverse audiences at home and abroad. By favoring individual experiences in the private realm, the latest wave of films from Latin America turn our attention away from structural issues (e.g., socioeconomic inequalities; the inefficacy of governmental institutions; racial discrimination) and the vital role of collective struggles to redress such problems.

Even a film like José Padilha's *Tropa de Elite* that deals directly with issues like police brutality, political corruption, and systemic poverty does so by recounting the struggles of its main character, military police captain Beto

Nascimento, to detach himself from the elite squad that he leads. In chronicling his search to find a successor among new recruits, his voice-over serves as a narrative filter, telescoping down from the structural to the particular. For its part, the jittery camera conveys both Nascimento's sense that he is losing control over his life and, in other moments, the fear and confusion of the young police recruits as the requisites of imposing order erode their their innocence. More generally, the film's formal choices work to convey the personal costs and subjective experiences of law enforcement officials facing urban violence on a daily basis. By the end, as Nascimento finds his replacement, the film has encouraged the audience to question facile moralizing about society's ills, most notably, assertions that policemen are all good (or all bad) and that corruption is the result of self-serving individuals. At the same time, *Tropa de Elite* avoids the type of structural critique present in Padilha's earlier documentary, *Ônibus 174* (Brazil, 2002) as well as the kind of historical contextualization that might help account for the social, economic, and political problems portrayed therein.[1] Given that *Tropa de Elite* was spun off into a PlayStation video game (as a variant of *Grand Theft Auto*), the film's stylistic virtuosity can certainly be questioned—less for its instrumentality as a marketing ploy, than for contributing to a culture of immediacy devoid of ethical concerns.

This chapter analyzes two other aesthetically innovative films that touch on sociopolitical issues through stories of personal struggles: Fernando Pérez's medium-length feature *Madagascar* and Alejandro González Iñárruti's *Amores perros*. Unlike *Tropa de Elite* and some of the other works mentioned earlier, these two narrative films address the 1960s and 1970s as subtext and quite deliberately examine the contemporary moment in light of the radical struggles of the recent past. Thus, the proposed analysis will deepen the discussion begun in the previous chapter about contemporary cinema's obsession with the era of dictatorship. Pérez's film chronicles the deteriorating relationship between Laura, a woman who came of age during the early years of the Cuban Revolution, and her teenage daughter, Laurita, who appears increasingly disengaged from her surroundings in 1990s Havana. As part of its interlocking narratives about life in contemporary Mexico City, the more well-known *Amores perros* features a homeless man who is trying to reclaim the daughter that he gave up to become involved in a guerrilla group in the 1970s. By highlighting the internal struggles of individuals, such films have been viewed by many critics as attempts to recast revolutionary projects in light of the dominant neoliberal paradigm of contemporary Latin America. According to Deborah Shaw and Ignacio Sánchez Prado, *Amores perros* delegitimizes calls for structural change by underscoring the ultimate failure of the left's utopian projects to create a more just and equitable society and, in so doing, is ultimately complicit in the neoliberal project whose alienating market logic the film seems to want to critique.[2] Scholarly commentary on Pérez's *Madagascar* has been less critical, but tends to see it as part of a larger shift in contemporary Cuban cinema toward more intimate storytelling. Commentators like Ann Marie Stock, Juan Antonio García Borrero, Ana Serra, and Jan Mennell all characterize *Madagascar* as a highly poetic exploration of personal identities and private relationships.[3] While praising Pérez's intimate cinema, Cuban critic García Borrero has expressed concern that, other contemporary Cuban filmmakers have lost the "collective poetics" that so distinguished Cuban cinema in previous decades.[4]

As in the previous chapter, this essay will demonstrate how the analysis of the films' sensorial appeals can enrich our understanding of the sociocultural work that they perform.[5] *Madagascar* and *Amores perros* address the relationship between the past and the present and between the public and the private not only on the level of narrative (by juxtaposing the struggles of today's youth with those of their parents' generation who came of age in the 1960s and 1970s)[6], but also through their invitations to feel—that is, by encouraging audience members to recognize in visceral ways the affective legacies of the recent past as well as newer sensibilities emerging in the contemporary moment. The films' tones are clearly distinct, as are the stylistic mechanisms each utilizes to convey that tone. *Madagascar*'s dreamy and hollowed out mise-en-scène attests to feelings of "*desarraigo,*" or uprootedness, while *Amores perros*'s frenetic pacing and tight compositions convey a pervasive sense of dread about impending violence.

In analyzing the films' sensation-laden evocations of the revolutionary past and the neoliberal present, the present chapter draws on the work of film scholar Thomas Elsaesser and cultural studies critic Raymond Williams. Elsaesser, along with Marcia Landy, has reexamined the relationship between affect, history, and the cinematic form in order to problematize the dominant tendency to denounce the evocation of emotion in films about the past as a trivialization of complex historical trajectories.[7] Elsaesser's work helps us understand how a film's sensorial appeals can, at times, perform political work by helping the audience to think about the past (and their own roles as historical actors) in fresh ways. For its part, Williams's notion of "structures of feeling" is useful for examining how the two films speak about the present. In coining the term, Williams was trying to get at experiences, consciousnesses, and sensibilities that manifest themselves in emergent artistic productions in structured ways.[8] Williams's concept will allow a more thorough discussion of how particular films and groups of films respond to larger sociocultural dynamics by conveying emergent sensibilities.

Elsaesser's lucid and complex essay "Subject Positions, Speaking Positions: From *Holocaust, Our Hitler,* and *Heimat* to *Shoah* and *Schindler's List*" is particularly relevant for the issues under discussion because he speaks of what has often been seen as the limit case of all social trauma (the Holocaust) and of the political and social efficacy of filmic and televisual texts that try to deal with that traumatic past. Elsaesser suggests that attempts to reckon with Germany's Nazi past have not been entirely successful in dealing with the issues of complicity, responsibility, and guilt and asks, "[w]hat kinds of affect might possibly 'unlock' numbness, apathy, indifference, and reconcile memory and hope, commemoration and forgetting, [and] mediate between pity, sentiment, and shame..."[9] Challenging conventional critical paradigms that oppose emotion to thought (and works like Steven Spielberg's *Schindler's List* to Claude Lanzmann's *Shoah*), he argues that the evocation of emotion in film (and television) can have a mobilizing effect and invokes the German term *"Betroffenheit,* which roughly translates as 'the affect of concern' but in its root-meaning includes 'recognizing oneself to be emotionally called upon to respond, act, react'." Elsaesser goes on to explain that the term "covers empathy and identification, but in an active, radical sense of being 'stung into action'."[10]

Clearly not all films evoke this "affect of concern" or "touch a point where the self itself knows and can experience otherness," and Elsaesser suggests that the ability to do so depends upon "the ambiguous or extreme subject positions [films] are able to sustain."[11] He is speaking not only of what is presented on screen, but also of the relationship established between the film and the spectator. He praises Marcel Ophul's *Hotel Terminus* (1988) and Lanzmann's *Shoah* (1985) for "fill[ing] the mind's eye and ear with voices and presences: they will forever speak of a history for which there is neither redemption nor exorcism."[12] At the same time, he argues that even as their multifaceted testimonials "suspend preconceived narrative and explanations" and underscore the incommensurability of having any (number of) representative(s) stand in for those who were killed (that is to say, the inadequacy of any representation to account for what happened), neither of the two films "threaten[s] the coherence of the viewer's identity." In this sense, they fail to revitalize the spectator's understanding of his or her engagement with the past, with the present as historical moment, or with the social body. Elsaesser contrasts the two documentaries to Joseph Losey's *M. Klein,* a much more mainstream film about the Holocaust, "carried along by the processes of fictional identification" between spectators and the central character that employs those very processes to force the spectator to acknowledge his or her own "impotence [as well as] collusion and complicity" in historical processes like the one portrayed—in other words, to destablilize the spectator's subject position.[13] For Elsaesser, such mainstream fiction films have a particular advantage in potentially reshaping the spectator's *cognitive* understanding of history and historical processes and of his or her own role in those processes.

Although Elsaesser's attempt to complicate the dominant understanding of the role of emotion in film responds to U.S. and European critical traditions and his understanding of the sensorial as emotion is somewhat limiting, his arguments have a special pertinence for recent Latin American cultural productions like Iñárruti's *Amores perros* and Pérez's *Madagascar*. Despite differences in tone and setting, these films are similarly preoccupied with contemporary urban life, personal as well as social losses, and the current generation of young adults caught between the politically charged, if corrupt, legacy of the 1960s and postmodern ephemera. Although neither film is an historical film per se (that is to say, one set in the past), they are vitally interested in engaging the recent past and its affective as well as political legacies. As films about the past set in the present, they offer provocative counterweights to the tradition of historical films about revolution specific to both Mexico and Cuba and to the ways in which those films deployed emotion. Classic Mexican films about the Revolution of 1910, like *Flor Silvestre / Wild Flower* (Emilio Fernández, 1943) and *Río Escondido* (Emilio Fernández, 1947) often employed melodramatic conventions to stress the affective ties binding the subject to the nation-as-family. In contrast, Cuban films like *La primera carga al machete* (Manuel Octavio Gómez, 1968) and *Lucía* (Humberto Solás, 1968) about revolutionary movements from the nineteenth and early twentieth century that seemingly anticipated the Cuban Revolution of 1959 frequently used hyperbolic on-screen acting and disjointed camerawork to disrupt conventional identificatory mechanisms; in so doing, the films hailed their spectator as performative subject-citizens who must embody their commitment to the nation-state inside and outside of the theater.[14] As discussed in greater detail later, *Amores perros* and *Madagascar* break with these respective representational conventions and frame their sensorial appeals quite differently to register the crises of the present in the context of perceived historical crossroads.

In exploring the way these films register contemporary social crises and resituate the past, I take a cue from Thomas Elsaesser to analyze their modes of address—specifically how they engage the spectator at the level of sensation. After an overview of *Amores perros*'s plot, basic themes, and historicizing thrust, I analyze the film's affective charge and suggest that it has less to do with what we see on screen than with its cyclical narrative and strategic framing of the action. Considering *Madagascar,* the film Pérez made before his acclaimed *La vida es silbar / Life Is to Whistle* (Spain-Cuba, 1999), it will be useful to examine the affective work carried out through its ingenious soundtrack and sparse mise-en-scène. In analyzing two films about the past that are set in the present, this chapter explores how affect participates not only in the construction of popular historical memory per Elsaesser, but also in the articulation of contemporary "structures of feeling." I argue that whether or not they destabilize the subject position of the spectator and his or her relationship to history, the two films register an epistemological crisis wherein the past functions as the site of reckoning for contemporary social breakdown. Finally, I will discuss the degree to which these films strengthen and/or question the moral economy underpinning the dominant neoliberal project. Thus, beyond its analysis of two important Latin American films, this essay reconsiders the so-called waning of affect and the death of history in contemporary society.

## Horrific Acts

Chronicling the sometimes intersecting lives of several residents of present-day Mexico City, *Amores perros* ostensibly has little to do with Mexico's turbulent past. The first episode ("Octavio y Susana") deals primarily with Octavio, a young man who gets involved in dogfighting as a means to get out of his violent neighborhood and liberate his battered sister-in-law from his abusive brother. Episode 2 ("Daniel y Valeria") picks up characters seen briefly in the earlier episode and traces the personal and professional crisis of Valeria, a rich and beautiful model who is united with her married lover Daniel and then loses her leg in a tragic car accident. The final episode ("El Chivo y Maru") examines the life of a tramp living off what he collects on the city streets and earns from contract assassination jobs. These are tales of tragedy, loss, and degradation about the transitory nature of love in the contemporary cityscape where connections between human beings are slowly eaten away in a dog-eat-dog world.

As with many Latin American films made since the 1980s, *Amores perros* pays great attention to the private sphere. These are intimate stories or, rather, stories about intimacy or the lack of intimacy, as evident in the careful detailing of personal habits and mundane routines: where people sleep, what they watch on TV, what they eat, and whether or not they clean their fingernails. The interior spaces of homes—whether Octavio's modest, working-class home or El Chivo's broken-down hovel—are depicted as dark, hermetic, seemingly airless places, rather than as tranquil locations protected from the hustle and bustle of the city streets. This is true even of Valeria's luxury apartment located in a high-rise far above street level and adorned with modern art and a lavish photo spread of Valeria herself.

Situated directly across from a huge billboard featuring Valeria in an ad for Enchant perfume, the light-filled apartment seems to be a testament to her rising success on both personal and professional planes. Yet, during her recuperation from the accident, her home turns into a claustrophobic jail cell where she must come to terms with her changed status in the world.

In these stories, the home is not an escape from the violence of the outside world, but rather the very site in which hostile actions and petty cruelties are carried out with excruciating familiarity. Although *Amores perros* opens with a fast-paced chase sequence of speeding cars, plenty of blood, and gunshots, the film quickly throws us into reverse, returning us to an earlier moment in Octavio's home. It is there, in that particular time and place where the chain of events begins that leads, seemingly inescapably, to the public confrontation we have just witnessed. In this originary moment at home, Cofi, the family dog, escapes onto the street; Octavio's brother Ramiro cruelly berates his adolescent wife, Susana, for letting the dog out; and Octavio tries to defend his sister-in-law. For his troubles, he becomes the object of his brother's wrathful harangues and his mother's admonition not to get involved. Taking place within the confines of their small kitchen (figure 3.1), the family conflict is situated between scenes of a dogfight taking place in a nearby building. This sequencing creates an interesting parallel between the two "combat zones" and characterizes Octavio and Ramiro as a pair of vicious dogs engaged in a meaningless battle to the death for the right to rule over an already disintegrating family home.[15]

Yet, as much as *Amores perros* focuses on the dynamics of family intimacy, the interlocking nature of its three episodes and their common dog motif

**Figure 3.1** The suffocating family environment in *Amores perros*

suggests that the film is an allegory depicting Mexico as a family in crisis—a trope traceable at least as far back as films and novels about the Mexican Revolution. While all three episodes discuss the disintegration of families, the first and last episodes pay particular attention to Cain-and-Abel conflicts between brothers. In the first episode, Octavio and Ramiro's fights escalate from daily verbal clashes into physical beatings. Frenetic montage sequences—like the one ricocheting between shots of Octavio at Cofi's dogfights, Ramiro robbing pharmacies, and Octavio having sex with Susana to the driving beat of a hip-hop song ("Dime qué te sientes...")—assault us with brutal acts and betrayals that belie myths about the agglutinizing role of the Mexican (and Latin American) family in times of crisis. A later montage sequence interspersing shots of Octavio and Susana making love on top of the dryer with others of Ramiro being beaten by a group of thugs contracted by Octavio demonstrates the complete breakdown of the brotherly bond.[16]

The conflict between Octavio and Ramirio finds a parallel in the final episode where a man named Gustavo contracts El Chivo to kill his swindling business partner Luis, who as it turns out is also his half-brother. The elevated economic status of Gustavo and Luis suggests that the decay of the Mexican family is not a result of growing levels of poverty as it occurs at all levels of society. The film may indeed be critiquing the moral bankruptcy and personal cowardice of Mexico's upwardly mobile middle class as it mocks Gustavo's inability to get his hands dirty and kill his brother himself. And, indeed, there are hints of intraclass warfare breaking out as a result of escalating greed and competitiveness in El Chivo's earlier assassination of an industrialist. Yet, given the parallels it establishes in the first and third episodes, the film's critique goes beyond a particular class or social group and is not primarily a denunciation of the current economic situation (in other words, the ravages of neoliberalism).

Rather, the film's critique is at once more diffuse and more specific, as can be seen in the final episode. Here we find out that El Chivo's estrangement from his own family (and specifically his daughter, María Eugenia [or Maru], whose apartment he has been haunting) was a result of his participation in a guerrilla group fighting to establish a more revolutionary and just society in the 1970s. Committed to his cause and jailed for his actions, El Chivo agreed to give up any claim to his wife and daughter. Rather than depicting his actions as heroic (as a sacrifice of personal security and happiness for a larger social good), *Amores perros* characterizes it as a solipsistic and futile act of personal hubris and political naïveté. El Chivo/Martín himself renounces his political past near the end of the film in a phone message he leaves for his daughter: "Back then I thought that I had to change the world before sharing it with you...As you can see, I failed."[17] As the final episode of the film, the story of this family breakdown is given special weight and a type of explanatory authority that casts the radical political struggles of the 1960s and 1970s and, more particularly, the reification of totalizing schemes of societal reform, as a major contributor (if not the source) of private and public decay and the breakdown of the Mexican family.[18]

To a certain degree, the film's reworking of Mexico's radical past is somewhat analogous to what occurred in classic films from the 1940s about the Revolution of 1910. By romanticizing revolutionary struggle just as the Mexican state initiated an industrialization process, a film like *Flor silvestre* (1943) helped entomb revolution as a necessary *antecedent* to contemporary modernization projects even as its melodramatic conventions became a conduit through which it articulated a generalized sense of longing characterized as the affective legacy of *past* losses (rather than as dissatisfaction with the transformation of contemporary socioeconomic structures). Whereas *Amores perros* dismisses revolutionary struggle outright, like *Flor silvestre* it ties uncertainties about contemporary life to past conflicts. Yet, Iñárruti's film is less interested in displacing concerns about contemporary society entirely onto the past than with utilizing its affective register to convey an epistemological crisis that has destabilized the subject's understanding of contemporary society and, perhaps, more importantly, his or her ability to make substantive proposals for a better future.

### *The Art of Horror*

As suggested earlier, the way in which *Amores perros* disconcerts the spectator has little to do with what is shown on screen. The moments of explicit, physical violence are startling and graphic, but often quite brief. Nor, I would argue, is the spectator overpowered by the faces of the characters contorted with physical pain or emotional grief (like those featured in the film's publicity campaign). These are certainly affecting elements, but they do not sufficiently account for the type of affective work performed by the film. What does is its narrative structure and inventive use of off-screen space.

As discussed earlier, the format of interlocking stories encourages us to view *Amores perros* as a film about Mexican society as a whole. Each subsequent episode further develops a character or characters depicted only briefly in an earlier episode and, at the same time, gives us brief glimpses of what has happened to the main characters from earlier episodes. For example, while we see brief shots of Daniel (in his car with his family or kissing his daughters goodnight) in Episode 1, his story only becomes fully developed in Episode 2, which begins as the continuation of a TV program first seen in Episode 1 by Octavio and his friend, Jorge. In Episode 3, we see brief glimpses of what has happened to Octavio, Susana, and Ramiro after the car crash that ends Episode 1. Less about three discrete groups, the film suggests that everyone's life somehow influences everyone else's life and that Mexican society itself is spiraling downward into a vortex of violence.

However, the significance of the film's narrative structure goes beyond establishing thematic parallels, as the stories from each episode are not only interlocking, but circular. We get to see the same events repeated later on --either from the same perspective (for example, we see Octavio and Jorge in the car chase at the beginning of the film and at the end of Episode 1) or from a different perspective (for example, we see the car crash from Octavio's perspective in Episode 1 and from Valeria's perspective in Episode 2). This narrative repetition of particular events has a different effect than in Orson Welles's *Citizen Kane* or even Quentin Tarantino's *Pulp Fiction,* to which many have compared the Mexican film. In *Amores perros,* this narrational technique not only transforms how we think about what we see (for example, what are the causes, what are the effects, who is responsible), but also substantively frames how we perceive those events on an affective level. Most specifically, it allows us to anticipate (not foresee as much as "forefeel") tragic events like Valeria's car crash. The circularity or looping nature of the narrative infuses the spectator with an ongoing sense of dread; having seen the tragic car crash once, then twice, then a third time, the film conditions the spectator to be wary, to assume that another encounter with violence is just around the corner, or just around the edges of the next frame.

The looping structure also instills the feeling that there is no escape from tragedy and loss and that any belief in redemption is futile and naïve. As the characters from earlier episodes appear again later on, the film initially suggests that they have survived earlier confrontations, both physically and emotionally , but quickly enough rips away that fantasy. In Episode 3, we see a seemingly reconciled Ramiro and Susana walking on the city streets only to soon witness Ramiro die in a failed bank robbery. We find out that Octavio survived the car crash despite serious injuries, but his attempt to reunite with Susana after Ramiro's death and dream of escaping with her to Ciudad Juárez is once again doomed to fail.

The way in which the film infuses the spectator with a sense of impending doom and lurking danger has a great deal to do with how it artfully toys with the relationship between what is observable and what is not or between different modes of perception. In a number of instances, the film draws a contrast between what we see and what we feel or "know" through other senses. As suggested earlier, the horrifying effects of *Amores perros* are less the result of what we see on screen than of what we intuit and the way in which the film directs our attention toward what cannot be seen but only detected by other means.[19]

The film's mechanisms for building suspense depart from the classic paradigm outlined by Alfred Hitchcock wherein a film reveals things to the audience that the characters don't see or "know" (like the villain placing a bomb under a table), and thus pulls us to the edge of our seat with the desire to "tell" the characters what we know. Suspense works differently in *Amores perros,* which teaches us to anticipate coming violence or lurking danger without providing us a privileged view. For example, having seen the image of a bloody dog in the car in the opening sequence and having then seen the initial moments of a dogfight, the spectator senses that Cofi's escape from Octavio's house in the next scene will only end in more violence. Something similar, but more diffuse, occurs in the scenes of El Chivo watching a variety of people. Having seen that he is a man who will defend his dog-family with a machete and having witnessed his ability to carry out a public assassination in the middle of a bustling street, the spectator learns to associate his watchfulness with impending danger. This, in turn, imbues the repeated scenes where he peers at his daughter, or visually stakes out the young businessman, with a sense of great unease.

One of the primary ways in which the film toys with the relationship between the knowable and the visible is through its ingenious use of off-screen space. In the sequence where Cofi escapes from the house, the camera presents a long shot that remains on the doorway to the house even after Susana runs off screen right to pursue Cofi. The shot's fixity frustrates our desire to travel with Susana, to see where Cofi is going. Possessing earlier evidence of injured and attacking dogs, the spectator can now only intuit what will happen next. A more sustained example of the unsettling use of off-screen space occurs in the second episode when Richie, Valeria's beloved Lhasa apso, becomes lost underneath the floor of her luxury apartment. Haunted by the periodic sounds of his muffled barks and scurrying feet over days at a time, Valeria eventually moves from worry to panic—an escalating emotional trajectory that threatens her relationship with Daniel. Her ability to perceive her dog's continuing predicament through aural means alone leads her to imagine Richie suffering not only gradual starvation, but also being eaten by marauding rats. Lost in a dark and fathomless maze, Richie comes to symbolize all of Valeria's latent fears about the end of her modeling career and the uncertainty of her relationship with the still-married Daniel. Through its deliberate manipulation of what we see and what we hear, the film manages to draw the spectator into Valeria's feelings of panic, suspicion, and paranoia and, in the context of the larger film, position the unseen events occurring beneath the floor as a metaphor for the ongoing suffering and violence underlying society as a whole (figure 3.2).

**Figure 3.2** The floor gestures toward latent dangers that lie off-screen in *Amores perros*

In his effort to understand culture as a process and not as something already crystallized and recognizable in particular "representative" objects (for example, paintings, novels, films), Williams proposed the notion of "structures of feeling" to suggest how emergent sensibilities (shared beliefs, thoughts, and feelings) manifest themselves in cultural productions in ways that are perceptible but not always initially *meaningful*. In other words, he was pointing to currents of thought-feeling that had not, as yet, been named, classified, and boxed up to serve a variety of aesthetic, social, and/or political purposes. Williams's examples include the works of Charles Dickens, Emily Bronte, and others that registered generalized emergent sensibilities dismissed by dominant Victorian ideology as deviations from the norm limited to sectors of the population affected by poverty, debt, or illegitimacy.[20] Williams was not arguing that the works of these authors articulated a working-class critique of the industrial change (which, according to Williams, emerged only later as an alternative ideology), but rather that at a particular moment of history, those novels became a privileged register for streams of latent, unsedimented beliefs and feelings.

Williams's concept draws us back to Deleuze and Guattari's suggestion that art can produce and help circulate affects, particularly in periods of sociohistorical upheaval. As noted in the Introduction, Deleuze linked the emergence of time-image cinema to the post–World War II period in which deep social, economic, and political ruptures "greatly increased the situations [to] which we no longer know how to react [...]."[21] In this context, new aesthetic forms emerged that invited different responses from spectators.

Unlike the previous movement-image cinema, time-image cinema did not channel the viewer's responses by fostering his or her identification with particular protagonists or, more broadly, by organizing the narrative into sequences and shots revolving around actions. Instead, the postwar cinema established a different relationship with viewers in ways that made manifest but did not direct or "fix" emergent sensibilities or "structures of feeling."

Iñárruti's film was made at a much different time and a much different location. While not in the aftermath of a war between nations, Mexico was undergoing a period of intense transformation, including the adoption of a neoliberal economic model, the outbreak of the Zapatista rebellion, and the final decline of the Partido Revolucionario Institucionalizado (PRI) as hegemonic party. In this context where the signs of radical change were not always evident (as in the ruined urban landscapes of postwar Europe), *Amores perros*'s aesthetic experimentation registers contemporary structures of feeling about the uncertainty of present-day society. Premiering in an age of escalating urban crime in Mexico City and growing economic inequalities, the film transmits the feeling that violence, loss, and conflict are constitutive elements of everyday life (think of the several scenes in which a shot of a violent act is directly followed by a close-up on a plate of food). This is a tale about the mundane—about people's pets and what they eat—not about state-sponsored terrorism, the ravages of current economic inequalities, political corruption, the breakdown of moral principles in a Catholic nation, or the artificiality of the media—though these are all touched upon. Without defending the film's "realism," I am arguing that it gets at the dreadful ache of lived experiences. As Claudia Schaeffer has suggested, by immersing the audience in intense experiences and "provok[ing] real, physiological agony," *Amores perros* manages to "make a culture's greatest fears become a visible part of the collective imaginary."[22] Moreover, as suggested in my analysis, these intense sensorial evocations are of indeterminate origin and exceed all promises of narrative resolution. Thus, these affective provocations cannot be contained by the film's ideological and political conservatism.[23] While we may leave the theater feeling sad for Octavio or uncertain about Valeria and Daniel's future, the pervasive sense of dread and unease articulated by the film is not easily assuaged by its implicit solution in calling for the restoration of stable families (and strong fathers).

### *Dead Spaces*

If the horrifying violence of *Amores perros* stirs up feelings of disgust, fear, and horror, a film like Fernando Perez's *Madagascar* (1994) works quite differently. It is a much quieter film chronicling a young girl's affective "disconnect" from family and society, as well as her mother's feeling that she has lost her ability to dream.[24] Unlike the stylistic flash and rapid pace of Iñárruti's film, *Madagascar* pursues a much more lyrical, contemplative aesthetic. Yet, like *Amores perros,* it is a story about a family on the verge of breakdown set against the backdrop of a decaying cityscape; it, too, is a personal story with social implications. Within the context of the family drama, both films question the meaning and legacy of the revolutionary projects of the 1960s and, most importantly, articulate structures of feeling. Within the context of Cuban cinema, *Madagascar* was one of several films from the early 1990s that became preoccupied with personal experiences or the interior life of the subject.[25] At the same time, it was also unique for suggesting, in lyrical ways, that psychic crises are linked to the process of instituting revolution as a collective struggle.

Perez's film focuses on the world-weariness of Laura, a university physics professor, and, more particularly, the growing tensions between Laura and her daughter, Laurita. As Laura is less and less satisfied with her professional life, her relationship with Laurita becomes more and more strained. Laurita shows little interest in school or her immediate surroundings and dreams of traveling to Madagascar because, as she tells her mother, "Es lo que no conozco" ["It's what I don't know"]. Her mania for rock music transmutes into a fixation with "great" art and, later, into a devotion to evangelical Christianity. Her changing obsessions and disjunctive emotions flummox her mother, who admits in voice-over that she doesn't understand why Laurita cries at some moments but not in others. Scenes showing Laurita's initial affective disengagement from her mother and surrounding social institutions (specifically her school and the nation-state) are followed by others where we see her sobbing uncontrollably as she listens to Puccini's aria "Nessun Dorma" ["None Shall Sleep"]) and peers at a painting in a museum.[26] Laura herself continually teeters on the edge of hysteria as she repeatedly screams at her daughter, in ever less successful efforts to penetrate Laurita's self-contained, somewhat solipsistic demeanor and seemingly selfish disregard of larger social norms.

The film avoids "diagnosing" Laurita's changing interests and wildly oscillating emotions, leaving any concrete explanation elusive. However, it does suggest that the tensions and affective disjunction present in Laurita's family are part of a larger social dynamic. At several points in the film, we see groups of people chanting the word "Madagascar" in unison—most notably in a sequence in which innumerable young adults stand with their arms outstretched on the roofs of apartment buildings throughout Havana. Pictured as crosses or as antennas, the people reach out for something unknown; their bodies are isolated, separate, but their words signal their common search for something beyond themselves and beyond their immediate surroundings.

To a certain degree, *Madagascar* locates this search as a generational issue felt most acutely by young adults—as visualized in the scene described earlier or as indicated in the final dedication of the film to the director's three children. However, the parallels it establishes between Laurita and Laura (who by the end have exchanged roles) as well as the presence of older adults (particularly Laurita's grandmother) chanting "Madagascar" suggest that the "problem" is not limited to a single age-group, but permeates Cuban society as a whole.

In quite specific ways, *Madagascar* is a meditation on the lost promise of the 1960s and the uncertainty of the future in the early 1990s. Laura frequently muses on the failings of fellow university professors like Mercedes, who was to have been the greatest investigator in her field, but now merely repeats the same lessons over and over again. As Laura ponders in voice-over, "¿Qué pasó? Nadie sabe lo que pasó." ["What happened? Nobody knows what happened."] Laura's growing disillusionment with what has been achieved in the last thirty years is most evident in a scene where she looks at an old photograph from the 1969 May Day celebration. Reminiscing with her mother about the fun she used to have with a friend (who later married an Italian billionaire and left the country), Laura's laughter abruptly stops when she is unable to locate herself in the crowded picture. Taking out a magnifying glass, she searches the photograph asking, "¿Dónde estoy yo? ¿Dónde estoy yo?, Díos mío" ["Where am I? In God's name, where am I?"] Framing the photograph in an extreme close-up through the distorting power of the magnifying glass, the film suggests that the self has been lost in the social and that the pursuit of greater equality overlooked personal fulfillment and, under the worst of circumstances, treated difference as deviance. (These themes are underlined in comic fashion in Perez's *La vida es silbar* when a teacher makes her young students recite the word "I-GUAL-DAD" again and again and again until they "get it right.") Although *Madagascar*'s lyricism and elliptical narrative discourage us from a narrow sociopolitical reading, its swipes at hollow revolutionary rhetoric are quite obvious as it defends Laurita's disinterest in "flags, emblems," or preaching about "conciencia."

The film attempts to capture and transmit the characters' alienation in two main ways: through the inventive use of asynchronous sound and a sparse mise-en-scène. Unlike *Amores perros* which engaged the spectator in a structure of feeling through the manipulation of off-screen space (or through what was not visible), *Madagascar* plays with what we can see and hear by "hollowing out" both the sound and image tracks. The film opens with a sequence that crosscuts between close-ups of people on bikes riding through the streets of Havana and extreme close-ups of Laura being examined by a doctor. Although Laura's voice-over accompanies the shots of her, only vague or muffled sounds of horns, voices, and music are perceptible during the shots of people on the street. In a subsequent shot showing the doctor examining Laura's ear, the film seems to link the distorted sounds on the street with Laura's "ailment," suggesting that we were perceiving the world as Laura does. At the end of the film, we return to the doctor's office, where Laura's statement that "everything has returned to normal" is undermined by her subsequent comparison of herself to a violin that is out of tune and can't quite catch on to what is being played (musical metaphors become central to Pérez's subsequent films *La vida es silbar* and *Suite Habana* (Cuba-Spain, 2003).

Our visual perceptions are just as important to drawing us into Laura's understanding of the world. Shot through a telephoto lens, the close-ups of the bicyclists in the opening sequence isolate the figures against a blurry foreground and blurry background. Like the emptied-out soundtrack, the images visualize Laura's sense of alienation as a feeling of distantiation from her contemporaries and of being out of touch with her surroundings. In other words, the opening sequence of the film plays with our sense of depth, a sense that is central to our understanding of reality and that is at once visual and auditory, to communicate the character's affective disjunction.

*Madagascar*'s arrangement of space is particularly important in this regard. As evident in a later sequence in which Laura is honored for her contributions to the university in an outdoor ceremony, the film presents Havana as a vacant wasteland and uses the mise-en-scène to unmask the celebratory language of officialist discourse during the so-called Special Period in Times of Peace. The final "frozen" moment of this scene manages to not only underscore the absurdity of declaring triumphs in the context of such obvious material devastation ("cuando hay empeño, hay logros" ["when there is effort, there is achievement"]), but also to amplify Laura's feelings of alienation by laying over the sonorous notes first heard at the beginning of the film. The vacant, decaying spaces in *Madagascar* are important registers of the deterioration of material conditions of Cuban society at large, but the devastated homes and public plazas also function as metaphors for the psychic impoverishment of individuals.

The deployment of the ruined cityscape as a metaphor for the contemporary crisis in Cuba can be seen in numerous films from the 1990s and early 2000s, including Pérez's *La vida es silbar* and *Suite Habana*, Gutiérrez Alea and Tabío's *Fresa y chocolate* (1993), and even Wim Wender's *Buena Vista Social Club* (1999).[27] However, the clearest use of this motif can be found in the work of younger filmmakers like Enrique Alvarez [*Sed* (1991) and *La ola* (1995)], and Jorge Luis Sánchez, who has served as Perez's assistant director on a number of films, including *Madagascar,* and whose short film *Un pedazo de mí* (1989) will be analyzed in chapter 4. To a certain degree, films like these might be seen as a response to contemporary economic conditions on the island and, more specifically, as an implicit critique of the increasingly visible disjunctions between urban renovation projects aimed at attracting more tourists and the increasing physical degradation of surrounding neighborhoods.[28] At the same time, the lyrical representation of space in the work of younger filmmakers like Sánchez (as well as in the more widely recognized films of Pérez) points to an emergent aesthetic interested in capturing not only people's thoughts about contemporary life, but also their emotional states, their sense of being spatially and temporally disengaged from their surrounding environment and society itself. This feeling of "*desarraigo,*" of being uprooted and afloat, is best captured in *Madagascar* by Laura and Laurita's constant movement from one house to another. Their inability to find a stable home or, more generally, a place in which they feel at home, gestures toward the unsettled and unsettling sensibilities undergirding Cuban "reality."[29]

While uprootedness has been a constant theme of numerous recent Cuban films like *Miel para Oshún / Honey for Oshun* (Humberto Solás, 2000) and *Video de familia* (Humberto Padrón, 2001), most of these works link this feeling to the issue of exile and to those living outside the island or to those on the island who feel the loss of friends and family who live abroad. *Madagascar* is unique in the way that it posits uprootedness (of which physical exile is one manifestation) as a constitutive element of the revolutionary experience wherein the individual has become unmoored during a restructuring process grounded in collective identity and solidarity. Its indictment of the Revolution is consequently much harsher than the critiques present in countless other Cuban films. Whereas it has become commonplace for Cuban films to poke fun at officialist discourses about revolutionary triumphs and to underscore what the Revolution has not yet achieved, *Madagascar* points to the Revolution's constitutive costs—in other words, to what may be the unavoidable loss of such commitment to the social good.

Rather than suggest that *Madagascar* is an antirevolutionary film, I am highlighting its humanism and the way its contemplative aesthetic and affective register interpellate the spectator as an historical subject differently from other Cuban films.[30] Cuban historical films have traditionally encouraged their spectators to see the Revolution of 1959 as the capstone of a long series of previous rebellions against injustice and to regard themselves as the guardians of this heritage. As Tim Barnard has argued, an unfortunate consequence of this otherwise refreshing effort to "sting" the viewer-subject into action has been an avoidance of the contentious issues of contemporary society.[31] In contrast, *Madagascar* invites the spectator to "tune in" to the affective dissonances of contemporary life and consider the consequences of muting the individual in any grand scheme of collective social transformation. While seeing dangers in contemporary Cuban cinema's concern for sensorial immediacy, García Borrero defends the invitations to feel present in Pérez's work, noting that films like *Madagascar* remind us that "el cine (igual que el corazón) tiene razones que la razón ignora. Que lo primero es emocionarse y, después, pensar" / "film (just like the heart) makes sense in ways that reason ignores. First you have to feel and then to think."[32]

## Sentio, Ergo Sum

I want to conclude by presenting some final thoughts on how the affective address of *Amores perros* and *Madagascar* responds to a sense of crisis about contemporary life and about cinema's ability to represent the social. The end of the twentieth century and the beginning of the twenty-first have been marked by incredible political, economic, and social changes, including the fall of the socialist bloc, the subsequent paralysis of the left, the rise of neoliberalism, the expansion of marketplace logic, and the appearance of new technologies with widespread influence on the everyday practices of many populations. The accelerated nature of these transformations has been breathtaking and has led many filmmakers to look for new aesthetic formulas to convey the density of what has been happening. How can one register growing economic inequalities without chasing the skirts of the latest neorealism?[33] How can one examine the reformulation of subjectivities without reinforcing the individualizing logic of the marketplace? How can a film offer sociopolitical critique without holding on to a notion of the avant-garde that is no longer tenable? These questions are crucial for filmmakers working in the rapidly transforming industries of Mexico, Cuba, and elsewhere. As direct and/or indirect forms of state support have been severely reduced or eliminated, directors have had to pay greater attention to commercial appeal as they look for new forms of private investment at home and abroad.

Notwithstanding the important differences that distinguish their work and their political perspectives, directors like Iñárruti and the older Pérez have responded in a similar way—by proposing an aesthetic of "presence" where sociopolitical critique is secondary to altering our perceptions. *Amores perros* gestures toward what is visibly inaccessible and, at the same time, detectable. It registers exhaustion with political debate and an extreme disenchantment with the paradigms of the left even as the film seemingly criticizes the inequalities and ephemeralities of neoliberalism. *Madagascar* is less definitive in its rejection of the political legacies of the past and yet forces us to address the affective price that has been paid for revolutionary change by hollowing out our perceptions and unmooring us from the immediacy of sensorial impressions, or common sense(s).

The films do not entirely unsettle the subject position of the viewer—at least not in the way theorized by Elsaesser. They do not shock the spectator into recognizing the inadequacy of his or her own moral economy or complicity in particular historical processes. Nor do they encourage the spectator to reimagine his or her relationship to the community. *Amores perros* in particular limits its articulation of the social to the recurrent metaphor of the family. While both films suggest that the path to the future is uncertain (*Amores perros* closes as El Chivo walks off into a hazy, sun-cracked mudflat; and *Madagascar* as Laura and Laurita walk their bicycles into a tunnel), only the latter engages the spectator in the process of imagining a different future through the lines of identification it has forged between Laura and the spectator.

Nevertheless, in their affective mode of address, both films problematize the very "knowable-ness" of the present by disrupting and reorienting the spectator's perceptions: *Amores perros,* by questioning the epistemological primacy of the visual realm and *Madagascar,* by playing with our sense of depth. The attempt by Iñárruti's film to recuperate the deep uncertainties it has articulated and thus, its complicity in the neoliberal paradigm, lies not in its gesturing toward past errors, but rather, primarily, in its moral economy—its call to honor one's family, one's brothers-in-the-nation, as the basis of future redemption. Although *Madagascar* also highlights family breakdown, it does not draw the same metonymic connection between family and society. Its historical sensibility is also different and goes beyond its critique of the limitations of revolutionary projects. The past is made present in Pérez's film in its residual liberal humanism, a stance that clashes both with the type of individualism promoted by neoliberalism (subject as constituted by the market) and with the Marxist formulations of Ché Guevarra and Julio García Espinosa, who argued that the fullest realization of man would occur through a true commitment to the revolutionary process and the social body.

The next chapter offers a point of comparison to the aesthetic of "presence" discussed herein by analyzing several films from Argentina and Cuba that are similarly concerned with shifting our modes of perception. Revolving around the lives of young adults, the works could be considered "youth films," a broad and somewhat problematic category or genre. Films about adolescents and twenty-somethings have proliferated in many Latin

American countries since the 1990s, responding to the perception of a growing niche market of young-adult consumers and, at the same time, to larger discourses about the "problem of today's youth." The films under consideration are intensely concerned with exploring the subjectivities of young adults and turn to formal innovation to convey their experiences of isolation and alienation from the larger society in ways that resonate viscerally with audiences.

# CHAPTER 4

# Alien/Nation: Contemporary Youth in Film

The past two decades have witnessed a proliferation of films from a variety of Latin American countries about disaffected youth, among them Víctor Gaviria's *Rodrigo D: No futuro* (Colombia, 1990) and *La vendedora de rosas / The Rose Seller* (Colombia, 1998), *Johnny Cien Pesos* (Chile/Mexico/United States, Gustavo Graef Marino, 1993), *Madagascar* (Cuba, Fernando Pérez, 1994), *Buenos Aires viceversa* (Argentina, Alejandro Agresti, 1996), *Como Nascem os Anjos / How Angels Are Born* (Brazil, Murilo Salles, 1996), *Pizza birra faso / Pizza Beer Cigarettes* (Argentina, Bruno Stagnaro/Adrián Caetano, 1997), *Amor vertical* (Cuba, Arturo Sotto, 1997), *Amores perros* (Mexico, Alejandro González Iñárruti, 2000), *25 Watts* (Uruguay, Juan Pablo Rebella and Pablo Stoll, 2001), *Vagón fumador / Smokers Only* (Argentina, Verónica Chen, 2001), *De la calle / Streeters* (Gerardo Tort, 2001), *Perfume de violetas, nadie te oye / Violet Perfume, Nobody Hears You* (Mexico, Marysa Sistach, 2001), *Nadar solo* (Argentina, Ezequiel Acuña, 2002), *Mil nubes de paz ... / A Thousand Clouds of Peace...* (Mexico, Julián Hernández, 2002), *Hoy y mañana / Today and Tomorrow* (Argentina, Alejandro Chomski, 2003), *Como un avión estrellado / Like a Plane Crash* (Argentina, Ezequiel Acuña, 2005), and *Cielo dividido / Broken Sky* (Mexico, Julián Hernández, 2006).[1] Although tales of youthful alienation have been a cinematic staple in many countries since the 1960s, many of these recent Latin American films depart from the older models by privileging the perspective of working-class and lower-middle-class subjects and, in so doing, harshly indict societies riddled by mundane acts of violence, exploitation, and emotional brutality. Whether in the form of *Rodrigo D*'s blaring punk soundtrack or *Cielo dividido*'s disconcerting long takes, these films attest to the affective charge of everyday life for young adults.

These films are part of a much larger discursive network and resonate with concerns voiced elsewhere by both conservative and leftist critics about the depoliticization of young people, the decreased moral authority of schools, and the deleterious effects of media culture. There are clear analogies here to critiques of the so-called Gen-Xers in the United States since the early 1990s. However, as numerous critics remind us, "youth" is a sociopolitical category constituted by a variety of intersecting discourses (legal, psychological, sociological, filmic) and solidified by the work of numerous institutions (the state, schools, families). Hence, discussions about youth and the representation of youth must be situated historically and geographically in particular times and particular spaces.

In Latin America, particularly in the Southern Cone, discussions of "today's youth" are often inflected with debates about the region's recent political history. In the mid-1980s commentators like Miguel Bonasso, Mario Marcel, and others noted the key role played by Latin American youth in redemocratization efforts. By the 1990s others would designate contemporary youth as a "lost generation" —a product or residue of the long years of dictatorship—and characterize youth culture, whether discussed in terms of the proliferation of video arcades and mall culture or the practice of "zapping" (quickly scanning TV programs with the remote control), as the most trenchant signs of the triumph of neoliberalism.[2] In Cuba, discussions about contemporary youth have been framed differently—but similarly situate today's youth as a measure of the legacies of the past, in this case, the promise (or failed promise) of the Revolution. The state's recent *Batalla de Ideas* initiative—which has involved renovating old schools, constructing new ones, launching an educational TV channel, and establishing facilities and curriculum for the acquisition of computer skills, among other things—was clearly designed to better integrate "wayward" youth into Cuban society.[3] This widespread concern for "the problem of today's youth" tells us less about young adults themselves and more about the way in which youth has functioned as a sociocultural category. As critical educator Henry Giroux points out, youth has long functioned as "a metaphor for historical memory and a marker that makes visible the ethical and political responsibility of adults to the next generation" and thus has served as a useful "symbol of how society thinks of itself and as an indicator of changing cultural values."[4] Given the recent proliferation of films about young adults in Latin America, it becomes quite productive to analyze these works to understand how they support or contest larger discursive positioning of youth as a sign of the times (and of what is to come).

When talking about youth and film, we are clearly discussing a wide range of productions. There are obvious differences between Argentine films like *Picado fino* (Esteban Sapir, 1993–96), a very low-budget, stylistically experimental film, and *No sabe, no contesta* (Fernando Musa, 2002), a more mainstream narrative; and between Mexican films like *Por la libre* (Juan Carlos de Llaca, 2000) and *Perfume de violetas*. The differences between films such as these derive not only from differing modes of production and formal characteristics, but also from their targeted audiences. While it may be less reasonable to talk about "youth films" as critics do in the United States (where 18-24-year-olds are an established niche market), there are signs that some Latin American producers have been trying to nurture a local equivalent.[5]

With these differences in mind, the central concern of this chapter is to examine the affective play of particular films that explore the subjectivities of young adults who feel alienated from family and society. I will briefly analyze four recent films from two different countries that in many ways depart from the representation of youth found in other contemporary films made in their respective countries: from Argentina, *Picado fino* and *La ciénaga* (Lucrecia Martel, 2000) and, from Cuba, *Nada* (Juan Carlos Cremata Malberti, 2001) and the short *Un pedazo de mí* (Jorge Luis Sánchez, 1989). Despite their many differences (on which I will comment in a moment), these films share a common discursive tactic; they inscribe contemporary affective disjunction in terms of depth perception and, in so doing, register structures of feeling that question (and at times disrupt) dominant discursive formations. As I will illustrate later, *Picado fino* is a film about surfaces, about the absence of "in-depth" affective connections between family members and between lovers. Although this film seemingly registers a postmodern "waning of affect", such an interpretation will require modification. Unlike *Picado fino*, *La ciénaga* is a film that studies what lies underneath the surface of the perceptible. With numerous deep-focus shots resplendent with color, Lucrecia Martel's film registers the pregnant emotions percolating below the surface of everyday life as they strain against their representational containment. The Cuban film *Nada* shares an interest in superficial reality with Sapir's *Picado fino*, but in Cremata's work it becomes a means to bring into relief the affective textures of everyday life and to bridge the communicative distance between its protagonists. In contrast, the short *Un pedazo de mí* characterizes the crisis of youth in terms of the hollowing out of emotional spaces, an articulatory practice also evident in the works of Ismael Peralta, a young Cuban painter, and, as argued in the last chapter, in Pérez's film *Madagascar*.

The comparative nature of this analysis serves a number of purposes. Among other things, it suggests some of the ways in which "youth" has been articulated differently in different parts of Latin America. Furthermore, it highlights how representations of youth (and the anxieties attached to that sector) relate to differential socioeconomic conditions, specific historical trajectories, and local institutional genealogies. In the case of Argentina, I will situate the films in relation to the "explosion" of films by younger directors (or the "New Argentine Cinema" that emerged in the mid-1990s), as well as to a particular discursive legacy in which youth were defined as guerrillas or subversives. In the case of Cuba, I will locate *Un pedazo de mí,* a film made under the auspices of the Asociación Hermanos Saíz, and *Nada* in relation to the institutional crisis of Instituto Cubano de Arte e Industria Cinematográficos (ICAIC), the state film institute that has been producing films about youth by "not-so-young" directors, and to a dominant trope traceable to the idea of Cuba as the site of the perpetual revolution: youth as eternal (and, at times, martyred) militant epitomized in the figure of Ché Guevara.

### *Of Surfaces and Planes*

Standing on the margins of the new independent Argentine cinema, Esteban Sapir's *Picado fino* is a unique film that gestures toward the past even as it distinguishes itself from both previous and contemporary films about young adults.[6] Set in the city of Buenos Aires, the story revolves around Tomás, a young man from a working-class family who is ostensibly looking for employment after he discovers that his girlfriend Ana is pregnant. Frequently shot in close-ups that cut across rather than frame his face, *Picado fino* tells a tale of societal disconnect in which every search lacks direction and human relationships are void of affective grounding.

Like other contemporary Argentine films about young adults, *Picado fino* resonates with the themes of communication and desire reminiscent of the "first" *Nuevo Cine*—that is, films from the early 1960s by directors like David José Kohon, Simón Feldman, and José Martínez Súarez.[7] The story line of Sapir's film bears a remarkable similarity to the first episode of Kohon's *Tres veces Ana* (1961), in which a young, unmarried couple grapples with news of the young woman's pregnancy. Both films utilize the urban mise-en-scéne to articulate the subjective constraints experienced by their protagonists. Yet their differences are also startling. Whereas in *Tres veces Ana* the problem of communication was a matter of finding words to bridge the affective distances between two lovers, in *Picado fino,* dialogue collapses into an affectless echoing between the two characters. In the opening café sequence of Sapir's film when Ana tells Tomás that she is pregnant, alternating frontal close-ups of each character articulate their affective isolation as their stilted, monotonal exchange underscores their disconnectedness:

> *Ana*: How quickly things change, Tomás. In a few days, the results. I'm not sure, but what are we going to do?
>
> *Tomás*: It's not important what we do. Today I've lived a hundred times. I'm tired of this monotony. What are we going to do? What everybody does.
>
> *Ana*: What does everybody do?
>
> *Tomás*: What everybody does. What does everybody do?[8]

This interchange is markedly different from the similar café sequence in *Tres veces Ana*. In the earlier film, a two-shot "held" the two young adults together even as their conversation about the impossibility of her having their child—continually overlaid by the sounds of clinking dishes, chatter about the most recent soccer match, and the honking of cars—signaled their unraveling as a couple. In *Tres veces Ana*, the young couple's desire for each other, frustrated by socioeconomic limitations, was unambiguously present. In *Picado fino*, desire is ephemeral, something that helps pass the time.

The differences between *Picado fino* and *Tres veces Ana* might suggest that the newer film (and others that are less formally experimental like *Sábado* or the appropriately titled *No sabe, no contesta*) articulate a postmodern sensibility. The alienation of the 1960s has been replaced by ennui and irritation and the subject has become fragmented (evident in the off-kilter framing of *Picado fino*). There is now a glory in surface play, rather than in plumbing the emotional depths of individuals—a difference visible in the film's proclivity for frontal shots, extreme close-ups, and overhead shots as well as in the absence of master shots to anchor the protagonists, and the spectator, in a given place. By cutting across the character's face and flattening out the profilmic space, *Picado fino* points to the fragmentation of the subject, while its lack of master shots speaks of the subject's dislocation. Thus, it might be argued that in its depiction of young characters as destabilized and directionless subjects, *Picado fino* registers the irrelevance of politics to Argentine youth and, even more broadly, the impossibility of future social transformation.

Yet, this explanation is not entirely satisfactory. In the first place, the apathy of *Picado fino*'s young protagonists stands in direct contrast to the insouciant playfulness of the film itself, which uses a variety of techniques, including graphic inserts and asynchronous sound, to comment ironically on the characters' actions. In the second place, *Picado fino* is one of many works by young filmmakers that have exploded onto the Argentine scene over the last decade to revitalize a somewhat stagnant national film industry. Many of these filmmakers have emerged from the numerous film schools that were established in the early 1990s. As noted by Argentine critics, their films are not united by a dominant stylistic tendency or by a larger political or filmic project (as with the New Latin American Cinema).[9] Indeed, when provoked in interviews to comment on their own work, the latest group of young cineastes strenuously disavows any interest in political or social commentary.

Rather than take the filmmakers at their word, we must situate their work in relation to the way in which youth has been constructed in Argentina since the 1960s. In his fascinating work on rock music in Argentina, Pablo Vila has discussed the way in which the category of "youth" became synonymous with "*lo sospechoso*" (the suspicious) starting around 1974–75, during the second Peronist administration.[10] In the following years, after the coup that would install the *Proceso de Reorganización Nacional* (1976–83), a hard-line military junta that carried out the campaign of terror known as the Dirty War, this association hardened to the point that "the social space occupied by young people in those terror-filled years was absent, negated, a 'no-place'."[11] According to Vila, this "no place" resulted not only from the actions of the military, but also from those of other institutions of civil society like political parties and trade unions.[12] While youth could not be represented by (or represent themselves through) such institutions, they also disappeared from other discursive sites. Advertising agencies removed all young adults from commercials and replaced them with young children "smiling, freshly scrubbed, and, of course, totally obedient."[13] In this context, the rock scene became the dominant site through which young people could construct and negotiate their identity as youth during the initial years of the dictatorship.[14]

Yet, by the mid-late 1980s, rock was no longer necessarily an alternative cultural space and, as big producers made inroads, many bands turned their attention for the first time to the "body, pleasure, and entertainment."[15] Around the same time, cable TV access increased, and mall culture took off. Commentators increasingly viewed these shifts as contributing to the depoliticization of young people and it became commonplace to characterize contemporary young adults as apathetic, indifferent to the horrors of the recent past, and lacking a sense of social solidarity or totalizing view of society.[16] It should be noted that many scholars do not "blame" young adults for their lack of sociopolitical commitment, but rather see this as a result of the failures of social institutions (schools, the family), larger political dynamics,[17] and the seductive powers of "post-modern culture," often linked to the unfettered power of the marketplace.[18]

While the increased commodification of all aspects of everyday life is certainly troubling, these analyses often display an underlying urge to resuscitate older models of the political and, in so doing, pay insufficient attention to the sociocultural work carried out by new "sensorially laden" cultural practices favored by young adults. Films like *Picado fino* and *La ciénaga* as well *Sábado* and *No sabe, no contesta* are part of a youth culture "constellation" that includes other affectively charged works—from the ironic politics of the punk-ska band Todos tus muertos to the grunted screels of the heavy-metal A.N.I.M.A.L. to the *escraches* practiced by HIJOS, a group of young adults who lost their parents during the Dirty War.[19] If the latter's street performances are more readily identifiable as political acts, their sensorially packed, tactical interventions are nonetheless, like recent films, remapping what might be considered political.[20]

If *Picado fino* is not political in a traditional sense (particularly when compared to the New Latin American Cinema), it does comment on class relations, globalization, and the legacies of the dictatorship. The film situates the emasculating, dead-end factory job held by Tomás's father in direct relation to the forces of globalization, evident in the omnipresence of U.S. media and entertainment products, from old reruns of *Batman* to Tomás's video games, whose English terminology ("Insert Coin," "Extended Play," "Round II," "Game Over") are appropriated by the film itself and used as graphic inserts to provide ironic counterpoint to the actions of the characters. Although *Picado fino* antedated the December 2001 meltdown of the Argentine economy, the film ably anticipated the critiques that would be leveled against neoliberal policies and globalization in the aftermath of the crisis that led to the downfall of five presidents in a number of weeks—namely their exacerbation of socioeconomic inequalities.

Perhaps even more significant, if more subtle, are the film's references to Argentina's past. In one of his job applications, Tomás lists his birthday as May 25, 1973, a date significant on several levels. May 25 is Argentina's independence day, a date commemorated in the name of the central plaza of the nation's capital: Plaza de Mayo. Born on that date in 1973, Tomás becomes a symbol of the failure of the dreams and promises associated with independence and, more succinctly, of the political failures of the second Peronist government (1973–76) as well as the infamous *Proceso*. By selecting 1973 (rather than, say, 1976) as the date of Tomás's birth and "hiding" the reference in the detail of a single shot, *Picado fino* eschews facile political denunciations to concentrate on the effects that such political legacies exert on contemporary urban youth. In Tomás's world, there are no "real" heroes, only dubbed, parodic imitations like Batman, and the signs of what must be done are mixed and ambiguous at best. This is quite some distance from the reification of the martyred Ché and the Manichean worldview expressed in the classic *La hora de los hornos / The Hour of the Furnaces* of the New Latin American Cinema. Yet, the call to "wake up" is ever present in the insistent ringing of an alarm clock and the persistent imagery of a crying baby. This call extends to the spectator. Having disrupted the spectator's alignment with particular characters and encouraged an ironic detachment through its playful intertextuality, Sapir's film nonetheless offers an overwhelming sensorial experience. The director himself has called *Picado fino* an "autistic film," noting that he "tried to overpower the spectator by saying, 'Don't think. Watch and feel'."[21]

Before discussing the sociopolitical potential of *Picado fino*'s affective play, it will be useful to examine the representation of young adults in another Argentine film: Lucretia Martel's much celebrated *La ciénaga*. Although Sapir worked as a cameraman on Martel's previous short *Rey muerto* (1995) while he was putting together his own film, *La ciénaga* notably differs from *Picado fino* in stylistic and narrative terms. Martel's film features exuberant colors instead of black-and-white footage and a depth of field almost entirely absent from Sapir's film. Whereas *Picado fino* centered almost exclusively on the experiences of Tomás, *La ciénaga* chronicles the lives of two families: one, led by Meche, owns La Mandrágora (The Mandrake), an estate that grows red peppers; the other, led by Tali, lives in the nearby town, La Ciénaga (The Swamp). Nonetheless, as in *Picado fino,* the subjective experiences of youth become the ultimate measure of more generalized social decay.

*La ciénaga* traces the interactions between the two families from the day of Mecha's accident by the side of the pool at the Mandrágora (where she falls on broken wine glasses in a drunken stupor) to the tragic death of Tali's youngest son Luciano (Luchi) in the patio of their home in La Ciénaga. Although the physical wounds on Mecha's chest are the most recent, her children have the most telling injuries and bear the most visible scars of familial and social decay. Joaquín, her youngest son, lost an eye while hunting in the nearby mountainside three years before; Vero, her teenage daughter, has a half-circle scar on her chin from some unknown accident in the past; and José, her eldest son, comes home bruised and beaten one night after getting into a fight during Carnival. Yet, the scars are more than signs of parental disregard. The film is quick to point to the children's own unthinking cruelties, which have contributed to their injuries: Joaquín's love of shooting small animals and his pitiless gaze on the dying cow; Vero's racist treatment of Isabel, one of the family's indigenous maids, and her boyfriend El Perro; and José's harassment of Isabel. Indeed, the film has a refreshingly unsentimental approach to the children and young adults who are at the center of the plot.[22]

Of all of Mecha's children, only Momi, her youngest daughter, exhibits no visible sign of injury, and it is precisely this character whose subjectivity is privileged by the film. As a film about the undersurface of daily life, about what is not immediately visible and yet is nonetheless detectable, *La ciénaga* characterizes the fifteen-year-old Momi as the only one to sense the latent forces ignored by the other characters.[23] In a key sequence, Momi dives into the family's stagnant pool as the other children lounge around the deck. Framed as a prolonged long shot from the other side of the pool, her plunge draws stupefied reactions from the other children who wait and wait for her to reappear, their lack of response underscored by a delayed reverse shot of the putrid surface of the water (figure 4.1). The scene functions as an effective metaphor for Momi's compulsion, unique among all the characters, to penetrate the surface of the dirty realities ignored by others. To some degree, the film's critique of familial and social decay is keyed to Momi's "psychic fall" from sensitive teen to emotionally numb young adult.[24]

Through the many scenes in which Momi stands as witness to the actions of others, *La ciénaga* suggests that the young girl somehow observes and feels more than the other characters. Momi's sensibility contrasts with that of her mother Mecha, whose willful blindness is symbolized by the sunglasses that she wears inside the house and by her failure to schedule the cosmetic surgery that would give Joaquín a prosthetic eye. Momi's sensorial acuity extends beyond the merely visual. Unlike her father Gregorio and her sister Vero who recoil from what they find to be offensive body odors produced

**Figure 4.1**   José, Vero, and the others wait for Momi to reappear in *La ciénaga*

by the oppressive summer heat, Momi rarely bathes. Told that she smells, Momi only showers after Isabel admonishes her for jumping in the fetid pool. In these and other ways, Momi functions as a key register of the film's "disquieting materiality."

As intimated earlier, one of the most notable means by which the film creates this sense of density or "materiality" is its soundtrack.[25] In a recent interview, Martel underscored the "youthful" perspective produced by the film's complex sonic density:

> Siempre tuve más clara la banda sonora que la imagen. Una cosa que me parece importante de *La ciénaga* es que aunque no haya un narrador definido, que era un riesgo muy grande, el punto de vista del narrador no iba a ser el mío de mi edad sino el de cuando yo era chica. Cuando uno es chico a lo mejor no entiende muchas cosas, pero es mucho más perceptivo... En el cine lo más táctil que uno tiene para transmitir, lo más íntimo, es el sonido. El sonido se mete en uno, es muy corporal. Y para ser fiel a esa perspectiva infantil, trabajé con la idea de que el sonido pudiera contar más que la imagen, incluso más que las palabras.

> [I always felt more confident with the sound than with the image. One thing that seems important to me about *La ciénaga* is that although there was no clearly defined narrator, which was a very big risk, the point of view of the narrator was not going to be me as an adult but me as a girl. When you're a child perhaps there are lots of things you don't understand, but you're much more perceptive . . . In cinema, the most tactile, intimate thing you have to convey is sound. The sound plunges into you; it's very physical. And to be faithful to that childlike viewpoint, I worked with the idea that the sound could tell more than the image, including more than the words.][26]

The point here is not that Momi is Martel's stand-in narrator, but rather that the film is trying to endow the spectator with the perceptive powers of the child. The soundtrack deliberately interweaves low-, medium-, and high-frequency sounds through the inclusion of distant thunder or airplanes, conversations, and the buzzing of different insects, respectively.[27] This density or multiplicity of sonic material "floods" the spectator and cannot ignored. As Martel says, "In the cinema, you can close your eyes but you can't stop listening.[28] Thus, the film's soundtrack "tunes" the spectator, like a piano, to vibrate in the correct key and to interpret the cadences being tapped out. The words of the characters become muffled and less distinguishable as the spectator, like a child, pays more attention to the tones and pitch of ambient sound to understand what is truly going on. Martel has said that *La ciénaga* "belongs to the genre of the 'desperate scream'."[29] It is this affective resonance that lasts beyond the film's tragic ending.

And, indeed, it is *there* in *La ciénaga*'s sensorial charge that one finds the politics in this ostensibly apolitical film about disaffected youth. Although references to the dictatorship are entirely absent from *La ciénaga,* its legacy is invoked in "[t]his tension between an ominous past and an indecipherable present."[30] Martel herself has noted that in films of the 1990s by first-time filmmakers the Dirty War and the "disappeared" is registered as "densities" or "knots."[31] Unlike films such as *La historia oficial* (Luis Puenzo, 1985) and *Sur* (Fernando Solanas, 1988) made immediately after the dictatorship that discussed the repression directly, more recent Argentine films eschew overt political denunciations. As Martel puts it:

> Lo que se siente es que la cosa ha perdido su carga política explícita y coyuntural y ha quedado la carga dramática humana, el peso de todo eso sobre la historia, la culpabilidad, la no expiación . . .La ausencia, porque a todo el mundo le falta un alguien, cercano o no. Todo eso tiene una presencia muy fuerte en lo que se está haciendo [. . .]"

> [What one feels is that the topic has lost its explicit, timely political charge and that what remains is the human, dramatic charge, the historical weight of all that happened, the guilt, the lack of atonement . . .the absence, because everyone is missing someone, whether someone close to them or not. All of that has a strong presence in what is happening today.[32]

By aligning the spectator with the child and her sensibility, not as a return to innocence but as a way of experiencing the affective legacies of dictatorship, *La ciénaga* reconnects us with the murkier depths upon which today's civil democracy floats.

Rather than putting forth a totalizing vision of societal reform, films like *Picado fino* and *La ciénaga* mobilize the affective legacies that have been ignored by the legalistic mechanisms of the so-called truth commissions and diverted by sensationalized public performances of commemoration. In Argentina, the trauma of the dictatorial past was "summed up" by the *Nunca más* report (1984) and "dealt with" when President Raúl Alfonsín declared the "Punto Final," an arbitrary date after which no further legal actions could be initiated for crimes committed during the military government. The enactment of the law of "Obedencia Debida" in June 1987 (granting immunity to low-ranking military officers who participated in the repression "under orders") largely put an end to state efforts to publicly recognize the crimes committed during the dictatorship. According to Claudia Feld, widespread public interest in the authoritarian past would only be reignited eight years later, during the presidency of Carlos Menem, through the appearance of former perpetrators on important political TV shows such as *Hora Clave* and *Tiempo Nuevo*.[33] This stage of public reckoning took place in an era of growing distrust in democratic institutions wherein television began to serve as the privileged arena for calls for justice.[34] Feld and others argue that this shift has not productively enhanced either remembering or accountability given the media's tendency toward spectacle and sensationalism. The Mothers of the Plaza de Mayo were turned into "stars" featured on the cover of *Gente* (Argentina's version of *People* magazine), a former torturer and his victim sat down to "chat" on a TV talk show, and repeated attention was paid to the bloodier aspects of the military's repression.[35] By focusing on the most sensationalistic aspects of the military's repression, such media reports complemented the earlier legalistic approach to the crimes of the Dirty War. The latter converted public reckoning into rational accounting, while the former channeled viewers' feelings about the recent past into "pre-established" emotions.[36] Both tendencies diverted attention away from messier affective legacies—including ongoing feelings associated with loss, mourning, guilt, complicity—that could not be easily "tamed" or untangled. Likewise, they forestall a more in-depth examination of Argentina's political history and ongoing economic inequalities. Although *Picado fino* and *La ciénaga* do not address such issues explicitly, their formal innovations "let loose" unsettling affects in ways that the thrillers discussed in chapter 2 cannot.

Both these Argentine films proceed along a fault-line between the disturbing past and new emergent structures of feeling. Rather than documenting a mere "waning of affect" or the "emotional paralysis" of young adults, these films register sensibilities associated with the renegotiation of modes of sociopolitical engagement. Joanna Page makes a similar point when she discusses how contemporary Argentine cinema's "retreat into the private sphere" marks a new form of politics. In her analysis , Page emphasizes how *La ciénaga* and other films gesture toward both the dictatorial past and the neoliberal present at the same time. Even films like *Picado fino* and *La ciénaga* that premiered before the December 2001 meltdown of the Argentine economy should "be read as . . . critical intervention[s], signaling the failure of a bankrupt, dysfunctional state and emphasizing the primacy of biological life in times of severe crisis."[37] Although Page's argument does not focus on the affective dynamics of the new cinema, she nonetheless underscores how *La ciénaga*'s narrative fragmentation—its tendency to cut away from shots of imminent danger to favor "the unresolved, the truncated, the elliptical"— constitutes ". . . a deliberate attempt to reproduce in the viewer the same feeling of abandonment and disorientation experienced by her characters."[38] As I have been arguing in this essay, the preoccupation of both *Picado fino* and *La ciénaga* with adjusting the spectator's depth perceptions has a similar effect: the films force viewers to adopt a new type of sensibility—one that cannot ignore the affective charge of history marginalized in the rationalized realm of neoliberal politics and, at the same time, one that does not subsume cognition to purgative outburst.

## *Of Sea Walls and Scaffolding*

Contemporary Cuban cinema offers a contrasting view of youth and their role in society. Whereas in Argentina there has been an explosion of filmmaking activity by younger directors since the mid-1990s, in Cuba these younger filmmakers have been both less numerous and less "visible" until recently. This "absence" is the result of a number of circumstances, among them, the economic difficulties starting in the 1990s that sharply curtailed ICAIC productions and, perhaps even more important, the production bottleneck at ICAIC. In the process, a whole generation of filmmakers who are slightly younger or contemporaries of "consecrated directors" like Tomás Gutiérrez Alea (1928–96) and Humberto Solás (b. 1941), including Juan Carlos Tabío (b. 1943) and Fernando Pérez (b. 1944), had extended "apprenticeships" and only began to make their first feature films while in their forties. Tabío (who collaborated with Alea on his last two films, *Fresa y chocolate* [1993] and *Guantanamera* [1995]) and Pérez have since inherited the mantle of Alea and Solás to become Cuba's most prolific and, in the case of Pérez, celebrated filmmakers. Curiously enough, many of the films of these two directors demonstrate a preoccupation with young adults: in the case of Tabío, *Se permuta* (1984), *Plaff* (1988), *Fresa y chocolate* (1993), and *Lista de espera* (2000); in the case of Pérez, *Clandestinos* (1987), *Hello Hemingway* (1991), and *Madagascar* (1994).

The structural bottleneck at ICAIC has had an even greater impact on the third generation of filmmakers that includes Jorge Luis Sánchez (b. 1960), Enrique Alvarez (b. 1961), Juan Carlos Cremata (b. 1961), Arturo Sotto (b. 1967), and Humberto Padrón (b. 1967). Although their work enjoys institutional support through the state-supported Escuela Internacional de Cine y Televisión in San Antonio de los Baños and alternative artistic organizations like the Asociación Hermanos Saíz, these "babies of the revolution" have had a hard time breaking into feature filmmaking. Despite many provocative shorts that emerged around 1990 like Enrique Alvarez's *Sed* (1989); Juan Carlos Cremata's *Oscuros rinocerantes enjaulados* (1990); and Jorge Luis Sánchez's *Un pedazo de mí* (1989), *El fanguito* (1990), and *Dónde está*

*Casals* (1990), it would be at least five to ten years before these no-longer-quite-so-young filmmakers would be given the opportunity to direct feature films. As recounted by Ann Marie Stock in her fine study of contemporary Cuban "street filmmaking," Cremata along with even younger directors like Esteban Insausti (b. 1971) and Pavel Giroud (b. 1972) are some of the few to maintain an active production schedule—in part as a result of their entrepreneurial efforts to form partnerships with nongovernmental organizations (NGOs) and state institutions other than ICAIC and to tap private financing and keep their budgets low.[39]

The unique production histories of these thirty- and now forty-year old directors have propelled them in different directions over the last ten years. Their works are neither stylistically similar nor do they share a common vision of Cuban society.[40] Nonetheless, according to Stock, these younger filmmakers demonstrate a preoccupation with questions of identity—"what it means to be gay, straight, sane, crazy, in love, alone, disenfranchised, an artist, and so on" as well as what it means to be Cuban in an "increasingly connected world."[41] In their explorations of identity, the place of young adults in Cuban society appears as a favored subject. Given that these younger directors do not subscribe fully to the "politically charged constructions of nation, utopia, revolution and [Ché Guevara's] 'New Man'",[42] it is not surprising that many of their films offer different perspectives on youth than those found in the films of older directors or problematize (and sometimes contest) dominant sociological discourses about the "crisis" of Cuban youth. Among social scientists from the island, it is commonplace to portray today's young adults as quite distinct from earlier generations, valorizing as they do access to dollars over professional fulfillment and rock stars over national heroes.[43] As discussed by María Isabel Domínguez García, demographic shifts and the slow-growing job market have created a series of problems for the incorporation of young adults into society.[44] Even as young adults (who by the late 1980s represented one-third of the total population) are better educated than ever before, they tend to be unqualified (or overqualified) for the types of jobs that are available—for example, those in the service sector oriented toward attracting foreign currency (tourism) and those in agriculture and fishing sectors.[45] The reorientation of the Cuban higher educational system toward professional and technical specialization has not occurred quickly enough to address this problem.[46] At the same time, the criteria for social mobility have been changing rapidly as those who have access to dollars (regardless of their educational background and job category) are viewed as more privileged.[47] Given these material conditions, the ideology of collective solidarity has lost traction among young adults, as well as others, who are drawn to individualistic pursuits and materialist values.[48]

Frequently tracing this generational shift to the difficulties of the Special Period, these studies define the "problem" of contemporary Cuban youth in economic terms. Nonetheless, they also unfailingly cast the issue in moral and emotional terms as a crisis in values and a question of dissident affective states.[49] Despite their apparent sympathy for the situation of young adults, many of the recent studies by social scientists reassert an older model of (sacrificial) youth and moral rectitude epitomized by the figure of Ché Guevara.[50] At the end of her article, Domínguez draws a distinction between three "types" of youth: those who are strongly nationalistic and tie their personal aspirations to those of society (like Ché); an "intermediary" sector who exhibit some social commitment, but who are pulled toward individualistic pursuits and react passively to the current situation; and, finally, an opportunistic sector characterized by deteriorating moral values and purposeful consumerism.[51] Domínguez's typology has been quite influential, drawing support from other scholars like Romero et al.[52] and reverberating in films like *Plaff* and *Lista de espera* with protagonists who are or become emblematic of the first category. Unfortunately, this type of "diagnosis of social ills" does not acknowledge either the failure of Ché's preferential model of moral over economic incentives (discarded by the Cuban state itself as a principle of economic policy by the late 1960s) or the possibility of a new politics that eschews systematic rupture in favor of the type of social mobilization imagined in Juan Carlos Cremata's *Nada*.

Like Arturo Sotto's *Amor vertical*, *Nada* reworks the broad gestures characteristic of Cuban comedies to depict alienated young adults in more subtle ways. The film follows the misadventures of Carla Pérez, a petty bureaucrat working in a neighborhood post office who spends her days stamping letter after letter with an official government seal. When a spilled cup of coffee leads her to open one of the letters in order to dry it off, Carla becomes fixated on the idea of rewriting the often tersely phrased missives that cross her desk to call forth all their affective potential and, in so doing, help people communicate with each other more effectively.

In this simple comedic plot, the film situates young people like Carla as the agents by which the fragmented nation can heal through the recovery and expression of "lost" or repressed emotion. Cremata's work juxtaposes Carla's editorial interventions, which infuse the letters with lyrical expressions of love and suffering, against the packaged emotionalism and stifling bureaucratic speech of the "older" generation: At home, Carla becomes drawn to the show of Professor Cruzado, a tele-psychologist who doles out trite advice and tells his audience to "paste on a smile" and move forward beyond their heartache; while at work each day, she confronts the empty rhetorical flourishes of omnipresent bureaucratic signage ("Don't monkey around, work" / "No mariposees, produce").[53]

In the interstices between bland officialist exhortations and the excessive emotional displays of absurd telenovelas,[54] Carla's acts of rewriting are figured as a type of guerrillalike, bottom-up insurgency. The film often crosscuts between scenes of Carla rewriting the letters in her apartment with those depicting the people who will receive them. In one such sequence, a close-up of Carla's hand tracing letters on a blank page dissolves into a medium long shot of an older man walking down a sidewalk staircase. Subsequent shots depict the man in his daily routine—playing dominoes with friends in the park, answering his door to receive his daughter's letter from the postman, picking up a bottle of milk and walking along the *malecón*—as Carla's breathy voice-over reads the words of heartfelt longing that she has written to replace the daughter's mundane complaints about her life in southern Spain:

> Tu vida y la mía sólo están en los recuerdos. Sólo se encuentran en ellos pero la vida de lo cotidiano, lo hastío, el placer y el tiempo que se va sin te dar tiempo para los recuerdos y aunque también es cierto que uno no los persigue, ellos se aparecen . . . Me duele no verte, papá. ¿Cómo estarás ahora? ¿Cómo serás sin mí? La memoria es un animal que . . . come, duerme y se despierta. Y cuando lo hace, sin querer, nos hiere el alma y con ella todo lo que le rodea...

> [Your life and mine only exist in memories. They only meet in memories, but [then there's] daily life, the boredom, the pleasure, the time that flies by without giving us time for our memories, and even if it's true that one doesn't go looking for those memories, they pop up again . . . It hurts not to see you, Dad. I wonder what are you like now, who you are without me there. Memory is an animal that . . . eats, sleeps, and wakes up and when it does, without wanting to, it wounds our soul and all that we are.]

In the middle of this montage, as the man reads the letter, an extreme close-up highlights a single teardrop rolling down the sheet of paper. In sequences such as this one, *Nada* depicts Carla's reformulations as liberating acts releasing authentic emotions sequestered by mundane routines and calcified familial bitterness.

Cremata's *Nada* articulates a clear, age-based critique of the older Cubans who have failed to address the affective costs of revolutionary struggle—particularly, though not exclusively, the pain of separation through immigration and exile. Like the older man in the aforementioned scene, Carla also feels the loss of family members—in her case, her parents, two opera singers who left Cuba for the United States and who now send her periodic postcards from Miami featuring overweight women on the beach, sirens of capitalism and symbols of complacent consumer culture. The film's opening sequence captures Carla in an overhead shot as she talks in voice-over to her absent parents saying, "You didn't do anything to me. Nothing at all" ("No me hiciste nada. Nada")—a claim that the film itself (whose very title echoes her words) questions.

In many ways, *Nada*'s attempt to revivify "true" or "authentic" emotion is an effort to respond to nothingness and disavowal. Yet, in contrast to traditional articulations that characterize authenticity in terms of depth, Cremata's film encounters what it is looking for in the surface of things. As mentioned in the opening of this essay, *Nada* shares *Picado fino*'s interest in surface play, albeit in a very different way. Whereas the Argentine film favored frontal shots and disjunctive editing, the Cuban film employs overhead shots and scratches the surface of the film stock. Among other effects, these devices tend to flatten the screen and play with the realism of the profilmic space.

Together with the film's black-and-white photography, they call attention to the tangibility of emotional states and the textures of reality. When the older man stands on the *malecón* at the end of the sequence mentioned earlier and the camera cranes up in slow motion to an overhead shot, the film encourages the spectator to perceive the textures of that moment. The chipped surface of the seawall and the pock-marked sidewalk stand in for the grating emotional wear of familial separation (figures 4.2–4.4). Yet, as the camera cranes down again to the other side, framing the man as he gazes out over the wall toward the oncoming waves and the distant horizon ("toward Spain"), the shot also suggests his underlying love and longing for reconnection that the rewritten letter has brought to the surface. Throughout the extended crane shot, we hear the continuation of Carla's voice-over:

Hay días en que tu cara se vuelve más dulce o más amarga pero allí está ella, escencial, callada, eternal, urgente. Hay días que me muero por hablar contigo, por oír tu voz . . . Hay días que eres Dios, papá, y eso ahorra la distancia entre nosotros . . .

[On some days your face appears more sweet; on others, more bitter, but it is always there, essential, silent, eternal, urgent. There are times when I'm dying to talk with you, to hear your voice . . . There are days when you are God, Dad, and that bridges the distance between us . . .]

**Figure 4.2–4.4** The textures of longing in *Nada*

Rather than attesting to the waning of affect, *Nada*'s preoccupation with the surface of things gestures toward the way in which emotion weighs on everyday life.

The film's call for "emotional mobilizations" to draw together the Cuban people—figured here not as a function of the nation-state, but rather as an imagined, paraterritorial, affective affiliation—appears to offer one solution to the dilemma of contemporary Cuban cinema as articulated by Cuban critic Juan Antonio García Borrero. In his 2002 book *La edad de herejía*, García Borrero characterized 1990s cinema as stylistically innovative, but plagued by individualistic navel-gazing.[55] Attributing such solipsism to a number of factors, including the crisis of the socialist bloc, the fall of utopian promise, and, on a more immediate level, the lack of vigorous debate among the island's filmmakers, García Borrero called on the younger filmmakers to recapture a sense of collectivity and to propose new utopias.[56] This is precisely what *Nada* accomplishes in the end when Carla renounces the lottery slot that would allow her to leave Cuba for the United States. In so doing, she acknowledges what her mail-carrier boyfriend César has written to her in a letter prior to her departure: "People leave without ever truly getting anywhere . . . If everybody leaves, nothing changes . . . nothing at all." Her decision to stay reconfirms the well-established revolutionary exhortation to find personal fulfillment through commitment to the larger social good and, at the same time, reasserts the joyfulness of such an endeavor. In the final sequence, a yellow butterfly scratched onto the surface of the film (a motif that has appeared recurrently in the film) flitters around the head of Carla and César as they sit on a hill overlooking the ocean and playfully discuss what it means to be Cuban. Even as Carla's decision to stay signals her recommitment to the collective body, the butterfly mocks the bureaucratic exhortation to work and not screw around ("No mariposees, produce"). Her pleasured sighs as César makes love to her remind us that to be Cuban is to laugh, have fun, and take it all in stride. Unfortunately, in this final gesture, *Nada* falls back into line with the recuperative moves of traditional Cuban comedies and fails to address seriously the shortcomings of the revolution, forestalling rather than challenging the siren call of global consumer culture.

Cremata's subsequent film, *Viva Cuba* (France-Cuba, 2005), continued in this vein. A road movie about two young children (Jorgito and Maru) who travel across the island from Havana to the east to find the girl's estranged father, thus eluding her mother's plans to migrate with Maru to the United States, *Viva Cuba* figures its young protagonists in quite traditional ways as "innocents" struggling against the blindness of their parents, themselves characterized as representatives of two "sides" of Cuban society: those who hold onto visions of a more refined life before the revolution (and to dreams of a more prosperous life in the United States) and those who dedicate themselves so thoroughly to the revolution that they foreswear their own families. For most of the film, Cremata's second feature invites spectators to root for Jorgito and Maru to reach their destination and suggests that the children's bravery in rebelling against their parents' intransigence has the potential to bridge the differences that separate the parents of the two families (and, by extension, the Cuban nation). The film's overarching efforts to call for(th) nationalist sentiment is only punctured in the final sequence. In that scene, crosscut shots isolate the two bickering sets of parents (and the state official trying to contain their ever more violent disagreement) from the two children, who stand together hugging each other tightly on a precipice overlooking the ocean. Instead of providing resolution, the last shot of the crashing waves spraying over the two children until the screen fades to white offers an open ending—perhaps suggesting, as many earlier Cuban films have, that the answers must be found outside of the film by the audience members themselves. However, the final shot also cuts against the sentimental thrust that has dominated the film up until this point by allowing for the disturbing possibility that the children's only option has been to jump.[57]

One of the most radical depictions of contemporary Cuban youth appeared eleven years earlier in Jorge Luis Sánchez's film *Un pedazo de mí*.[58] The film offers a refreshing perspective on young adults by examining the subjectivity of that "third" sector critiqued by Domínguez and written out of most mainstream films. This fifteen-minute short presents interviews with a number of so-called *frikis* (freaks), young men marginalized by society who love heavy metal and other types of hard-driving English-language rock music. In key moments, as the soundtrack plays Jimi Hendrix, Pink Floyd, and other rock legends, the film uses black-and-white footage and a revolving handheld camera on wildly dancing bodies to capture the liberating promise of the music. As counterpoint, the sparse mise-en-scéne marks the young men's sense of alienation and marginalization as they walk through half-finished apartment buildings or construction scaffolding on the streets of the city. Attesting to the economic hardships experienced by these young men (immediately prior to the Special Period), the film's hollowed-out urban landscape speaks, in quite poetic ways, about their feelings of emotional isolation and abandonment and about the absence of affective ties to their own families or to the larger society. In another particularly lyrical sequence, a slow tracking shot leads us down a hallway and into a room with a rocking chair and crib void of human presences.

Youth here—unlike in other Cuban films—functions metonymically, rather than an allegorically. In other words, *Un pedazo de mí* does not offer us a totalizing trope of Cuban society wherein young adults function *merely* or *primarily* as a symbol of future possibilities and potentialities. Nor does it suggest that the experiences of this marginal(ized) sector of young adults is somehow representative of all Cuban youth. Rather, the documentary situates the young men as an important, if ignored, part of a larger whole. The film's vacant cityscape and unoccupied buildings recall the symbolism of Sara Gómez's now classic *De cierta manera* (1974), yet in the context of forty years of revolution gestures at less sweeping proposals for change. In registering the young men's feelings of emptiness and thwarted yearnings, the mise-en-scène simply asserts the importance of minding one's house and the individuals who occupy it.

*Un pedazo de mí* does not "recuperate" the young men by showing their recommitment to the revolution. Although it documents their love of homeland in their testimonies ("I'd never leave," insists one of the young men), the film does not offer a tale of redemption through their eventual incorporation into the social body. Instead, *Un pedazo de mí* labors to deepen the spectator's understanding of the young protagonists' painful disconnect from society and to validate their truncated desires for familial affections. The film does not subsume personal desire under one's commitment to the social good, nor does it dismiss the affective resonance that rock music holds for young adults as an expression of superficial consumer desire or antirevolutionary activity (a perspective held over from the radical nationalism of the late 1960s and early 1970s when all rock music was considered inherently neocolonialist). In its dogged attention to subjectivities, it rallies against the dominant articulation of youth as eternal militant.[59]

\*   \*   \*

I want to conclude by taking a brief look at similar debates about contemporary U.S. youth cultures that will help clarify the specificity of Latin American youth formations. In his article "...And Tomorrow Is Just Another Crazy Scam," Ryan Moore examines the "progressively nihilistic, exhausted, and ironically distanced character of much of [U.S.] youth culture and link[s] that 'structure of feeling' with the downward mobility of the middle class and the cultural condition we have come to know as 'postmodernity'."[60] According to Moore, the weakening of the white middle class has unsettled the narratives of progress and upward mobility that have dominated U.S. culture since the World War II and deeply influenced the socialization of white, suburban youth.[61] This discursive break has been accompanied by a "fundamental rupture between affect and ideology" that has made the investment of affective energies in larger ideals "arbitrary at best."[62] The recent focus on the apathy or "aggressive indifference" of young adults can also be seen as the result of the contemporary influence of prosperous Baby Boomers who were in their twenties in the 1960s, as suggested by Lawrence Grossberg. Now in their sixties, the Boomers wish to retain the characterization of youth that emerged in the 1960s as the template through which all subsequent generations of youth should be viewed.[63] The lack of faith in political commitments and social causes exhibited by Gen-Xers conflict with the narratives of progress and social mobility that were embraced by the 1960s counterculture as much as by the mainstream "conservative" culture it rebelled against.[64]

The U.S. case provides several interesting contrasts to the situation in Latin America, where the legacy of earlier generations of youth, and the revolutionary 1960s, is quite distinct. While there are clear differences between Argentina and Cuba, the Latin American revolutionary movements of the 1960s and 1970s, which to a great degree defined youth at that time, had greater structural influence on their respective societies than did the U.S. counterculture. If only in the case of Cuba did the insurgency lead to a full-scale revolution, armed guerrilla movements in Argentina and elsewhere successfully destabilized political institutions and, more indirectly, economic structures. At least this was the dominant perception that right-wing groups appropriated to justify the numerous military coups that took place in Brazil (1964–85), Chile (1973–90), Argentina (1976–83), and elsewhere. Thus, today's critiques of contemporary Latin American youth may be traceable to the shared revolutionary legacies or, more to the point, to the worries of a revolutionary generation who are now in their sixties and seventies and are looking back on the failures or limitations of their own youthful projects. Given this often bloody historical past, it is much more problematic for the Latin American contemporaries of the U.S. Baby Boomers to lay claim to a heroic past of transformative "resistance."

Recent Latin American films about young adults (often made by young or "youngish" filmmakers) clearly respond to earlier representations of youth chrystallized in the preceding revolutionary generation. The Cuban films respond to the notion of youth as eternal militant symbolized by the figure of Ché Guevara and the moralistic orientation spawned in the early days of the revolution that continue to inform contemporary discussions of society. In a markedly different context, newer Argentine films engage historical legacies and contemporary political realities tangentially, through gestures and metaphors. Unlike recent U.S. films, these Argentine films and others from Mexico and Brazil do not manifest a simple nostalgia, but rather a "nostalgia for nostalgia."[65] Taken together, these representations of Latin American youth are quite different from the ones in the United States, which, according to Moore, are marked by "the inability to locate oneself or even one's class in a historical, narrative fashion."[66] As Moore (via Frederic Jameson) notes, the sense of "temporal fragmentation" evident in U.S. youth culture "is directly related to the crisis of affect in postmodernity insofar as history and narrativity are precisely the type of 'depth models' whose apparent evaporation has paved the way for the contemporary liberation of feeling."[67] Whether through the "presence of depth" (*La ciénaga* and *Un pedazo de mí*) or "surface play" (*Picado fino* and *Nada*), these Latin American films of disaffected young adults measure the weight of history even as they contest, to greater and lesser degrees, the legacies of earlier formations of youth.

# CHAPTER 5

# Migrant Feelings: Global Networks and Transnational Affective Communities

> [W]e might aspire to engage a theory and practice of mapping for "traveling cultures," a cartography beyond the cognitive, open to webs of ethno-cultural movements in a way that accounts for the motion of emotion embodied therein.
>
> – Guiliana Bruno

In the prologue to her wonderful 2002 study *Atlas of Emotion*, Guiliana Bruno reminds readers that the word "cinema" comes from the Greek *kinema*, connoting "both motion and emotion," in order to encourage us to rethink film as a means of "transport in the full range of its meaning, including the sort of carrying which is a carrying away by emotion." Bruno is particularly interested in the first decades of filmmaking when formal experimentations offered "the modern subject [...] a new *tactics* for orienting herself in space and for making 'sense' of this motion, which includes the motion of emotions."[1] At the end of the twentieth century, when Latin American cinemas began to enjoy a renaissance, film was no longer a revolutionary technology. What once were dislocating aesthetics that held the potential to disrupt the viewer's temporal and spatial orientation (e.g., scalar shifts in framing in the early twentieth century; jump-cuts by the mid-late century) had become routine. Likewise, the historical and technological context in which audiences went to the movies had radically changed. In the Internet era, the cinema has become but one means by which contemporary subjects "jump" from where they are to someplace else—and it is not a particularly agile one at that.

Nonetheless, Bruno's explorations can be fruitful for discussions of filmmaking in the late twentieth and early twenty-first century. After all, in an era often understood as sensorially taxing and ethically exhausted, the cinema still serves as a favored form of transport. Identifying the formal means that encourage today's savvy viewers to be carried away requires further analysis, as does comprehending the social and political significance of this type of cinematic conveyance. As always, one must be aware of differences between divergent filmic traditions and cultural contexts—between Hollywood and Latin American cinemas—as well as differences within specific traditions and contexts.

Driven by the perceived potential of new digital technologies (particularly computer-generated imagery [CGI]), Hollywood companies have invested millions of dollars and enjoyed great commercial returns transporting viewers to other planets and exotic, alternate landscapes (*Star Wars* I–III, *Crouching Tiger, Hidden Dragon*; the *Harry Potter* films; *Avatar*). While certainly the result of their ability to astound us with heart-stopping spectacles, the popularity of such films (with audiences in the United States and in many other countries) may also be attributed to their ability to move us in other ways. As deftly argued by Karen Whissel, these films have utilized the possibilities of CGI to create a new verticality—one in which characters are poised atop the precipice (whether a sinking ship, a mountain top, or a wizard's tower) on the verge of tumbling over. For Whissel, narratives about highly stratified societies utilize this "vertical screen" as a means of commenting obliquely on new social hierarchies. Invoking Bruno's arguments about film's ability to serve as a sensuous map, we might speculate that in carrying us up dizzying heights (and, sometimes, over the edge), such films attract audiences by mediating the vertiginous feelings being spawned by the reformulation of social relations in an economically volatile time.

Certainly this type of high-tech travel is somewhat unique to Hollywood films. However, upon surveying contemporary Latin American cinema, one also finds new forms of cinematic routing, not least of which is the plethora of road films that have emerged since the mid-1990s: *El viaje* (Argentina-Mexico-Spain-France-UK, Fernando Solanas, 1992), *Guantanamera* (Cuba-Spain-Germany, Tomás Gutiérrez Alea and Juan Carlos Tabío, 1995), *Terra Estrangeira / Foreign Land* (Brazil-Portugal, Walter Salles and Daniela Thomas, 1996), *Central do Brasil* (Brazil-France, Walter Salles, 1998), *Bajo California* (Mexico, Carlos Bolado, 1998), *Por la libre* (Mexico, Juan Carlos Llaca, 2000), *Sin dejar huella / Without a Trace* (Spain-Mexico, María Novaro, 2000), *Y tu mama también* (Mexico, Alfonso Cuarón, 2001),

*Diarios de motocicleta* (Argentina-United States-UK-Germany-Mexico-Chile-Peru-France, Walter Salles, 2004), *Viva Cuba* (Francia-Cuba, Juan Carlos Cremata, 2005), *Que tan lejos / How Much Farther* (Ecuador, Tania Hermida, 2006), and *El camino / The Path* (Costa Rica, Ishtar Yasín Gutiérrez, 2007).[2] The majority of these films are coproductions and one of their most notable aspects is an interest in traversing often arduous national (and sometimes continental) landscapes in ways that are appealing to audiences located both at home and abroad.[3] If less technologically and formally innovative than Hollywood's CGI-laden fantasy films, many of these Latin American films have resonated with audiences and enjoyed commercial success. Speaking of dislocations and uprootedness, the road films cast these uncertainties as part of a journey toward self-realization made possible through establishing horizontal alliances.

The road films are merely one example of a broader trend in contemporary Latin American cinema toward exploring "unknown" territories or underrepresented regions of a given nation or foreign land. Equally noteworthy are the films being made by Latin American filmmakers working outside or alongside their home industries, including Brazilian director Walter Salles's *Diarios de motocicleta* set in Argentina, Chile, Bolivia, and Perú; Mexican Luis Mandoki's *Voces inocentes / Innocent Voices* (Mexico-United States-Puerto Rico, 2004) set in El Salvador; Brazilian Fernando Mereilles's *Constant Gardener* (UK-Germany, 2005) set in Kenya; Cuarón's *Children of Men* (Japan-UK-United States, 2006) set in a futuristic Great Britain; and Alejandro González Iñárruti's *Babel* (France-United States-Mexico, 2006) set in Morocco, Japan, and the United States-Mexico borderlands. Certainly, there is a long history of Latin American filmmakers leaving their countries of origin to work in Hollywood or in Europe for brief or extended periods.[4] What is new about these recent ventures is their geographic scope (in setting and location shooting); their ambition to speak of/for "other" cultures; and their efforts to reach pan-Spanish-speaking and/or English-language audiences by, among other things, harnessing the power of U.S./global distributors. Only recently could a Brazilian director make a film in Africa using well-known English-language actors or a Mexican director shoot a futuristic movie set in an apocalyptic Great Britain that slyly comments on contemporary immigration issues and the dangers of state repression.

How have these directors been able to travel so far? And how have their films and the previously mentioned road movies been able to attract such sizeable audiences? One could surmise that the mobility of these films (and of certain filmmakers) depends on their skill in mimicking the formal conventions of hegemonic cinemas (principally Hollywood) and their ability to call for(th) what are understood as universal emotions. The popularity of Latin American road films might be attributed to their appropriation of a genre long understood as quintessentially "American" with its attendant emotional scripts that align the viewer with the personal epiphanies of the protagonist(s) during their travels. The works by Salles, Mandoki, Mereilles, Cuarón, and González Iñárruti might be seen as updated and transnationalized "social problem films," a category that would also include *Hotel Rwanda* (UK-United States-Italy-South Africa, Terry George, 2004), *Syriana* (United States, Stephen Gaghan, 2005), and *Blood Diamond* (United States-Germany, Edward Zwick, 2006).[5] Zooming in from scenes of mass suffering to track specific characters touched by genocide, civil wars, and epidemics, such films call on audiences (sitting in theaters comfortably removed from sites of struggle) to act as compassionate global citizens. Akin to earlier films such as *Under Fire* (United States, Roger Spottiswoode, 1983) and *Salvador* (United States, Oliver Stone, 1986), the resurgent humanitarianism evident in the more recent works is bolstered by the public performances of Hollywood celebrities who speak in telethons, press conferences, and the pages of *People* magazine of the sufferings of "our" global neighbors and implore us to open up our pocketbooks for the latest relief efforts.

It is tempting to see the type of "global human bonds" promoted by these films as highly problematic. As Lauren Berlant, Marjorie Garber, Kathleen Woodward, and others have carefully argued, the sociopolitical effects of such calls for compassion are not always salutary. Often cast as a form of solidarity, the dynamics of compassion tend to rely on and reinscribe differential power relations between someone's suffering "over there" and the until-then-untouched viewing subject.[6] In its worst guise, compassion involves the appropriation of the suffering of others to affirm the moral superiority of the compassionate. Even at its best, compassion's individualizing dynamics move us away from the recognition of structural inequalities.[7]

While convincing in many ways, this argument is overly general. Without suggesting that Latin American directors avoid these traps entirely, it is noteworthy that a number of the aforementioned "social problem" films were coproductions targeting English-language or pan-Latin American audiences, directed by filmmakers born in Latin America working outside or alongside their home industries. What does it mean that the drive to speak of and feel for "other" cultures located "elsewhere" comes from Latin American directors?[8] As I hope to demonstrate, the analysis of such films reveals the shortcomings of the arguments of Berlant and others, that, however illuminating, ignore cultural variation—that is, the possibility that 1) traditions of feeling vary from culture to culture; and 2) such traditions are registered in discursive habits and performative practices. In this essay, I explore how Latin American directors sometimes encourage audiences to feel *through* (rather than feel *for*) others by "poaching" traditions of feeling that have emerged from other cultural formations. My point of departure will be two quite different films that plunder the traditions of the Mexican melodrama and the *crónica roja*/sensationalist crime press: Alejandro González Iñárruti's ficitonal *Babel* and Chicana director Lourdes Portillo's documentary *Señorita extraviada* (United States, 2001). Deeply concerned with morality, justice, guilt, and feeling, these popular genres are certainly not unique to Mexico. However, they have developed there in particular ways that are pertinent for the present discussion. I examine how *Babel* mines the particularities of Mexican melodrama and how *Señorita extraviada* plunders the docudrama and, in the process, tutors non-Mexican audiences in other ways of feeling in the world.

My analysis will pay particular attention to the textual strategies by which these films make their sensorial appeals. However, in the conclusion, I will broaden my discussion to offer a more complex model for how (and when) films can move us in unexpected ways to unexpected places by acknowledging the significance of the sociohistorical contexts in which such films are produced and circulated as well as the ways in which they address and help constitute particular communities. In so doing, I want to propose the possibility that films (along with other forms of cultural production) can help promote transnational "communities of sentiment."[9]

Let's begin by acknowledging the many differences between *Babel* and *Señorita extraviada*. The first is a large-scale, commercial work by a globe-trotting auteur (Alejandro González Iñárruti) starring famous actors (Brad Pitt, Cate Blanchett, Gael García Bernal); the second is a documentary made by a well-known Chicana filmmaker (Lourdes Portillo) and backed by public media (Corporation for Public Broadcasting [CPB]) and a number of private philanthropic foundations. Iñárruti's big-budget film was shot in Morocco, Japan, Mexico, and the United States by three production teams.[10] Portillo's low-budget work was filmed in and around Ciudad Juárez in the northern state of Chihuahua (Mexico) by Portillo herself and a small crew.[11] While *Babel* was dismissed by many critics as an overwrought paean to the shared humanity of diverse peoples, *Señorita extraviada* was lauded for bringing public attention to the plight of hundreds of poor young women who had "disappeared" from Ciudad Juárez and spotlighting the ineptitude and corruption of Mexican authorities.[12]

The films also have important similarities, most notably a common concern about violence and the role of the law in an era of globalization. In *Babel*, Abdullah (a poor man in Morocco) purchases a gun to keep scavengers away from his goats. He gives it to his sons, as they are charged with overseeing the herd. While on guard, the boys' rivalry leads them to test their marksmanship and in the process, Abdullah's youngest son, Yusef, accidentally shoots an American woman (Susan) who is traveling with her husband (Richard) in Morocco. This event sets off a series of chain reactions that ultimately lead to two other tragedies: 1) the death of Yusef's older brother Ahmed at the hands of Moroccan police; and 2) a terrifying walk through the California desert by Amelia (Richard and Susan's Mexican nanny) and their two children (Debbie and Mike) after being abandoned there by Amelia's nephew following a run-in with the U.S. border police. In tracing out these stories set in Morocco and the U.S.-Mexico borderlands (as well as a third story set in Japan), *Babel* contrasts the emotionless tenacity of law enforcement officials with the traumatic suffering of everyday people, whom the police are presumably charged to protect.

In its exploration of the unsolved murders of hundreds of young women in the border city of Ciudad Juárez, *Señorita extraviada* casts the law as more corrupt and inept than impassive. Nonetheless, the film similarly showcases the limited range of understanding (if not willful ignorance) of public officials, from the state governor and assistant attorney general to the special prosecutor assigned to the cases. Structured itself as an investigation into the disappearances, Portillo's work offers an indictment of the local police and politicians, rather than a single, clear-cut "solution" to the crimes. The film frequently juxtaposes the emotionally charged testimonies of the victims' families with the public pronouncements of prosecutors and elected officials and, in the process, questions the validity of the authorities' seemingly detached and objective analysis of the situation. In the end, *Señorita extraviada* points the finger at various culprits and suggests that the ineffective response of legal and political institutions is, to a certain degree, deliberate given their complicity with larger economic actors—drug traffickers, more "legitimate" transnational business corporations, or both—whose power (and impunity) is expanding in a free-trade era.

Beyond their shared interest in questioning the justness of the law in an era of globalization, both films engage their subject matter with feeling. That is to say, *Babel* and *Señorita extraviada*'s preoccupation with questioning the cold logic of the law becomes the impetus for formal experimentation as they appropriate sensational cultural forms (namely, melodrama, the tabloid press, and the docudrama) to move their viewers in unexpected ways. Moreover, by deploying particular manifestations of those cultural forms traceable to Mexico, the films not only push their viewers to explore how we are touched by globalization, but also tutor non-Mexican viewers in other protocols of feeling in the world.

Analyzing Iñárruti's *Babel* alongside Portillo's *Señorita extraviada* allows us to recognize links—on the one hand, between Latino/a and Latin

American film; and, on the other, between documentaries and fiction films. As noted by many scholars, Latino/a visual artists have long drawn inspiration from Mexico as well as from other Latin American countries. This is certainly the case with Lourdes Portillo. As documented by Rosa Linda Fregoso and other scholars, the Chicana filmmaker found in the New Latin American Cinema (NLAC) a source of inspiration.[13] Her early documentaries were conceived as political and aesthetic acts of solidarity with the peoples of Latin America.[14] *After the Earthquake / Después del terremoto* (1979, codirected with Nina Serrano) explores the life of a young Nicaraguan woman who immigrates to the United States after the 1979 earthquake in her country, while *Las madres: The Mothers of Plaza de Mayo* (1986, codirected with Susana Muñoz) chronicles the efforts of the Mothers of the Plaza de Mayo in Argentina to protest state repression during and after the right-wing military dictatorship of 1976–83. While the characterization of Portillo's documentaries as part of a Latino/a American tradition of politicized filmmaking is convincing, her work also draws on and honors popular traditions of feeling (from popular mourning practices to melodrama) for their ability to provide cultural continuity across national boundary lines—as evident in *La ofrenda: Days of the Dead* (1988), *The Devil Never Sleeps / El Diablo nunca duerme* (1994), *Corpus: A Home Movie for Selena* (1999), and *Señorita extraviada*.[15] She has exhibited a savvy awareness about how to best exploit those traditions to make highly entertaining documentaries that appeal to a wider public—a tactic that has proven particularly effective in winning funding from public media institutions, such as CPB, as well as from private foundations. Portillo's concern for reaching audiences in visceral ways echoes Iñárruti's preoccupation with "emotional logic" and suggests that her films might also be fruitfully studied in relation to the sensorially charged contemporary Latin American cinema.[16] In sum, such seemingly perverse comparisons can help us map the trajectories of Latin/a American cinemas in terms of genealogies that recognize affinities as well as divergences, rather than in terms of distinct historical horizons and modes (fiction vs. documentary) that all too often ignore or brush away ambivalence.

### Feeling out the Law

*Babel* encourages its viewers to recognize what the law does not: the affective weight of human existence in both its most banal and extreme moments. As in their previous two films, in *Babel,* Iñárruti and scriptwriter Guillermo Arriaga posit feeling as the essence of what it means to be human. The filmmakers rework the biblical tale of the tower of

Babel. The linguistic (and cultural) divisions separating nations are not the result of arrogant human designs to reach the heights of the divine. Rather, according to *Babel,* the origin of the schism between peoples lies in the sin of misrecognizing and ignoring the suffering of others. Their film is an effort to restore a sense of shared humanity by celebrating acts of solidarity—in part, by leading its viewers to acknowledge what many of its characters do not...until it is too late. In sum, *Babel* promotes knowing-feeling, a form of recognition that moves us beyond the rational to promote understanding between people who initially halt in the face of difference.

One means by which the film accomplishes this is by scrambling the order of story events and moving the plot forward and backward in chronological time. Somewhat reminiscent of *Amores perros, Babel's* plot is organized through a series of narrative loops—in this case, moving back and forth from Morocco to the two other locations. This time, however, multiple national settings add a layer of complexity. As outlined in figure 5.1,[17] most of the plot unfolds in Morocco; eleven of the film's twenty-three sequences take place there, and these are divided between those dealing with Yusef's family and those dedicated to Susan and Richard. The first sequence begins in Morocco with the arrival of a man named Hassan, who sells the gun to Abdullah, and ends when a distant bus stops in the middle of the road and Yusef and Ahmed realize that their boyish shooting contest has had tragic consequences. From then on, sequences alternate between those taking place in Morocco and those set in southern California/northern Mexico (six total scenes) or in Japan (six total scenes). This plot structure has a number of effects; most notable among them is the attenuation of causal links between narrative events. While a subsequent sequence is often loosely connected to the prior scene, the nature of that relationship is initially unclear. For example, the second sequence is set in Richard and Susan's house in southern California where Amelia answers a phone call from Richard who reassures her that his wife is better but awaiting surgery. Amelia's employers have not yet appeared on screen; however, the plot sequencing suggests that it was Susan who was shot by Yusef. The third sequence opens with quick shots of tourists in a desert town before settling on a two-shot of Richard and his uninjured wife sitting in a restaurant in Morocco, an event that must have taken place *before* either of the other two previous sequences. Sequence 4 shifts to Japan where a girl (Chieko) is playing volleyball and then takes a short drive with her father, before going to a J-Pop with her friends. Sequence 5 returns to Morocco where Yusef and Ahmed are running back to their home to hide.

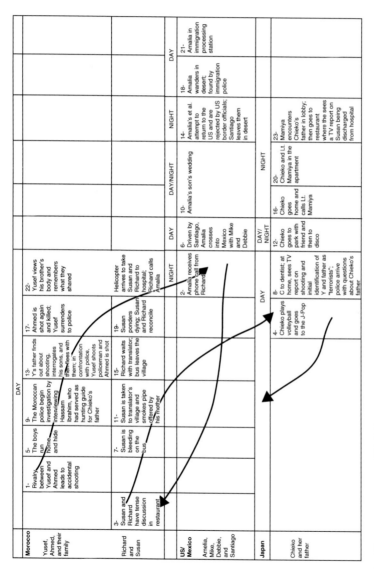

**Figure 5.1** Plot segmentation of *Babel*

In the initial half-hour of the film, the relationship between sequences is increasingly difficult to discern. While alluding to the consequences of the shooting for Richard and Susan, the second sequence places greater emphasis on exploring the impact on Amelia (who was planning to attend her son's wedding the following day) and on her loving relationship with Richard and Susan's two children, Mike and Debbie. The third sequence, in turn, diverts our attention further away from the aftermath of the shooting to provide us with information about the precarious state of Richard and Susan's marriage (in part, a result of the death of their youngest son). Lacking any reference at all to the previously seen event, the significance of the fourth sequence (set in Japan) is even more puzzling.

*Babel* does not function as a narrative of detection; we are not interested in finding "who did it" (indeed, from the first sequence onward, we already know). Nor does the film seem interested in exploring the characters' actions as crimes or in assigning guilt—at least not in a legal sense. Rather, by scrambling narrative continuity, *Babel* encourages viewers to turn away from the search for cause-and-effect connections as a privileged hermeneutics and to embrace other means of decipherment. Clearly, many other recent films feature this type of narrative looping—from *Pulp Fiction* (1994), to Iñárruti and Arriaga's own *Amores perros* (2000), to Paul Haggis's *Crash* (2004). What makes *Babel* more akin to the latter two than to Tarantino's film is its exploration of what Iñárruti has called "emotional logic." *Babel* reorders story events and juxtaposes sequences in particular ways as a means to reveal what it deems to be the true, affective connections between its characters—linkages that are concealed or covered over by attempts to find a strict line of causation (a method preferred by the police detectives in Morocco and the United States).

The first and second sequences are edited together through a match-cut juxtaposing the running feet of Yusef and Ahmed as they flee the hilltop overlooking the bus stopped on the road below to those of Mike and Debbie as they play hide-and-seek with Amelia. Even as the edit suggests a connection between these children living in opposite hemispheres, the film also underscores the differences: how childhood in less economically privileged environments entails greater responsibility (work over play) and how an innately "childish" desire for play can lead to calamity in specific contexts. This idea about the precarious innocence of childhood is further developed at the end of the second sequence when Mike, settled in his bed at night, asks Amelia to leave the light on so that he won't die in his sleep like his baby brother Sam did, presumably from sudden infant death syndrome (SIDS), as well as in the third sequence, when Richard and Susan's tense exchange alludes to Sam's death. Taken together, these initial sequences are intertwined less by their loose temporal relation than by a shared concern for death, depicted here as a haunting event that can happen suddenly and unexpectedly for uncertain reasons. The ghostly figure of death that appears in these three scenes further fosters a sense of low-grade foreboding. At the end of the third sequence, when Santiago asks his aunt Amelia, "Estás segura, tía" ["Are you sure, Aunt?"] about taking Mike and Debbie across the border to Mexico, the film intimates that danger is indeed imminent.

The "emotional logic" governing *Babel*'s plot structure differs from the ongoing dread of *Amores perros* (as discussed in chapter 3). Indeed, the foreboding developed in the first three sequences dissipates with the seemingly incongruent shift to the fourth sequence set initially at Chieko's volleyball match in Japan. *Babel*'s affective play is less cumulative than punctual or episodic. However, it fulfills a similar function of rerouting the viewer's hermeneutical wiring to acknowledge other circuits of knowledge. As seen in the shift from the first to the second sequence (i.e., from Yusef and Ahmed fleeing the mountaintop, to Mike and Debbie screaming in delight in their game of hide-and-seek), emotional extremes such as excitement and fear often serve as the hinge between key scenes set in divergent locales. By attenuating causal linkages, *Babel* encourages the viewer to concentrate on affective c(l)ues.

Approximately midway through the narrative (sequences 13 and 14), the film again shifts abruptly between Morocco and the U.S./Mexico borderlands to insist upon the shared experiences of common people and to indict the law's inhumanity. In Morocco, having confessed to their family about what they had unwittingly done, Yusef, Ahmed, and their father attempt to flee through the hilly terrain, but are unsuccessful when they are spotted by police in patrol cars on a nearby road. In the ensuing confrontation, after the police open fire and hit Ahmed in the leg, Yusef picks up his family's gun (seemingly to defend his bleeding sibling and his father) and shoots a policeman. At that moment, the film suddenly cuts to the Mexican village late at night, where in the aftermath of the wedding Amelia, Mike, Debbie, and a less-than-sober Santiago get in the car for the return trip to the United States. The abrupt edit ensures that the emotional pitch of the prior sequence in Morocco carries over into the subsequent sequence, which then recounts Santiago's drunken drive to the border in pitch-black darkness and the tense encounter with the border police, as well as Santiago's explosive decision to flee from the scene and abandon Amelia, Mike, and Debbie in the desert.

As in the film's first two scenes, the events depicted in sequences 13 and 14 ostensibly are causally unrelated. Yet, through the juxtaposition of the two sequences and their shared tone of urgency and anxiety, *Babel* encourages us to see other types of connections—most notably, how police officials' misrecognition of the underlying innocence of their "suspects" can lead to perilous outcomes. Both scenes depict the Moroccan and U.S. officers as implacable and tenacious. Having beaten Hassan (the man who originally sold the gun to Yusef's family), the Moroccan police forcibly place his wife in their car and compel her to help identify Yusef's father. Their single-mindedness finds a parallel in the actions of the U.S. guard encountered by Santiago and Amelia at the border station. After reviewing their passports and seemingly finding them in order, the officer responds to Santiago's awkward joking and Amelia's nervous acquiescence by asking for the children's paperwork. When Amelia cannot produce what she does not have, the border guard reacts to Santiago's increasing jitteriness by asking if he is drunk and then demanding that he get out of the car. Using a medium shot from within the car, as if from Amelia's perspective, the film shows the officer placing his hand on his side-arm, unsnapping the holster, and repeating his demand with implacable authority.

Although highlighting the harshness of their methods (particularly those of the Moroccan police), these sequences do not figure the police as corrupt. After all, both the Moroccan officers and the U.S. border guard are correct about the illegality of Yusef and Amelia's actions. However, the film clearly wants to question the moral underpinnings of their actions by highlighting the true and unjust suffering of Yusef and Amelia at the hands of these uncomprehending policemen. The two conjoined sequences help set up even more spectacular scenes of recognition and disavowal. In this drive toward the recognition of moral injustice and undeserved suffering, *Babel* betrays its melodramatic proclivities.[18]

While a full engagement with the notion of melodrama lies beyond the reach of this chapter, it will be helpful to review a few key arguments about its nature and function before discussing its differential historical trajectory in specific geocultural contexts, such as Mexico. In his masterful, pioneering work about the emergence of melodrama in late -eighteenth and nineteenth-century France, Peter Brooks contends that the melodramatic mode distinguished itself from other aesthetic formulations through its insistence on moral legibility in a nonsacred age. How melodramatic works achieve that goal (e.g., through a Manichean narrative order, the use of *tableaux vivant* and/or music to express hypostatic emotional states) would vary according to the particular work, time period, and cultural context. However, the compulsion to make moral categories utterly transparent in a post-Enlightenment era would remain a constant, as would the acknowledgement that such clarity had to be found or uncovered. Scholars of melodrama have often seen its narratives of misrecognition and revelation as a response to the anxieties produced by fluctuating political, social, and economic structures. As those structures have experienced tremors or undergone tectonic shifts, melodrama has insisted upon transcendent moral values as civilizing pillars anchored in the foundation of Christianity.[19]

In her lovely 1998 essay "Melodrama Revisited," film scholar Linda Williams discusses melodrama's utopic project, arguing that it "is structured upon the 'dual recognition' of how things are and how they should be."[20] In a similar way, speaking of televisual forms of melodrama, Jesús Martín Barbero argues that the telenovela is about "a struggle *to be recognized by others*."[21] Melodramatic narratives often revolve around the misreading of a given (main) character (and perhaps situation) as morally suspect by other characters. Such misrecognition is often sustained until the very end of the narrative when (a) climatic scene(s) reveal(s) his or her underlying innocence. The dramatic tension of melodrama arises, in part, from the conflict between the characters; however, equally important is the disparity between the limited understanding of particular characters and the more wide-ranging knowledge of the audience/reader, who is always aware of the essential innocence of the victim-hero.

Pathos, melodrama's most celebrated characteristic, is central to these dynamics of recognition. As Williams notes (following Franco Moretti's arguments about "moving literature"), the tears of pathos are generated by scenes of belated recognition, by the realization that "something important has been lost" and that this recognition has come "too late."[22] The tears spill over "when what one character knows is reconciled with what another knows, but 'too late'."[23] After such reconciliations, "tension is released, and at this point only [can the character, and we,] cry."[24] The relationship established between the aggrieved character(s) and the viewers is more complex than it might at first seem. Addressing those who have disparaged melodrama's emotional appeals and the tears of their presumably female audiences, Williams responds with the following corrective: "Pathos in the spectator is [...] never merely a matter of losing oneself in 'over-identification.' It is never a matter of simply mimicking the emotion of the protagonist, but, rather, a complex negotiation between emotions and between emotion and thought."[25]

This overview of the mechanics of melodrama allows us to better understand how (and why) *Babel*'s affective dynamics work to indict the law. Throughout the film, there is a disjuncture between what the police believe and what the audience "knows." This becomes particularly acute in the previously discussed sequences 13 and 14. The Moroccan police are working under the assumption that Yusef and his family are terrorists; the U.S. border guard seem to suspect that Amelia and Santiago are kidnapping the two children. In contrast, we know that the shooting was an accident and that Amelia's motivations for having taken the children to Mexico were not nefarious. These sequences help to build tension and to create pathos as the film encourages us to understand the actions of these law officers as unjust given the "true" innocence of Yusef and Amelia.

Yet, these scenes do not invite tears as there is no reconciliation of their different understandings of the same situation. That occurs later, near the end of the film, in another group of sequences. In scene 17, the film returns to Morocco and the shoot-out with the police, where Ahmed is shot again (this time fatally) as he tries to take cover from the police fire. Watching his father sob over Ahmed's body (figure 5.2), Yusef surrenders to the police and tearfully confesses to having shot the tourist, claiming all of the blame for the incident. The sequence tells us quite a bit about how the film frames the act of recognition. The low-angle reaction shot after Yusef's confession emphasizes the police detective's stunned expression as he realizes his/the law's mistake, and his sudden insight is underscored by the removal of his sunglasses. This shot is set up by the previous close-up of Hassan's wife who has served as an unwilling accomplice and whose gaze underscores the tragic nature of the events that she/we have just witnessed; the "reconciliation" of the law with those it mistook for "suspects"/"terrorists" has come "too late."

While this scene calls for tears, the film lets them fall elsewhere by cutting to the following sequence in Mexico, in which Amelia and the children wake up to find themselves (still) abandoned in the desert. Mike's question to Amelia ("Why are we hiding if we didn't do anything wrong?") neatly synthesizes the film's own perspective on their situation. Here, as in the previous sequence in Morocco, the film utilizes the plight of the child to question the hard logic of the law. At the same time, although Mike and his sister Debbie are situated as the ultimate innocents in the scenes set in the U.S./Mexico borderlands, *Babel* also insists upon the disproportionate nature of Amelia's suffering. The sequence includes numerous shots of her wandering through the arid landscape searching for the road, first carrying Debbie in her arms, and then stumbling on alone to find help after having left the exhausted children under a shaded tree. The often handheld camera jerks along with Amelia's stumbling gait and its angle mimics her dazed stare downward at the parched earth or upward at the glaring sunlight. These subjective shots alternate with medium close-ups capturing Amelia's shoeless feet, ripped hose, matted hair, sweaty face, smeared makeup, and stooped body. The disjunctive editing documents Amelia's increasing disorientation and, at the same time, makes Amelia's intense suffering visible to the viewer.

The prolonged duration of this sequence showcasing Amelia's perilous trek through the desert is absolutely key to what happens next. When she finally flags down a border patrol car, the officer's terse response and singular interest in arresting her ("Attention, dispatch, I think we got the suspect")—rather than heeding her terrified cries about the need to find the children—serves to deepen our sympathy for Amelia. Unlike the encounter with the police in Morocco, this one does not end in reconciliation nor does it invite our tearful relief. Rather, the conclusion of the sequence accentuates the pathos of the situation by underscoring the police officer's lack of understanding and lack of vision; the sequence ends with Mike and Debbie still lost in the desert as a couple of officers stand around their patrol cars asking Amelia if she came with "the others." Through the inclusion of three brief shots of adults and children (presumably illegal immigrants) behind bars inside a police vehicle , the film invites us to consider how Amelia's situation may be representative of that of "the others."[26]

The narratives set in Morocco, the U.S./Mexico border, and Japan indict the legal system in all three countries for ignoring "true" innocence. Yet, *Babel* seems to take particular aim at the United States. Whereas the detectives in Morocco eventually recognize the truth, those in the United States never do. The scene of recognition in Morocco where the detective appears to acknowledge Yusef's innocence finds a parallel in Japan, but not in the United States where there are three separate sequences (14, 18, 21) of official misrecognition.[27] Indeed, *Babel* characterizes the unjust actions of the police both in Morocco and on the U.S./Mexico border as the outcome of misguided American politics. As tensions escalate in the scene set on the border, a long shot of the patrol station (framed through the window of Santiago's car) includes photographs of President George W. Bush and Vice President Dick Cheney. Their faces smile down upon the border guards who emerge from the building to search Santiago's car. In an analogous fashion, in sequences featuring Richard and Susan's travails, there are numerous references to the culpability of the U.S. government, for the mischaracterization of the shooting as an act of terrorism, the subsequent rush to judge those responsible as dangerous fanatics (thus, to use whatever means necessary in their apprehension), and the exacerbation of Susan's plight/suffering.[28]

If *Babel*'s deployment of the melodramatic promotes a reconsideration of the law (and U.S. policies toward the rest of the world), what is particularly noteworthy about this effort is the recourse to a particular articulation of the melodramatic mode, which can be traced to Mexican cultural formations. The most obvious influence is the Mexican telenovela, which is distinguishable from Brazilian, Colombian, and Venezuelan varietals in a number of ways, including its moral absolutism anchored in (and validating) a particularly conservative brand of Catholicism and its proclivity for exhibiting ecstatic emotion.[29] *Babel* is infused with a Catholic sensibility, first and foremost, through its depiction of innocence and of the family as a sacred unit. Key to this is the film's privileging of the perspectives of children—Chieko, Mike, and, most notably, Yusef —who by their very nature are understood as "unknowing." Here *Babel* draws on a key distinction in Catholic doctrine between venial and mortal sin—that is, between less serious transgressions of God's law and grave violations of the central commandments ("do not kill"; "do not commit adultery"), in which the acts were committed with "full knowledge" and "deliberate consent" of the perpetrators. The film takes great pains in its first sequence to depict Yusef's actions (i.e., his shooting of Susan) as the result of a childish rivalry with his older brother, rather than a deliberate act of malevolence. He clearly does not intend to injure anyone. Moreover, he eventually "atones" for his sin after his brother is fatally shot when he falls down on his knees in front of the police to confess and take all the blame in order to protect his father from injury.[30]

In contrast, Amelia is clearly an adult who knowingly decides to take Mike and Debbie across the border to Mexico without their parents' explicit consent. Nevertheless, the film does not characterize this decision or her actions as sinful, despite the fact that they contribute to a nearly tragic outcome. Indeed, the film includes a sequence in which Amelia makes various attempts to find trusted friends to watch over the children for the day and dismisses Santiago's suggestion that they leave Mike and Debbie with one of his (girl)friends. In other words, *Babel* depicts Amelia as a loving caretaker who does not carelessly disregard her charges' well-being and characterizes the motivation behind her decision as a rather understandable desire to attend her own son's wedding (i.e., by her sacred duties as mother).[31] In these ways, Catholic doctrine subtends the delineation of innocence in Iñárruti's work.

*Babel*'s ties to Mexican melodrama go beyond this moral framework to include the way it highlights ecstatic emotional states—most notably, suffering, which is showcased with frequency and often at great length, in ways that call to mind Catholic iconographic traditions.[32] As the narrative progresses, these scenes of suffering occur more frequently. In sequence 16, after Lt. Mamiya rejects Chieko's attempt to seduce him, she begins to sob and we watch as he comforts her by holding her close and witnessing her pain (figure 5.3). The film then cuts to Morocco where (in sequence 17) we watch Yusef's father sob over his son's body (figure 5.2); and soon thereafter to the U.S./Mexico border (sequence 18) to Amelia's agonizing walk through the desert (figure 5.4). A short while later, sequence 21 begins

**Figures 5.2–5.4** The iconography of ecstatic emotion in *Babel*

with two fairly long takes of a distraught Amelia sitting before the customs official, whose initially blurred figure and remorseless tone underscore the brutally impersonal nature of the law.[33] The sequence ends by cutting from a close-up of Amelia's tearful face as she is being embraced by her son on the border (after having been thrown out of the United States), to Morocco where we first see Ahmed's body being carried down the mountain by the police and then a close-up of Yusef's tear-stained face framed through a slow track to the left.

Only a very few shots in these sequences visually fixate on the suffering body in a manner akin to the iconic representations of the tormented Christ or martyred saints that populate Catholic churches—that is, through static shots and immobile/ized bodies. Nonetheless, *Babel* evokes this representational tradition and the viewing protocols it entails through, respectively, 1) the prolonged length of scenes of suffering, which position that ecstatic state of feeling as a transparent sign of moral good; and 2) the frequency of their utilization to call on the viewer to serve as witness to this suffering.

Clearly, these types of close-ups are not unique to Mexican melodrama. They can also be found in older U.S. films—in the silent period and in 1940s women's films—as well as in contemporary U.S. soap operas.[34] Nevertheless, *Babel* deploys such moments of hypostatic or "overly ripe" emotion differently, as they tend to be performative in nature. This interest in "exhibiting" emotion—as a worthy enterprise in and of itself—is characteristic of many melodramatic forms from Mexico, including the *canción ranchera,* a musical form traceable to early-twentieth-century Mexico during the period immediately following the outbreak of the Mexican Revolution. In her essay "Unruly Passions: Poetics, Performance, and Gender in the Ranchera Song," anthropologist Olga Nájera-Ramírez characterizes the *canción ranchera* as a "form of melodrama—a discursive space characterized by the intensity of emotion in which issues of profound social concern may be addressed."[35] Her analysis moves beyond the discussion of the representation of emotion in the lyrics to consider emotional excess as a preferred performative style, noting that "[t]he singer's ability to engage the audience depends on his or her ability to invoke a broad range of emotions"—a dynamic made possible through "singing style, costuming, gestures, and other theatrical devices, as well as the sites of performance."[36] It is this performative style that has allowed the music and lyrics to resonate with Mexican audiences "on both sides of the border."[37] As Nájera-Ramírez herself insists, this is not an essentialist claim about the "passionate nature" of Mexicans as expressed in their cultural forms. Rather, her argument "recognize[s] emotional excess as a deliberate aesthetic quality of the ranchera" as well as of other melodramatic forms that developed in Mexico in particular ways.[38]

What, then, might it mean when such aesthetic (representational and performative) traditions show up in a film produced and distributed by Paramount Vantage whose top billing was given to its two English-language stars (Brad Pitt and Cate Blanchett)? Might not such a film, geared in large part toward an English-language audience, serve to school it in other ways of feeling in the world? To develop this part of my argument, I want to return to the propositions of Williams, Martín Barbero, and others about the goals of melodrama. For her part, Williams argues that it aims for "the achievement of a felt good, the merger—perhaps even the compromise—of morality and feeling" as experienced by readers, theatergoers or movie audiences.[39] If the nature of that "felt good" relates in part to the moral values exalted therein,[40] it also is the product of a particular (path)way of feeling as carved out and expressed in culturally and historically situated ways. Commenting on the nineteenth-century novels of French authors Sue, Hugo, and Balzac, Thomas Elsaesser seems to confirm this when he writes that melodrama has "served as the literary equivalent of a particular, historically and socially conditioned *mode of experience*."[41] In discussing the telenovela, Latin American communications scholars have made a similar argument, suggesting that such programs house "cultural matrices" understood not only as "mental schemes, but also habits of knowledge and behavior" / "esquemas mentales, sino como 'prácticas de conocimiento y comportamiento'."[42] But how might we define that mode of experience or embodied understanding of the world being advanced through *Babel*?

Aside from the privileged moral valence attributed to suffering, the film also insists on making such anguish not only visible, but palpable. Again and again the film showcases the ecstatic or "high-key" emotional states of its protagonists and positions spectators to act as sympathetic witnesses. When abrupt edits "carry over" these feelings to a subsequent sequence, *Babel* pushes viewers to be moved in unexpected ways. In so doing, the film does not promote a politics of compassion—at least not as theorized by Berlant. For her, compassion depends upon a type of visual regime that maintains a separation between the spectatorial subject and the scene of suffering "over there," regardless of the way in which such scenes are "brought home and made intimate by sensationalist media."[43] It is my contention that *Babel* does something different. Through edits that move (us) from one "global locale" to another, the film establishes contact zones wherein scenes of suffering intermingle. More importantly, through its formal mechanisms, the film invites its Anglo-American viewers to feel otherwise by glorying in the overt display of "excessive" emotion—something generally discouraged by cultural traditions in the United States, whether as a result of its Protestant heritage (Puritanism and/or Calvinism) or the collective experience of specific historical conjunctures (the Great Depression, World War II).[44] Iñárruti and Arriaga are drawing on and "publicizing" other traditions wherein being emotionally demonstrative is not merely acceptable, but rather laudable—a sign of authenticity and sociability.[45]

They may also be tapping into more recent shifts in this mode of experience tied to the effects of globalization as lived on a mundane basis in what was formerly understood as "the periphery." As argued by Martín-Barbero, Carlos Monsiváis, and others, whether in Mexico or other parts of Latin America, melodramas have served to mediate social transformations. In the twentieth century, *radionovelas*, cinematic tearjerkers, and then telenovelas eased the cognitive-affective transition of rural denizens to city life, allowing them to, among other things, "appropriate modernity without abandoning their oral culture."[46] In the late twentieth and early twenty-first centuries, Latin American melodramas may be functioning to reconcile tensions that have emerged between national traditions and global flows. This is clearly a vast topic that goes beyond the parameters of this chapter. What I hope to suggest is that *Babel*'s intensity, its ecstatic, disruptive aesthetic, may also be reverberating with the accelerated destabilizations experienced by those living in Mexico and other parts of Latin America—an awareness of rupture already registered in contemporary Mexican telenovelas with their fractured, accelerated narratives and penchant for the startling.[47]

As I will discuss further in the conclusion, moving emotions is not merely a matter of textual *tac*tics or maneuvers that invite audiences to expand their communicative competencies and repertoires of feeling, but also of sufficiently dense receptive communities and production-distribution circuits. However, before exploring these issues in greater detail, I want to look at how Lourdes Portillos's *Señorita extraviada* plunders another Mexican popular form, the *nota roja*, to denounce the murders in Ciudad Juárez and their sensationalist depiction in the local press.

### Making Sense of Globalization: Tabloid Appeals and the Politics of Mourning

*Señorita extraviada* (2001) offers a different type of affective mapping of the violence of globalization. Unlike *Babel*'s globe-trotting structure, Portillo's documentary focuses on a single place, the Mexican border-city Ciudad Juárez, as a microcosm of a world gone askew. A key sequence near the beginning of the film features Portillo's voice-over reciting information that seemingly defines the city: with the signing of the North American Free

Trade Agreement (NAFTA), "multinational companies flooded into Juárez to open assembly plants, called *maquiladoras*. Eighty percent of them are American-owned"; "the *maquiladoras* around the border generate around 16 billion dollars revenue per year"; young women from Mexico's poorest regions looking for work "earn 4 to 5 dollars a day." Images of the *maquiladoras*, workers getting off buses, and computer parts give way to fast-motion shots of workers buzzing around a restaurant kitchen and cars whizzing through the city's streets. Day becomes night and the colors of neon lights blur together. Through this aural-visual overlay, the film effectively undercuts the traditional function of such an introductory sequence. Instead of helping to anchor the viewer in a particular, locatable, and thus *understandable* place, the accelerated motion and frenetic movement characterize Juárez as a city that is no longer legible, a "city of the future" that is menacing and anxiety-producing.

From its opening sequences, *Señorita extraviada* casts the massacre of young girls there as the outgrowth of a larger economic, social, and political restructuring, rather than as a "mere" crime traceable to specific culprits. The film situates itself as a response to globalization, understood as social trauma.[48] It sets out to accomplish this goal by combining two disparate approaches. On the one hand, *Señorita extraviada* hooks into Mexican traditions of mourning in order to represent the grief of family members and to work through the social trauma being experienced by many people living in Ciudad Juárez. On the other, Portillo's film poaches the conventions of tabloid journalism (particularly the Mexican tradition) in order to give voice to social anxieties and popular forms of knowledge about the contemporary moment. As this latter contention goes against most previous interpretations of the film, I will begin my argument here.

When discussing *Señorita extraviada*, most commentators agree that the film offers an effective indictment of the salacious depiction of the killings in Ciudad Juárez by the press on both sides of the border. Among other things, critics have pointed to the film's refusal to "make a spectacle of sexual violence against women" as well as its insistence on portraying women as agents rather than as mere victims.[49] Such characterizations are convincing in their efforts to distinguish Portillo's film from the exploitative traditions of tabloid journalism. Nonetheless, as detailed in this next section, in the rush to celebrate the film as socially conscious and politically engaged, these critical perspectives have overlooked the ways in which *Señorita extraviada* actually mines sensationalist media forms for many of their prized formal tactics, including framing itself as a response to an unsolved mystery, incorporating interviews with people whose testimonies have been ignored by the police, recontextualizing materials through juxtaposition (or through what scholars of tabloid journalism have called "rearticulation"), and deploying dramatic re-creations in calculated ways to reenact key moments in a crime.[50]

The move by critics to distance *Señorita extraviada* from tabloid journalism is noteworthy, as scholarship on her earlier films has recognized and celebrated their appropriation of other "lowbrow," sensorially rich media forms such as telenovelas and noir. Rosa Linda Fregoso, Yvonne Yarbo-Bejarano, and many others have recognized the recourse to melodrama, in particular, in films such as *Después del terremoto* and *El Diablo Nunca Duerme / The Devil Never Sleeps*, as a means to honor culturally situated traditions of making sense of social realities.[51] Drawing on the feminist revision of melodrama that emerged in the 1980s through the work of Christine Gledhill, Linda Williams, and others, they underscore Portillo's critical and reflexive use of such forms.[52]

Portillo's *Señorita extraviada* does something similar with tabloid journalism (in general) and *la nota roja*, Mexico's crime press (in particular), giving voice to other forms of knowledge and subverting the empirical epistemologies upon which the state's legal apparatus depends. As noted by Kevin Glynn, "[t]hat tabloids include and amplify voices and popular knowledges that are otherwise excluded from the dominant regime of truth can be seen to account for both their wide circulation among relatively disempowered social formations *and* their rampant demonization by those with easy access to the structure of power and its distributive mechanisms."[53] Thus, it will be helpful to better understand how *Señorita extraviada* employs many of the formal tactics of tabloid journalism and, in so doing, "appeals to feelings of alienation and exclusion from the circulation of information."[54]

### "I Came to Juárez to Track Down Ghosts… "

With this initial voice-over, Portillo situates her film as an attempt to solve a mystery that has seemingly flummoxed law enforcement officials. As a counterinvestigation, her efforts at detection forgo the type of empirical evidence favored by the law. Instead, the film "draw[s] on the domain of common sense and lived experience"[55] by privileging interviews with family members of several of the disappeared girls (namely Silvia Arce, Sagrario González, and María Isabel Nava) along with conversations with Victoria Caraveo and Judith Galarza, two local activists; Irene Blanco, a lawyer defending Sharif Sharif, (the man that state officials long identified as the mastermind behind the murders); and María, a woman who was raped by the local police. Forming the structural backbone of the film, these interviews serve several functions. In their loving descriptions, the family members reanimate the individual lives of their daughters and sisters and, in emphasizing their particularities, counterbalance the discursive tendency of the mainstream media (as well as of the documentary form itself) to treat the disappeared women as statistics.

At the same time, the family interviews bracket those with state officials and help to deconstruct their patriarchal discourses and undercut their empirical methods. Early on, the film problematizes the position of the governor of Chihuahua (Francisco Barrio) and the state's assistant attorney general (Jorge López), who initially dismissed the disappearances as crimes against "mere prostitutes," through a tactic of double enclosure. Whereas family members and others appear in medium shots speaking directly to the camera or to an off-screen interviewer, the two male officials speak within the borders of a television screen (as part of previously recorded programs). The composition portrays the men as distanced from the tragic events they so coolly discuss and out of touch with those who have suffered. The film further undercuts their authority by recontextualizing or rearticulating these archival interviews between shots of activist Judith Galarza speaking directly to an off-screen interviewer (presumably Portillo). This calculated juxtaposition privileges Galarza's impassioned (and speculative) arguments and situates the male officials as little more than talking heads.

Later on, the film continues its indictment of the state by taking aim at Zully Ponce, the female prosecutor brought on board in 1996 to head a special unit dedicated to solving the crimes. Unlike the two male officials, Ponce appears directly in an interview with an off-screen Portillo and speaks of the errors committed by the police before her arrival (including the mishandling of key evidence) before touting the "new scientific rules of investigation" introduced during her tenure. But rather than celebrate these empirical methods, the film quickly debunks their efficacy by cutting to an interview with Guillermina González, who recalls that officials attempting to carry out a DNA test on her murdered sister exhumed the wrong body from an adjacent tomb. In discussing the matter, González notes that when confronted with their mistake, the officials insisted that despite the error in the paperwork (listing the wrong tomb number), they had exhumed the right body and, thus, that the DNA test was valid evidence. In these and other sequences, *Señorita extraviada* rejects "dominant meaning-systems" as well as their bureaucratic guardians.[56] Through the judicious juxtaposition of the two interviews, Portillo's documentary reveals scientific rationalism to be less an objective mode of knowledge than a tool deployed by state institutions in selective ways in order to bolster official, patriarchal narratives.

In the process of discrediting the cool, distanced certainty of the law, the film makes a case for the alternate explanations of activist Galarza and lawyer Blanco, as well as popular knowledges of the family members and of María.

The two professionals supply overarching theories, both of which accuse the Mexican state of protecting the perpetrators. In her various appearances, Galarza argues that the *maquiladoras* serve as "hunting grounds" for the murderers and that the government has ignored what has been happening in order to avoid angering the foreign companies who own the assembly plants and to ensure Mexico's growth in the global economy. For Blanco's part, after effectively undercutting the state's insistence on Sharif Sharif's guilt despite the accumulation of new evidence indicating other culpable parties, the lawyer suggests that the murders are tied to the drug trade and that the state has failed to investigate the murders in order to safeguard the profits it earns in payoffs. By returning again and again to interviews with these two women experts, the documentary favors their hypotheses as valid possibilities whose explanatory powers are, at the very least, superior to the conjectures of state officials.

While interested in the overarching theories of Galarza and Blanco, Portillo pays particular attention to the testimonies of family members, who tend to eschew master explanatory narratives. The parents and siblings speak of many things, including the overall character of their daughters or sisters, the events surrounding their disappearance, and the family's efforts to overcome the incompetency of local law enforcement officials in order to locate their loved ones. It is alongside these interviews that *Señorita extraviada* deploys reenactments, a familiar formal tactic of tabloid journalism, to validate alternate popular knowledges that are felt or embodied. For example, immediately after the title sequence, *Señorita extraviada* features the voice of an (initially) unidentified woman who speaks of her kidnapping and rape at the hands of unidentified (and ultimately unpunished) assailants. As she recounts her ordeal, the image track alternates between shots of the woman herself (in the present in what appears to be her home) and scenes that seemingly re-create her past experience: a long shot of sand dunes lit by automobile headlights ("Corrí entre los arenales" / "I ran through the sand") and another long shot of a deserted road, similarly illuminated, as seen from the backseat of a car ("Duró toda la noche conmigo y no me decía nada" / "He kept me all night. He didn't say anything"). Both her compelling words and the expression on her face hint at the harrowing nature of what happened. However, it is the reenactments that animate her testimony by helping viewers envision her experience. As noted by Alejandro Enríquez, when the woman (Eva Arce) reveals "[t]owards the end of the scene...that [her] daughter, Silvia Arce, is one of the contemporary victims," the film shocks the viewer into recognizing that the recent murders are "symptomatic of the long-standing historical violence against women."[57]

Portillo's documentary offers another reconstruction during the second interview with María in which she recounts her decision to report her rape at the hands of the police. Following a brief commentary by Zully Ponce ("We believed her, but it was out of our hands"), insinuating the inability (or unwillingness) of the special prosecutor to punish police abuse, the film offers a re-creation of the night that the officers came and threatened María at her home. While her voice-over narrates the events, the image track features a long shot of her house from the point of view of the car, a Black Marquis described by María in her oral testimony. While mimicking the menacing perspective of the men who stalk María, the voice-over recasts the shadowy composition as an illustration of María's feelings of being threatened. The reconstruction is a key means by which the film endows her testimony (ultimately dismissed as unproveable by a local judge) with a legitimacy that is tangible to viewers.

This dramatized re-creation sets up her two later appearances in the documentary (taken, according to Portillo's voice-over, from a second interview María did with the filmmaker two years later in 2000). In these later sequences, María reveals the full story of what happened to her. During the time that she was held by the police at the Carcel de Piedra, they showed her a photo album of the other young women that they had abused, including explicit photos of a gang rape. In contrast to the earlier interview, this one does not include a reenactment, but rather medium shots of María recounting in detail what she saw in the photos. By placing her subsequent testimony *after* the earlier dramatization, which positioned the viewer as sympathetic "witness" to the threats María faced after her initial complaint against the police, Portillo provides a reasonable explanation for María's hesitancy to disclose this part of her experiences. Thus, the film counters official discourses that often characterize later disclosures by witnesses as signs of untrustworthiness.

In its judicious use of reenactments, *Señorita extraviada* demonstrates a kinship not only with reality news shows from the United States, but also with Mexican traditions of tabloid journalism dating back to the first decades of the twentieth century. While deploying many of same formal tactics, the *nota roja* or *crónica roja* (crime report or crime chronicle) is distinguished from its U.S. penny press counterpart in terms of the differential relation to modernity experienced in "peripheral" Mexcio (vs. the United States), and for its closer ties to popular and artistic traditions of representing death graphically. Portillo's film draws on this tradition to give voice to uncertainties about globalization, while distancing itself from the media's tendency to exploit violence and objectify women's bodies.

The *nota roja*'s role in mediating the affective charge of the moderniza-tion process has a long history in Mexico. According to Carlos Monsiváis, the *nota roja* emerged in the early 1900s, a time of fast-paced urbanization and incipient industrialization, as a "prolongation of Catechism" in a more secular era. The graphic depiction of traffic accidents and horrific crimes in broadsheets produced by Guadalupe Posada and others offered moral-izing lessons that helped calm a public unsettled by the rapidly changing cityscape.[58] According to Monsiváis, in the *nota roja*'s exaggerations and inexactitudes, "el morbo adquiere calidades de 'pesadilla tranquilizadora'" / "morbid fascination becomes a kind of 'tranquilizing nightmare'."[59] While in some ways heightening feelings of uncertainty by pointing out the dan-gers of everyday life, the broadsheets made the novelties of urban existence (bustling trolley cars, automobiles, and chaotic traffic patterns), as well as shifting social norms, more palatable by casting their dangers as morality lessons within existing moral frameworks.

In his illuminating study *The Shock of Modernity: Crime Photography in Mexico City*, Jesse Lerner goes further than Monsiváis by arguing that crime photography in particular "played a decisive role in creating and defining the anxiousness with which Mexico entered the modern world."[60] According to Lerner, the new technology was used in different, yet complimentary ways by the Mexican state and by local entrepreneurs. For the former, photogra-phy served as a mechanism of social control. As early as the mid-1800s, law enforcement officials began to take photos of convicts for identification pur-poses.[61] Photography also became a means to record evidence and to docu-ment the proper handling of "police, judicial, and penal procedures." The state had such faith in the new technology's ability to produce "impartial documentation of visible evidence, of scientifically verifiable facts" in the early part of the twentieth century that judges began to order photographic reconstructions of crime scenes to "determine the credibility of conflicting accounts of the crime."[62]

To a certain degree, the state's use of photography was at odds with com-mercial motivations of photographers such as Agustín Víctor Casasolas and his associates. If, for the state, photography was a means to confirm order, the commercial press used it to underscore how rapidly times were chang-ing, showcasing both the exciting possibilities and troubling uncertainties of the period.[63] Whereas shots of political pageantry, fancy shops, and auto-mobile factories might solicit a sense of wonder, photos of crime scenes were a means to "titillate and shock" by placing "violence at the center of the modern, urban experience."[64] Yet, state and commercial traditions of crime photography also overlapped in significant ways. The court-ordered recon-structions of crime scenes were shot by commercial photographers, and the effort to showcase the medium's possibilities as a dispassionate scientific instrument often produced documents that were highly "theatrical, even hyperbolic" in nature.[65] The dramatic nature of bodily gestures (an arm pointing a gun, a torso twisting away from a weapon) was often at odds with the bored or neutral facial expressions of the "actors." In adhering so closely to the medium's promise of impartiality, crime scene reconstructions actually underscored photography's status as artifice. For its part, the commercial crime press foregrounded the fascinating possibilities of modern science in ways that blended together the factual and the fictional. Specialized journals like *Argos* (est. 1929) aimed at policemen included photographic lay-outs "displaying corpses from the latest unsolved mysteries" and "didactic texts of the criminological laboratory" alongside translated fiction by English-language mystery writers such as Nick Carter and Edgar Allen Poe.[66] Similarly geared toward policemen, *Seguridad Pública* (est. 1939) balanced information and entertainment by combining editorials on crime and virtue with crime fiction and hyperbolic illustrations.[67] Publications aimed at a wider public were not markedly different. During the trial of artist Tina Modotti for the murder of her lover, *El Gráfico de la Mañana* published a photographic reconstruction of the crime done by a member of the Casasola team.[68] The more lowbrow *Magazine de Policía* included a *fotonovela*-like series of captioned photographs "dramatiz[ing] a fictional crime, providing enough clues for the attentive reader to discover the identity of the perpetrator."[69]

This blending together of the sensational with the didactic was a key formal means by which the *nota roja* mediated the affective charge of modernization. On the one hand, by envisioning the dark side of that process through the vivid depiction of violent crime, the crime press acknowledged fears about the rapid changes taking place in Mexican society. On the other hand, the crime press also encouraged the public's fascination with the possibilities of modern scientific methods through informative articles showcasing particular scientific methods and procedures and also through the indexical precision of photographs. The inclusion of fictional elements interpellated readers as participants in the project of modernizing Mexico. By positioning them as detectives, the stories and *fotonovelas* helped readers imagine themselves as capable empiricists, utilizing contemporary tools to find order in a chaotic world.[70]

The economic and political changes taking place today in Mexico are equally profound. The privatization of state-run enterprises, the inauguration of free-trade policies, and the growth in foreign investment have radically altered the labor market as well as consumer imperatives. The end of the seventy-year dominance of the Partido Revolucionario Institucionalizado

(PRI) in national (and state) government has encouraged talk about a more democratic political culture—even as continuing charges of governmental corruption demonstrate the limited nature of that change. In this context, the traditions of the *nota roja* continue to play a meditational role. According to communications scholar Daniel Hallin, the 1990s have witnessed the tabloidization of the larger media culture.[71] The shift has been particularly evident in television with the emergence of tabloid news programs in the mid-late 1990s like *Ciudad desnuda* (Azteca, 1995–97), *Fuera de la ley* (Televisa), *Duro y Directo* (Televisa), and *Visión Urbana* (Azteca). Featuring "a primary focus on street crime, a fast pace, breathless tone, dramatic visuals, and a high level of emotion" as well as the showcasing of interviews with ordinary people, such programs have been remarkably popular and now influence the format of mainstream newscasts.[72] In the past, Mexican newscasts often featured an authoritative anchorman, whose reports tended to more or less "summarize" the official, governmental rhetoric about particular policies or events "without interpretation and certainly without skepticism."[73] Today, the television news is characterized by "breathless headlines, sound effects, dramatizing narrative devices, reconstructions, slow-motion videos, and moralistic condemnations of criminal suspects by the journalists."[74]

Hallin argues convincingly that the tabloidization of Mexico's media culture responds to "two deep changes in Mexican society and Mexican media"—on the one hand, the privatization of the latter and its increasing concern for the commercial viability of its "products" (e.g., print and online editions of newspapers and magazines; particular types of television programs); on the other, the public desire for democratization and the audience's coincident "passion for 'vox pop'."[75] We can push Hallin's explanation a bit further by placing these recent shifts within the longer historical trajectory of the *nota roja*. In this context, the popularity of crime stories, sensationalist appeals, and the tendency toward moralizing can be understood in relation to their ability to mediate feelings of anxiety and uncertainty about larger social, economic, and political transformations taking place in Mexico and about its changing position in the world.

Like contemporary Mexican media in general (and tabloid news in particular), *Señorita extraviada* expresses deep cynicism about the role of the state in Mexican society. As noted earlier, the documentary repeatedly characterizes government officials (whether governors, mayors, prosecutors, or police officers) as bumbling, corrupt, misogynistic, and, in certain instances, homicidal. While skepticism about the government is also visible in the U.S. press (particularly in the tabloids), the level of distrust expressed in Portillo's film is proportionally distinct. It takes aim not only at the government agents themselves, but also at the state's structural complicity with furthering the interests of elites. In so doing, Portillo's work questions whether state officials can ever serve as faithful representatives of the people's interests. In this sense, *Señorita extraviada* amplifies the doubts long expressed by the Mexican crime press about the country's ability to successfully modernize.

But Portillo's film also breaks from the *nota roja* tradition in that it betrays none of the fascination with "modern" scientific methods evident in the crime press from the 1920s through 1940s. Indeed, the documentary insinuates that the state's use of such methods (which today include DNA testing) never really improves the lives of its citizens. Rather than mediate anxieties about the contemporary moment by holding out the possibility of Mexico's successful transition to First World status, *Señorita extraviada* concludes by exacerbating the uncertainties of modernization. "Who was it?" Portillo's voice-over intones near the end of the film, "Sharif? The 'Rebels' gang? The bus drivers?..." Instead of providing a definitive response and "solving" the mystery, the film positions itself as a testimony to an ongoing horror: "During the eighteen months it took to make this documentary, fifty more women were killed."

## Working Through Globalization as Social Trauma

Up until this point, I have been arguing that *Señorita extraviada* poaches the techniques of tabloid journalism to counter state rhetoric, give voice to alternate (often incomplete and embodied) knowledges, and recognize social anxieties. However, in order to more fully understand the film's affective charge and transformative potential, it is necessary to broaden our analytical framework to explore how Portillo's documentary engages Mexican and Chicano traditions for expressing grief and for mourning. This section argues that Portillo's film *socializes* bereavement as a communal (rather than individual) practice and *mobilizes* sorrow as the basis of a political praxis that crosses cultural and political borders.[76] My analysis invokes the theoretical work of trauma studies—particularly the distinction made by Dominick LaCapra between the acting out and the working through of trauma, the latter understood as more psychically healthy (for the subject) and, potentially, more politically productive for the social body.[77]

In "A Social Context for Mourning and Mourning's Sublimation" (the final chapter of his 1995 book *Rethinking the Borderlands: Between Chicano Culture and Legal Discourse*), Carl Gutiérrez-Jones argues that grief and mourning have played a particular role in Mexican and Chicano cultures, both having related histories marked by violence, rupture, and displacement. For Mexicans, colonization as a traumatic process had immense social, cultural, and psychic implications.[78] He notes that Chicanos have incurred similar historical wounds at the hands of an Anglo society that has repeatedly repressed, displaced, and marginalized peoples of Mexican descent. In cases where these injuries have gone unacknowledged (such as those inflicted on Mexican Americans in the aftermath of the servicemens riots of the 1940s), he argues that the psychic wounds have served as the "basis for an on-going melancholia."[79] While underscoring the psychosocial costs of these festering wounds, Gutiérrez-Jones also recounts the ways in which Mexican Americans have sought recognition of past wrongs by making mourning visible to Anglo society. In one example, the widow of a Mexican American serviceman who died in World War II fought to have her husband buried in a veterans' cemetery in his hometown of Three Rivers, Texas, over the objections of the Anglo elite. The publicity campaign she engineered led to an investigation by the Texas House of Representatives and an offer by then-Senator Lyndon B. Johnson to bury her husband with full military honors at Arlington National Cemetery. According to Gutiérrez-Jones, her quest for social acknowledgment of her loss was successful in large part because her efforts eventually mobilized a sense of grief and sorrow that was shared by both Anglo and Mexican American communities in postwar society.[80]

Rather than an isolated case, the contestatory response of this widow to the circumvention of her mourning would find echo, he suggests, in the work of Chicana activists and artists in the ensuing decades. As efforts to work through the long-standing collective trauma of displacement and marginalization, Helena María Viramontes, Sandra Hahn, and Patricia Preciado Martín foreground Chicano mourning practices as a means to bind together a community and to contest Anglo sociopolitical dominance. In their stories and short films, Viramontes and Hahn draw on and rework cultural icons such as La Llorona and traditions like the Day of the Dead, while Preciado Martín sketches out a revisionist historiography to suggest how one generation of Chicanos honors an earlier one.[81] According to Gutiérrez-Jones, these efforts to "hold...up representations of loss" have been effective in countering Anglo strategies of containment and disenfranchisement in part because Mexican and Chicana/o mourning practices differ from Anglo-Protestant traditions, which from the early colonial period to the twentieth century have increasingly constrained the public expression of grief.[82]

While Gutiérrez-Jones alludes to Portillo,[83] her work is actually paradigmatic of this tendency, as death and loss haunt almost all of her films. As noted earlier, her first works, *After the Earthquake* and *Las madres* (the documentary cited by Gutiérrez-Jones), deal with the aftermath of devastating loss experienced by a young Nicaraguan woman and Argentine mothers respectively. Another early film, *La ofrenda*, chronicles the Day of the Dead as practiced both by Mexicans and Mexican Americans.[84] In *El Diablo nunca duerme,* Portillo investigates a personal loss (the somewhat mysterious death of her beloved Tío Oscar), and in *Corpus: A Home Movie for Selena,* the murder of the pop icon becomes an occasion to examine her impact on Mexican American communities, particularly on young girls. Clearly there are many important differences among these films in terms of how they approach the issue of death and the degree to which they directly or indirectly examine bereavement and mourning practices. Nonetheless, considered together, these films demonstrate Portillo's long-standing concern for making death and loss as experienced by Latin/o American communities visible and recognized.

Of all of Portillo's films, *Señorita extraviada* may be her most touching attempt to work though collective trauma—in part because of the way in which the documentary evokes loss as a visual and tangible presence. Throughout its chronicle of the state's mismanaged investigation, the film insists on making the murdered girls visible as ghostly traces by going beyond long-standing Mexican visual traditions for representing death (not only those of the *nota roja* mentioned earlier, but also of canonical artists from José Guadalupe Posada to David Alfaro Siqueiros) to incorporate more recent ones from the Argentine context. Drawing on the tactics utilized by the Mothers of the Plaza de Mayo (the subject of one of her earlier films), Portillo's work marks the disappearance of specific girls through the use of individual photographs, often seen in close-ups. Each shot includes a graphic title, listing the name of a particular young woman and the year of her disappearance. Appearing throughout the documentary, the photographs mark the passage of time (from the early to the late 1990s) and the accumulating number of unsolved murders. While attesting to the government's ineptitude, the photos also insist on the individuality of each young woman and, in so doing, contest the tendency of public officials and the media to treat the murders in terms of disembodied statistics.

The photographs are only one means by which the film makes absences (the disappeared) visible. Reminiscent of the work of Argentine artists who left silhouettes of the disappeared (each with a name and date) on the walls of public buildings in downtown Buenos Aires,[85] *Señorita extraviada* includes recurrent close-ups of shoes without feet and a dress being laid out on a bed. The shots are incredibly effective in calling to mind the missing bodies who used to breathe life into the now-inert clothing and footwear. Equally evocative are the numerous shots of young girls whose images appear as moving reflections in windows—marking them as animate yet insubstantial beings—or as refractions through a prism—their bodies vanishing in the blink of an eye. Such doubly mediated images find a parallel in other shots of young women looking directly at the camera, their movements captured in slow motion. These latter shots portray the young women who still wander the streets of Juárez as unearthly creatures out of sync and haunted by death. Through these tactics, Portillo's documentary insists on making perceptible the lives of young women whose worth has been devalued by the Mexican government and by the transnational companies that employ them as cheap labor. Aside from their role as part of the film's political critique, the recurrence of these ghostly images serves another important function by gesturing toward the unsettling nature of grief. The shots align viewers with family members as witnesses to "what-was-but-is-no-longer-there." In so doing, the film tries to convey the dual sensibility of grief as a liminal state—on the one hand, registering loss; on the other, longing for presence.

In calling on the viewer to grieve alongside the families of the missing young women, *Señorita extraviada* suggests that mourning is a communal practice that can be the basis of political action. The suggestion that bereavement is a public process of collective recognition is evident throughout the documentary in numerous shots of black crosses being painted on pink rectangles on telephone poles and through the sonic motif of a haunting requiem. The film's effort to mobilize sorrow becomes manifest at the end of the documentary when it reveals that the crosses have been the work of Voces sin Eco, a community group formed by the victims' families and their allies. As noted by Guillermina González, the sister of Sagraria (one of the missing girls), in an interview featured in the last several minutes of the film, Voces sin Eco emerged out of the families' frustration with the government's response and their desire to keep public attention focused on their missing loved ones by marking the city streets with crosses and by marching on public thoroughfares.

Casting itself as part of this effort to mobilize sorrow for social action, *Señorita extraviada* works to amplify the efforts of Voces sin Eco and other grassroots organizations. Broadcast on public television in the United States as well as in select theaters, Portillo's documentary aimed not only to inform U.S. viewers, but also to move them in new ways. By tying the disappearances of hundreds of young women to the *maquiladoras*, the film implicates U.S.-based corporations like Philips and RCA, whose logos are repeatedly showcased in shots of the buildings where the young women worked. By establishing that connection, *Señorita extraviada* encourages U.S. viewers to see the murders in Juárez as something that also touches their lives and to consider what they might do as U.S. citizens to support the work of human-rights groups in Juárez, including questioning the role of U.S.-based multinationals that locate assembly plants located abroad. At the same time, the documentary's psychosocial charge exceeds those specific goals. In evoking deep feelings of uncertainty about the contemporary moment through its tabloid tactics and encouraging (Anglo) viewers to mourn alongside Mexican families, *Señorita extraviada* attempts to forge affective alliances. As acknowledged more fully later, such bonds can be unstable and may lack durability if not reinforced. Nonetheless, the strong feelings evoked by Portillo's film (and *Babel*) do not function as calls for compassion—at least not in the sense outlined by Berlant, Woodward, and others wherein the summons to "feel for the other" reinscribes and thus, consolidates established power structures.

### *Of Migrant Feelings and Affective Communities*

If the textual tactics of particular films are not enough, what other factors need be in play for filmmaking to contribute to the transformation of how feelings circulate or "travel" across cultural zones, and thus toward the expansion of viewers' repertoires of feeling and social action? First, there must be a critical mass of production—in other words, a sufficient number of "traveling" filmmakers (directors, screenwriters, perhaps cinematographers, editors, and sound producers) who work across different cultural traditions and who have a penchant for the type of formal infiltrations outlined earlier in this book. Obviously, the reach of their works must also be supported by wide distribution and exhibition circuits. Thus, when analyzing such films as a whole, it will be important not only to trace how particular elements or formal mechanisms conform or depart from particular national conventions or industrial protocols, but also to examine how they relay specific traditions of feeling. Obviously, we must also understand the reach of these works by discussing their target audiences and how the films circulate.

Second, it is essential for critics and film scholars to think about reception and to consider different types of receptive communities. How do such films help constitute, hook into, and/or amplify transnational communities of feeling—a notion that utilizes Appadurai's concept of "communities of sentiment" as a point of theoretical departure? For Appadurai, "emotions are discursive public forms whose special power...draw[s] on embodied experience..." anchored in "existing forms of performance in particular cultural settings [as well as in] alternative topographies of the self' rather than in "any parsimoniously describable biological substrate."[86] How might the increased mobility of peoples and cultural forms on macro and micro scales in the contemporary moment allow for the intermingling of repertoires of feeling emerging from different cultural formations? How might existing networks of solidarity facilitate the proliferation of these forms of attachment?

I am thinking, for example, of communities defined less by their ethnicity and/or transgenerational experiences of migration than by their particular political (liberal) sympathies, which allow for the transfusion of alternate traditions of feeling,[87] as well as of (younger) sectors that might be (pre)disposed to respond to the proposals of particular films and define themselves as part of a global village because of their existing engagements with interactive, digitally based networks. In his account of a screening of *Señorita extraviada* that took place at the University of Minnesota in 2001, Alejandro Enríquez's article provides an example of how a film's ability to move audiences can be amplified by their political inclinations and prior practices of solidarity. According to Enríquez, "the shocking documentary prompted a group of students, community activists, teachers, and women's advocates to form the Committee in Solidarity with the Women of Juárez." In the ensuing years, they dedicated themselves to collecting and disseminating information about what was happening on the U.S.-Mexican border to the U.S. public and to raise funds to help support women's groups in Juárez.[88] Without in-depth reception studies, we can only speculate about the role of the film's affective appeals in stimulating activist responses. Nonetheless, such anecdotal accounts point to the usefulness of taking seriously the notion of a sensate politics—in other words, the possibility that making sense of contemporary networks of power is not only a matter of cognitive mapping, but also of forging affective alliances.

Other critical and investigative methods might be crafted to investigate the role of commercial films like *Babel* in forming and consolidating alliances and attachments. An initial survey of online responses to *Babel* (and a review by A. O. Scott) published on the website of *The New York Times* is quite enlightening in this regard.[89] In their comments, the respondents frequently spoke of *Babel*'s sensorial impact, describing the film as "gripping and dazzling," "heart-breaking," "moving," a "heartfelt tear jerker," an "aria for compassion," or, alternately, as "needlessly emotional," "draining," relentlessly "heavy-handed," or overly "sentimental." Such visceral reactions often became a fundamental criterion by which these on-line reviewers evaluated the film as worthy or not. Nearly as common were remarks celebrating or criticizing the film's thematic concerns and worldview—most commonly identified as the universality of human experience and the problems of miscommunication in a globalized world.[90] The reviewers' characterization of *Babel*'s emotional effects often correlated with their evaluation of the film's political goals and aesthetic merit. Those who responded favorably to *Babel*'s visceral appeals frequently commented on the effectiveness of its humanist impulses calling for greater understanding between people from different cultures. Conversely, reviewers who portrayed the film as overwrought dismissed Iñárruti's work as either "an overly orchestrated attempt at expressing both the global and personal problem of communication" or as formally contrived and derivative.

This analysis of online posts by "reader reviewers" could be developed further, but this initial overview offers food for thought. It suggests two possible interpretations for how emotion and politics interact in terms of reception. On the one hand, the effectiveness of a film's sensorial appeals may help to determine how viewers respond to its political propositions. On the other hand, viewers' existing political inclinations may (also) function as an aperture, permitting or excluding emotional appeals. Furthermore, as several entries commented on the reaction of other reader-reviewers, the posts also hint at how *Babel*'s visceral appeals may have helped to open up a dialogue between people located in diverse cultural spaces. Such cybersites may offer an initial (if imperfect) means to chart the emergence and trajectory of microcommunities, however ephemeral and tenuous they may be.

\*   \*   \*

While offering some final thoughts on the films and issues discussed in this chapter, it also will be useful to situate them within some of the overarching arguments made throughout this book. Here and in previous chapters, I have argued that films' sensorial dynamics should be located culturally and historically in an effort to offer fuller accounts of the relationship between emotion, affect, aesthetics, and politics. Filmmakers like González Iñárruti and Portillo, for example, mine older Mexican discourses of feeling found in popular genres. Earlier chapters underscored the usefulness of analyzing films within specific temporal band horizons, as responses to recent historical traumas that have remained unacknowledged and unresolved.

In arguing for the importance of considering cinematic emotion and affect, I have questioned the tendency to characterize a film's sensorial dynamics as determined by its ideological stance—whether understood in terms of the filmmakers' stated political inclinations, specific textual or formal mechanisms or features, a film's position within particular aesthetic and industrial currents, or their commercial viability. As acknowledged earlier, there is no doubt that the ways in which films evoke and route sensorial responses carry an ideological charge and can exert political effects. This is evident in films such as *O Que É Isso, Companheiro?*, which taps into unsettling affective currents and then attempts to harness or channel them to "resolve" authoritarian legacies (as suggested in chapter 2), as well as in others like *Babel*. As noted by Deborah Shaw and others, there are immense limitations to the film's humanist impulses; even as Iñárruti's film "de-centre[s] the white male gaze of classical Hollywood cinema," it fails to divest itself of an Orientalist "tourist gaze."[91] Thus, while the nature of the political has changed, it remains productive to understand the degree to which films offer structural critiques of institutions, question discursive frameworks, and unsettle formal conventions that normalize particular ways of looking at the world.

Nonetheless, while recognizing the continuing relevance of ideological readings, this book has argued for the importance of situating film's sensorial dynamics as a semiautonomous level distinct from the medium's political and aesthetic dimensions. As discussed in chapter 1, a film's formal innovations do not preclude its reliance on "packaged" emotional appeals. *Rio 40 Graus* drew on established currents of sentimentality to revivify nationalist sensibilities even as its neorealist inclinations challenged domestic audiences to imagine their national community in new ways. As argued in several chapters, the affective charge of particular films can also *exceed* the narrative armature that imbues the works with political meaning, whether they are generic thrillers like *O Que É Isso, Companheiro?* or avant-garde experiments such as *La hora de los hornos*. Only in analyzing the sensorial, the aesthetic, and the ideological as separate but related aspects of film art can we more ably understand the multifaceted nature of cinematic appeals as well as the often complex and sometimes contradictory manner in which they intervene in larger sociocultural processes.

# Notes

## Introduction

1. This was "only the second time in that festival's fifty-eight year history that a Latin American film ha[d] scored top honors." *Central do Brasil* won the Golden Bear in 1998. Numerous Latin American films had won the Silver Bear, including two other Brazilian films: *Os Fuzis* (Rui Guerra, 1964) and *Brazil Ano 2000* (Walter Lima, 1969). See the annual archive on the festival's website: http://www.berlinale.de/en/HomePage.html.

2. Randal Johnson notes that "[a]fter experiencing one of the most severe crises of its history in the early 1990s..., [the Brazilian industry] recaptured the rhythm of the 1980s, with [the production of] 20 to 30 films per year" ("Departing Central Station," *The Brazil e-Journal* (a publication of the Brazilian Embassy in Washington, DC). http://www.brasilemb.org/br_ejournal/cinebras.htm (accessed on September 28, 2000). For a similar discussion of the other industries, see Horacio Bernades, Diego Lerer, and Sergio Wolf, eds., *New Argentine Cinema: Themes, Auteurs and Trends of Innovation / Nuevo cine argentino: temas, directores y estilos de una renovación* (Buenos Aires: Tatanka/FIPRESCI, 2002); Tamara Falicov, "Latin America: How Mexico and Argentina Cope and Cooperate with the Behemoth of the North," in *The Contemporary Hollywood Film Industry*, eds. Paul McDonald, et al. (Malden, MA: Blackwell, 2008), 266, 272. For a comparative treatment, see Luisela Alvaray, "National, Regional, and Global: New Waves of Latin American Cinema," *Cinema Journal* 47.3 (Spring 2008), 49–51.

3. See sources listed in the previous note, as well as Tamara Falicov, "Argentina's Blockbuster Movies and the Politics of Culture under Neoliberalism, 1989–98," *Media, Culture & Society* 22.3 (2000).

4. Stephen Hart, *A Companion to Latin American Film* (Woodbridge, UK: Tamesis. 2004), 13. Randal Johnson and Tamara Falicov are more nuanced in their assessment of the new financing structures in Brazil and Argentina, respectively. However, they laud the new arrangements for ending the stultifying nature of the state-supported film industries. For their part, Alberto Elena and Mariana Díaz López situate the contemporary cinema as a watershed,

recapturing the utopic promise of the NLAC [*The Cinemas of Latin America* (London: Wallflower Press, 2004), 11].

On the other end of the spectrum are critics like Diego Batlle who have been quite vocal about who benefits from the new industrial arrangements. In his essay, Batlle reflects on the shifts that occurred in the Argentine industry from the mid-1990s to the early 2000s and notes, among other things, that Argentine films were still at a disadvantage as the new multiplexes favored Hollywood imports (even when certain Argentine films had greater box-office appeal). See "From Virtual Death to the New Law: The Resurgence" in *New Argentine Cinema: Themes, Auteurs and Trends of Innovation / El Nuevo cine argentino: temas, directores y estilos de una renovación*, eds. Horacio Bernades, et al. (Buenos Aires: Tatanka/FIPRESCI, 2002), 24.

5. The notable exception is Cuba. The changes that are occurring in that industry have been less spectacular and less noted outside of Cuba until recently. See Ana López, "Cuba," in *The Cinema of Small Nations*, eds. Mette Hjort, et al. (Edinburgh: Edinburgh University Press, 2008); Ann Marie Stock, *On Location in Cuba: Street Filmmaking during Times of Transition* (Chapel Hill: University of North Carolina Press, 2009), and Cristina Venegas, *Digital Dilemmas: The State, the Individual, and Digital Media in Cuba* (New Brunswick: Rutgers University Press, 2010).

6. Monsiváis was particularly concerned with how such films deceptively package their depiction of Mexican society as raw realism. Near the end of his essay, he remarks: "la franqueza, que es uno de los puntales del éxito del 'nuevo cine mexicano', es la seña de la adaptación belicosa de lo local a las leyes conductuales de la globalización" ("Lo local y lo global," *Público*, October, 21 2001, 21).

7. Ivana Bentes, "The *sertão* and the *favela* in contemporary Brazilian film," in *The New Brazilian Cinema*, ed. Lúcia Nagib (London: IB Tauris, 2003), 124–25.

8. Other critics agree with the filmmakers, including Sergio Wolf, "Las estéticas del nuevo cine argentino: el mapa es el territorio" and Quintín, "De una generación a otra: ¿hay una línea divisoria?" in *Nuevo cine argentino: Temas, autores, estilos de una renovación*, eds. Horacio Bernades, et al. (Buenos Aires: Ediciones Tatanka/FIPRESCI, 2002).

9. *The Charlie Rose Show* (PBS) December 20, 2006.

10. In the introduction to their edited volume *Passionate Views: Films, Cognition, and Emotion*, Platinga and Smith argue that "the dependability of movies to provide emotional experiences for diverse audiences lies at the center of the medium's appeal and power" [(Baltimore: Johns Hopkins University Press, 1999), 1]. Noel Carroll agrees, saying "one of the primary reasons that... movies are so popular is undoubtedly their potential to arouse us affectively" ["Affect and the Moving Images," in *The Philosophy of Motion Pictures* (Malden, MA: Blackwell, 2008), 147]. Following a scholarly trajectory quite different from that of these cognitivists, Linda Williams nonetheless agrees: "We go to the movies not to think

but to be moved" ["Melodrama Revised," in *Refiguring American Film Genres: History and Theory*, ed. Nick Browne (Berkeley: University of California Press, 1998), 61].

11. Paul Gormley, *The New-Brutality Film: Race and Affect in Contemporary Hollywood Cinema* (Bristol: Intellect, 2005), 8. Gormley cites Linda Williams's pioneering essay "Film Bodies, Gender, Genre, Excess" originally published in *Film Quarterly* VXLIV.4 (1992).

12. Several commented on the films' "overheated emotions" and the way in which they "grab...you by the throat." See, for example, Elvis Mitchell, "From Mexico, 3 Stories and an Array of Lives United by a Car Wreck," *New York Times*, October, 5 2000, E5; Jay Carr, "With violent 'Amores perros,' a stunning directorial debut," *The Boston Globe*, April 13, 2001, D6.

13. Jorge Ayala Blanco, "González Iñárruti y el neotremendismo chafa," *El Financiero-Cultural*, June 19, 2000, 108. While praising the film overall, Julia Elena Melche knocked Iñárruti for the overuse of "video-clip-like sequences and editing" ("Entre amores y perros," *Reforma-Magazzine*, June 25, 2000, 15). In discussing his subsequent film *21 Grams* (United States, 2003), Guillermo Vaidovits and David Lida reiterated Ayala Blanco's critique of Iñárruti's telenovela aesthetic; see Vaidovits, "La levedad del ser," *El Informador-Espectáculo*, November 23, 2003; and Lida, "Unos gramos más," *Reforma-Cultural*, November 30, 2003, 7.

14. See the essays "Video-games" and "Zapping" in Beatriz Sarlo, *Escenas de la vida posmoderna: Intelectuales, arte y videocultura en la Argentina* (Buenos Aires, Ariel, 1994).

15. Starting in the late 1980s, in an effort to bolster their respective national economies, the administrations of Salinas de Gotari (Mexico), Menem (Argentina), Fujimori (Perú), and Collor de Mello (Brazil) privatized state-owned companies, lowered trade barriers, and instituted other policies designed to promote foreign investment. These economic tactics proclaimed faith in the ultimate rationality of the free market to improve the economic outlook of all citizens. In Chile, the process had begun under the military junta run by General Augusto Pinochet (1973–90).

16. Franco, "Obstinate memory: Tainted History," in *The Decline and Fall of the Lettered City: Latin America in the Cold War* (Cambridge: Harvard University Press, 2002), 240.

17. Ibid., 239.

18. Ibid., 247. Snaith's article "La muerte sin escena" appeared in *Debate feminista* 11.21 (April 2000): 3–41.

19. Richard, "Cites/Sites of Violence: Convulsion of Sense and Official Routines," in *Cultural Residues: Chile in Transition* (Minneapolis: University of Minnesota Press, 2004), 17.

20. Ibid., 17–18n8. Richard's commentary on Guzmán's film originally appeared in *Revista de crítica cultural* 15 (November 1997): 54–61. See also Franco's recap of Richard's argument in "Obstinate Memory," 251.

21. At times, it seems that Franco and Richard (and others like Idelbar Avelar and Francine Masiello), consider literature to be the ultimate, if not only textuality able to process mourning in ways that enable more critical (and productive) views of the past and the present. Franco notes Avelar's contention that the society of spectacle inaugurated by the Chilean military dictatorship and concretized by President Aylwin's "Concertación de Partidos por la Democracia" "'reproduced itself by relentlessly annihilating the aura of the literary, unveiling that aura as a remnant of a moment still incomplete in the unfolding of capital'" (from Avelar's *The Untimely Present* as cited by Franco, 259). For her part, Richard's celebration of literature and performance as sites of critique coincides with her overall wariness of the visual arts. Despite Franco's suggestion that Richard sees the critical potential of Carlos Altamirano's 1996 installation "Retratos" ("Obstinate Memory," 252), at the end of her own essay Richard denounces Altamirano's work for his complicity in glossing over historical complexities, saying it "reproduce el cinismo de los procesos de *igualamiento del valor*" ["El drama y sus tramas: memoria, fotografía y desaparición," in *Espacio urbano, comuicación y violencia en América Latina*, ed. Mabel Moraña (Pittsburgh: Instituto Internacional de Literatura Iberoamericana, 2002), 200]. Franco was citing an earlier version of Richard's essay that appeared as "Memoria, fotografía: drama y tramas" in the Argentine journal *Punto de vista* 68 (December 2000).

22. Michael Hardt, "Foreword: What Affects Are Good for," in *The Affective Turn: Theorizing the Social*, eds. Patricia Ticineto Clough, et al. (Durham: Duke University Press, 2007), ix.

23. See, for example, the studies of Ann Douglas and Jane Tompkins on Anglo-American fiction. Christine Gledhill's *Home Is Where the Heart Is: Studies in Melodrama and the Woman's Film* (London: BFI, 1987) is one of the foundational critical works on film melodrama.

24. See, for example, Cathy Caruth, *Unclaimed Experience: Trauma, Narrative, and History* (Baltimore: Johns Hopkins University Press, 1996); Dominick LaCapra, *Writing History, Writing Trauma* (Baltimore: Johns Hopkins University Press, 2001); and (in terms of film) E. Ann Kaplan and Ban Wang, "Introduction: From Traumatic Paralysis to the Force Field of Modernity," in *Trauma and Cinema: Cross-Cultural Explorations* (Hong Kong: Hong Kong University Press, 2004).

25. Eve Kosofsky Sedgwick, *Touching Feeling: Affect, Pedagogy, Performativity* (Durham: Duke University Press, 2003), 18–19.

26. "Shame in the Cibernetic Fold: Reading Sylvan Tomkins," in *Shame and Its Sisters: A Sylvan Tomkins Reader* (Durham: Duke University Press, 1995), cited by Elspeth Probyn, *Blush: Faces of Shame* (Minneapolis: University of Minnesota Press, 2005), 28. Sara Ahmed notes that Tomkins's work is attractive for "its emphasis on how emotions are not simply located in the individual, but move between bodies" [*The Cultural Politics of Emotion* (New York: Routledge, 2004), 10].

27. Kosofsky Sedgwick herself notes the potential problem of invoking Tomkins's work in relation to "cross-cultural analysis" (*Touching Feeling*, 117). In *Blush*,

Elspeth Probyn responds to this issue by citing anthropological studies of shame in different cultural groups in order to distinguish between universal affects and their differential manifestation among varied cultures (xiv, 29–34).

28. Lisa Cartwright, *Moral Spectatorship: Technologies of Voice and Affect in Postwar Representations of the Child* (Durham: Duke University Press, 2008), 22–24, 35, 44–46.

29. Ibid., 36–44.

30. Ibid., 36–37.

31. Cartwright takes particular aim at the distinction between identification and empathy offered by Robert Stam, Robert Burgoyne, and Sandy Flitterman-Lewis in *New Vocabularies in Film Semiotics: Structuralism, Post-Structuralism, and Beyond* (New York: Routledge, 1992), 150–51 as cited in Ibid., 23.

32. Ibid., 37.

33. Ibid., 23, 24.

34. Ibid., 35, citing André Green, *The Fabric of Affect in the Psychoanalytic Discourse*. Trans. Alan Sheridan (London: Routledge, 1999), 268; italics in original (*Le Discours vivant*, 1973).

35. Among other things, the cognitivists attack psychoanalytic theory for its inadequate account of the process of identification, its relatively exclusive focus on the visual, and, most pertinent to this study, its inattention to the question of filmic emotion and film's emotional appeal in favor of the issues of desire and pleasure. See Greg Smith [*Film Structure and the Emotion System*, (Cambridge: Cambridge University Press, 2003), 5, 85, 102] and Murray Smith [*Engaging Characters: Fiction, Emotion, and the Cinema* (Oxford: Clarendon Press, 1995), 73–79]. Greg Smith also presents a lucid critique of the limitations of cognitivist approaches to emotion in film, including his own (65–81, 171–72).

36. Greg Smith, *Film Structure*.... 12.

37. Cognitivists themselves have noted their own lack of enthusiasm for social constructivist approaches to emotion. See Platinga and Smith, *Passionate Views*, 9 and Greg Smith, *Film Structure*..., 9–10. Carroll justifies this lack of interest in sociohistorical specificity by noting film's remarkable ability to "elicit—across diversified audiences—roughly the same or converging general emotional responses to fictions on screen" ("Affect and the Moving Images," 156–57).

38. See Platinga and Smith, *Passionate Views*, 7–9 and Greg Smith, *Film Structure*... 17–18, for an overview of the psychological studies that undergird the work of film cognitivists.

39. Carroll, "Affect and the Moving Images," 149.

40. Carroll, "Film, Emotion, and Genre," in *Passionate Views: Films, Cognition, and Emotion*, eds. Carl Platinga, et al. (Baltimore: Johns Hopkins University Press, 1999), 21–22.

41. Despite their insistence that cognition and emotion "are not necessarily enemies [but rather] cooperate to orient us in our environment and to make certain objects more salient," the film cognitivists still privilege the former as determinant (Ibid., 2). The scientific underpinnings of their work ignore alternative

models like that of neuroscientist Antonio Damasio whose dynamic feedback loops between different areas of the brain (including both the cortical and sub-cortical structures) and the surrounding environment suggest that emotion is, in fact, absolutely essential for reasoning and decision-making.

In summarizing the work of the (male) film cognitivists, I am reminded of Isobel Armstrong's analysis of the way in which male literary critics tended either to bracket off emotion (as did new critics like I. A. Richards) or master it like Stanley Fish. Armstrong ingeniously observes that both tendencies demonstrate an interest in dominating or "conquering" the (feminine) emotional appeal of the text using the (masculine) analytical tools of literary analysis [*The Radical Aesthetic* (Oxford: Blackwell, 2000), 85–91]. I do not think it excessive to note that when the (largely male) cognitivists challenge the adequacy of psychoanalytic theory, they take particular aim at the work of (female) feminist scholars.

42. Originally published in 1996 as part of Paul Patton, ed. *Deleuze: A Critical Reader*, the essay was later incorporated into Massumi's *Parables for the Virtual: Movement, Affect, Sensation* (Durham: Duke University Press, 2002).

43. Ibid., 27–28.

44. Deleuze and Guattari, *What Is Philosophy?*, 173 as cited in "Percept, Affect and Concept," in *The Continental Aesthetic Reader*, ed, Clive Cazeaux (London: Routledge, 2000), 472.

45. Deleuze, *Cinema 2: The Time-Image*, trans. Hugo Tomlinson, et al. (Minneapolis: University of Minnesota Press, 1989 [1985]), xi.

46. Ibid., 7.

47. Psychoanalytic film theory is a complex set of propositions. Since the publication of Laura Mulvey's groundbreaking essay "Is the Gaze Male?" in 1975, many feminist scholars have questioned the success of such interpellations.

48. Moira Gatens, "Privacy and the Body: The Publicity of Affect," *ASCA Yearbook* (2000), 7 as cited in Probyn, *Blush*, 141.

49. For a more developed discussion of Deleuze and Guattari's understanding of subjectivity in relation to the cinema, see Barbara Kennedy, *Deleuze and Cinema: The Aesthetics of Sensation* (Edinburgh: Edinburgh University Press, 2000), 90–91.

50. In *Cinema 2*, Deleuze makes this argument specifically in relation to time-image cinema (59). For further discussion, see also Kennedy (*Deleuze and Cinema*, 110, 114) and Bennett [*Empathic Vision: Affect, Trauma, and Contemporary Art* (Stanford: Stanford University Press, 2005), 43–44], who examines how contemporary visual art promotes an understanding of trauma.

51. Massumi takes pains to locate the potentiality of affect not in texts, but rather in communicative events. In other words, while asserting that "[t]he mass media are massively potentializing [and that] [m]edia transmissions are breaches of indetermination," Massumi argues that affect emerges in utterances (actor-president Ronald Reagan's "jerky" mime), media streams (televised soccer games), and performances (French artist Stelarc's mediated installations), only to be closed down as those flows are captured at a site of reception. It is in the receptive act that potentiality is "qualified [and] given content" as "[r]eceiving

apparatuses fulfill [...] the inhibitory, limitative function [and] select [...] one line of movement, one progression of meaning, to actualize and implant locally" (*Parables of the Virtual*, 41, 43).

52. The limited development of this historicizing impulse in Deleuze's own work can be attributed to his interest in film primarily as a means to expand his philosophical proposals, as opposed to approaching film as a historically situated aesthetic text or industrial product.

53. Laura Marks, *The Skin of the Film: Intercultural Cinema, Embodiment, and the Senses* (Durham: Duke University Press, 2000), 185.

54. Guiliana Bruno is another scholar interested in the haptic or how film touches us in particular historical moments. Taking a broader approach linking film to long-standing currents in the visual arts, Bruno argues that in its first decades "[f]ilm provided the modern subject with a new *tactics* for orienting herself in space and for making 'sense' of this motion, which includes the motion of emotions. By the way of its site-seeing, it offered a sensuous orientation to cognitive mapping, creating a spatial architectonics for mobile, *emotional* mapping" [*Atlas of Emotion: Journeys in Art, Architecture, and Film* (New York: Verso, 2002), 251.] Like Marks, Bruno turns to an alternative theoretical apparatus (in her case, ranging from eighteenth-century tracts on "sentient aesthetics" to the work of Rudolf Arnheim and Deleuze)—a genealogy that allows her to rethink the medium's mapping potential, particularly its ability to move us in ways that can facilitate intersubjective encounters as well as in those that merely reaffirm our place in the world.

55. Gormley, *The New-Brutality Film*, 13.

56. I am thinking particularly of cultural theorist Frederic Jameson's famous suggestion that postmodernism was characterized by a "waning of affect" in his 1991 book *Postmodernism, or the Cultural Logic of Late Capitalism*.

57. The few essays on Latin American cinema that take a Deleuzian perspective share this tendency with Marks and Gormley. See the work of Christian Gunderman, "Entre observación desprendida y dinamización emocional: algunos comentarios sobre los Nuevos Cines latinoamericanos en Argentina, Brasil y Cuba," *Estudios Interdisciplinarios de América Latina y el Caribe*. 22.1 (2007), http://www1.tau.ac.il/eiai (accessed on December 29, 2009) and "The Stark Gaze of the New Argentine Cinema: Restoring Strangeness to the Object in the Perverse Age of Commodity Fetishism," *Journal of Latin American Cultural Studies* 14.3 (2005); and Hermann Herlinghaus, "Affectivity beyond 'Bare Life': On the Non-Tragic Return of Violence in Latin American Film," in *A Companion to Latin American Literature and Culture*, ed. Sara Castro-Klaren (Malden, MA: Blackwell, 2008).

58. Social scientists are not the only ones to acknowledge the viability and importance of contextualizing collective states of feeling. In the 1990s, U.S. historians such as Peter Stearns began to publish studies that historicized emotion. In his groundbreaking study *American Cool: Constructing a Twentieth Century Emotional Style* (New York: New York University Press, 1994), Stearns tied shifting emotional standards to larger economic and social changes and was

careful to limit his study to specific socioeconomic classes and geographic sub-regions—in his case, to middle-class whites in the northeastern United States.

59. Appadurai situates his discussion primarily in relation to the experiences of populations in what used to be known as the "periphery," whereas Bauman tends to speak from/about the anxieties of those in the United States and Europe.

60. Zygmunt Bauman, *Liquid Times: Living in an Age of Uncertainty* (Cambridge: Polity, 2007), 1–3, 14–24.

61. Ibid., 9–11.

62. As evident in news reports, the public expression of feelings of fear tended to coalesce around worries over urban violence, new forms of criminality, the dangers of errant youth, and the "problem" of street children. In some Latin American countries, these shared uncertainties became more generalized in the aftermath of the severe economic downturns that ruptured public faith in the adequacy of neoliberal policies (e.g., Mexico in the 1980s and again in the 1990s, Brazil in the 1990s, Argentina in 2001). In other countries, fears were tied to more specific circumstances (e.g., drug trafficking in Colombia, Perú, and Bolivia). While the sense of apprehension quite likely exceeded the reality of conditions, it fueled misgivings about the sustainability of the recent economic growth and the long-term consequences of globalization for Latin American societies, given the region's long legacy of economic dependency. See the essays in *Citizens of Fear: Urban Violence in Latin America*, edited by Susana Rotker (Rutgers University Press, 2002). In their discussions of other countries, Appadurai and Bauman note the same disjuncture between people's perceptions and the statistical evidence about crime rates, and so on. As noted by Bauman, "[C]ontrary to the 'objective evidence,' it is precisely the cosseted and pampered 'we' of all people who feel more threatened, insecure and frightened, more inclined to panic, and more passionate about everything related to security and safety than people of most other societies on record" (Ibid., 55).

63. See the essay "Ciudad" in Sarlo, *Escenas de la posmodernidad*, 15–23.

64. Martín Hopenhayn, *No Apocalypse, No Integration: Modernism and Postmodernism in Latin America*, translated by Cynthia Margarita Tompkins and Elizabeth Rosa Horan (Durham: Duke University Press, 2001), 11. See the epigraph to this chapter for the original in Spanish taken from Martín Hopenhayn, *Ni apocalípticos ni integrados: aventuras de la modernidad en América Latina* (México: Fondo de Cultura Económica, 1994), 29.

65. Jesús Martín Barbero, *Al sur de la modernidad: comunicación, globalización, y multiculturalidad* (Pittsburgh: Instituto Internacional de Literatura Iberoamericana, Universidad de Pittsburgh, 2001), 173–75.

66. Ibid., 118.

67. Franco, "Obstinate Memory," 240–41

68. Martín Barbero, *Al sur de la modernidad*, 113.

69. Martín Barbero, "La ciudad que median los miedos," in *Espacio urbano, comunicación y violencia en América Latina*, ed. Mabel Moraña (Pittsburgh: Instituto Internacional de Literatura Iberoamericana, 2002), 26. See also "Mediaciones

urbanas y nuevos escenarios de comunicación," in *Las ciudades latinoamericanas en el nuevo [des]orden mundial*, eds. Patricio Nava, et al. (Mexico: Siglo XXI, 2004), 80–82.

70. Marks, *The Skin of the Film*, 162. She defines intercultural cinema as those works that move "between one culture and another" and mediate "between different cultural organizations of knowledge" (6–7). Although she does not exclude commercial films from this category, her analyses privilege experimental works made predominantly by second generation (im)migrants.

## 1   Of Passion, Aesthetics, and Politics: Rethinking the New Latin American Cinema

1. Although other personal friends like filmmaker Pablo Perelman, Guzmán's uncle Ignacio Valenzuela, and Dr. Alvaro Undurraga are also featured recurrently in *La memoria obstinada*, Malbrán is given more screen time, and it is his poetic voice that summarizes the meaning of the Allende years at the end of film.

2. He notes that "recordar" comes from the prefix *re* (again, to return) and the root *cord* (heart).

3. The notion of "working through" (vs. "acting out") comes from intellectual historian and critical theorist Dominick LaCapra, whose work on the Holocaust built on concepts first deployed by Sigmund Freud. E. Ann Kaplan and Ban Wang characterize the notion of working through trauma as "an attempt to breakout, not by completely freeing oneself from the trauma, but in facilitating the subject's freedom by offering a measure of critical purchase on problems and responsible control in action which would permit desirable change' " (citing LaCapra in "Introduction: From Traumatic Paralysis to the Force Field of Modernity," 5–6).

4. One Catholic University student argues that the coup was warranted because Allende could not control his supporters, adding that the popular support shown in *La batalla de Chile* was totally false. The response of the students' professor goes even further to illustrate the instrumental rationality promoted by the Pinochet government; he argues that the small number of disappeared (a mere couple of thousand) demonstrates the efficiency of the Chilean dictatorship in comparison to similar regimes and the junta's superiority to the United States in the fight against communism. The professor's response stands in sharp contrast to that of the female teacher at the girls' school who quietly and deliberately speaks of her own shame and culpability for having initially supported a coup that quickly demonstrated its monstrous nature.

5. The trope of radical utopia as dream is invoked by Ernesto Malbrán, who characterizes the revolutionary project of the Allende years as a "nave de sueños" or "nave de locos." Yet, for all his warnings about the dangers of being trapped in the mirror-play of memories, he serves as the most insistent voice

that revolutionary dreams have not been swept away by the waves of repression. At the end of the film, looking directly at the camera, Malbrán intones that the "ship of fools" has not been shipwrecked, but rather merely tossed about.

6. Ruffinelli says the film serves as "una descarga emocional profunda, perturbadora y contagiosa" / "a deep, disturbing and contagious unburdening of emotion" [*Patricio Guzmán* (Madrid: Cátedra/Filmoteca Española, 2001), 284].

7. In *La batalla de Chile,* individuals often stand in for larger social classes. The film often identifies individuals through their dress and surroundings as in the much-commented sequence in which Müller's wonderful roving camera documents a middle-class woman's material wealth as she pratters on about her support for the conservative Partido Nacional [López, "The Battle of Chile: Documentary, Political Process, and Representation," in *The Social Documentary in Latin America*, ed. Julianne Burton (Pittsburgh: University of Pittsburgh Press, 1990), 279–80; Ruffinelli, *Patricio Guzmán*, 138–39). See López for one of the earliest analyses of this sequence and one of the most insightful discussions of how the film used long takes to subtly comment on the profilmic events. See also Ruffinelli, *Patricio Guzmán*, 139 for similar observations on a scene with a working woman on the street in which the camera gradually tracks back to reveal her shirt with a hammer-and-sickle insignia.

8. Ruffinelli calls this sequence one of the "most impressive" in Part I and notes that in Guzmán's initial plans for *La memoria obstinada*, the filmmaker had hoped to include a present-day interview with the woman (*Patricio Guzmán*, 283).

9. Fernando Birri cited in Chanan, "Rediscovering Documentary: Cultural Context and Intentionality," in *The Social Documentary in Latin America*, ed. Julianne Burton (Pittsburgh: University of Pittsburgh Press, 1990), 38.

10. Taking a cue from the manifestoes of filmmakers like Glauber Rocha, Julio García Espinosa, Jorge Sanjinés, and Fernando Solanas and Octavio Getino themselves, critics like Daniel Díaz Torres, Enrique Colina, Michael Chanan, and Peter B. Schumann have traditionally characterized the NLAC as a cinema of ideological rupture and formal innovation—one that eschewed the "cheap" emotional entrapments of the melodramatic mode of filmmaking that dominated local productions and Hollywood imports from the 1930s to the 1950s. Instead of allowing their spectators to "escape" into a fictional world or to experience an emotional catharsis that could "buy off" their suffering and frustration, the new films confronted their spectators with national realities that had been barred from the screen and stimulated a new consciousness about the underlying structural causes of the nation's (and/or the region's) socioeconomic woes. Most importantly, the films' formal innovations encouraged contemporary audiences to be more engaged, both as spectators and as citizens.

11. Walter Achúgar, "Using Movies to Make Movies," cited in John King, *Magical Reels* (London: Verso, 2000 [1990]), 99. The original citation comes from Burton's *Cinema and Social Change: Conversations with Filmmakers* (Austin: University of Texas Press, 1986), 223–24.

12. In "Hacia un tercer cine" (1969), Solanas and Getino note that "each screening for militants, middle sectors, activists, workers and university students became, without us having proposed it that way beforehand, a sort of meeting of an amplified cell; the films formed part of the event, but they weren't the most important one" [In *Hojas de cine: testimonios y documentos del nuevo cine latinoamericano* Vol. I. (México, D. F.: Fundación Mexicana de Cineastas : SEP : Universidad Autónoma Metropolitana, c1988), 57].

13. "La hora de la censura" in *Cine, cultura y descolonización* (Buenos Aires: Siglo Veintiuno, 1973), 24. In "Hacia un tercer cine," Solanas and Getino recounted that in Mérida and Caracas, students took to the streets singing "La internacional" after *La hora de los hornos* was screened there (44).

14. "Apuntes sobre la experiencia realizada" in *Cine, cultura y descolonización*, 180.

15. Juan Antonio García Borrero ["La utopia confiscada (De la gravedad del sueño a la ligereza del realismo)," in *La edad de herejía (Ensayos sobre el cine cubano, su crítica y su público* (Santiago de Cuba: Editorial Oriente, 2002)], Christian Gunderman, and Darlene Sadlier ["Nelson Pereira dos Santos's *Cinema de lágrimas*," in *Latin American Melodrama: Passion, Pathos, and Entertainment* (Urbana: University of Illinois Press, 2009) are among the few scholars who have addressed the emotional appeals of the NLAC. Interestingly, while analyzing some of the same films addressed here (namely *Rio 40 Graus* and *La hora de los hornos*), Gunderman arrives at different conclusions—a point that I discuss in a later note.

16. From the 1980s until fairly recently, the NLAC was treated as the gold standard of Latin American filmmaking, particularly by U.S.-based critics, and served as an implicit (and, at times, explicit) point of comparison in the interpretation of contemporary works. This is evident in the tendency to analyze contemporary Latin American cinema in terms of its politics. See B. Ruby Rich "An/Other View of New Latin American Cinema" *Iris* 13 (1991); M. Chanan, "Latin American Cinema in the 90s. Representational Space in Recent Latin American Cinema," *Esudios interdisciplinarios de América Latina y el Caribe* 9.1 (1998); and Marvin D'Lugo, "Authorship, Globalization, and the New Identity of Latin American Cinema: From the Mexican 'Ranchera' to Argentinian 'Exile,'" in *Rethinking Third Cinema*, ed. Anthony R. Guneratne ( New York: Routledge, 2003) for examples of very smart, illuminating articles about films from the 1980s and 1990s that nonetheless utilize the NLAC as a political (if not aesthetic) yardstick. The interest demonstrated by scholars like Ana López in the early 1990s in reexamining the "old" Latin American cinema through the lens of Anglo-American feminist film theory on the melodrama was one of the earliest efforts to shift the terms of analysis.

In Latin America, scholars have had a more liberal approach to Latin American film history. Nonetheless, into the mid-1980s, there were endless debates at the Havana Film Festival about whether or not the NLAC had ended. More recently, several of the articles in Lucia Nagib's lovely anthology *The New Brazilian Cinema* (London: I.B. Tauris/Centre for Brazilian Studies/Oxford University Press, 2003) make explicit comparisons between contemporary productions and those of Cinema Nôvo, often to the former's detriment. Cuban critic Juan Antonio García Borrero makes similar, albeit more nuanced, comparisons between contemporary Cuban cinema and works from the 1960s and 1970s in *La edad de la herejía*.

17. *The New-Brutality Film*, 18.

18. Gutiérrez Alea, "Beyond the Reflection of Reality," in *Cinema and Social Change: Conversations with Filmmakers*, ed, Julianne Burton (Austin: University of Texas Press, 1986), 127.

19. Johnson, *Cinema Novo x 5: Masters of Contemporary Brazilian Film* (Austin: University of Texas Press, 1984), 166; Burton, *Cinema and Social Change*, x–xi; Rich, "An/Other View of New Latin American Cinema," 7, 8–9; King, 69–70.

20. Keating, "The Fictional Worlds of Neorealism," *Criticism* 45.1 (Winter 2003), 24. She discusses the emotional appeals of Luchino Visconti's *La terra trema* (1948) and other films in terms of Benjamin Harshav's theory of internal and external fields of reference (11). Her main interest, however, concerns how the film's fictional aspects do not compromise neorealism's "realist agenda." For their part, scholars such as Geoffrey Nowell-Smith and, more recently, Vincent Roccio have discussed the histrionic emotion of some of Visconti's work as "degenerate melodrama."

21. Hess, "Neo-Realism and New Latin American Cinema: *Bicycle Thieves* and *Blood of the Condor*," in *Mediating Two Worlds: Cinematic Encounters in the Americas*, eds. John King, et al. (London: BFI, 1993), 104. See also Keating, who notes that *Bicycle Thieves*'s humanism encourages the spectator "to appreciate that all humans are worthy of our emotional concern" (Ibid., 24).

22. Hess, "Neo-Realism and New Latin American Cinema," 106.

23. Scholars also note the influence of John Grierson and Jorge Ivens's "leftist humanism" on dos Santos and Birri. See Helidoro San Miguel, "Rio, 40 Graus," in *The Cinema of Latin America*, ed. Alberto Elena (London: Wallflower, 2003), 71 and Pick, "Social Inquiry and *Los inundados*," in *The New Latin American Cinema: A Continental Project* (Austin: University of Texas Press, 1993), 104.

24. Here I recall Massumi's understanding of emotion as "the socio-linguistic fixing of the quality of an experience which is from that point onward defined as personal...[a] conventional, consensual point of insertion of intensity into semantically and semiotically formed progressions, into narrativizable action-reaction circuits, into function and meaning" (*Parables of the Virtual*, 28).

25. This age-based divide breaks down when considering the cases of Julio García Espinosa (b. 1926) and Tomás Gutiérrez Alea (b. 1928), who were born in the same decade as Birri and dos Santos. As detailed in the following section of the chapter, Alea made films more akin to those of filmmakers born in the subsequent decade; a similar case can be made for the often experimental work of García Espinosa.

26. Greg Smith speaks of "emotional scripts" in *Film Structure and the Emotion System*, 34–35.

27. Classic melodramas like *Nosotros los pobres* and *Mercado de Abasto* also include moments of unrestricted narration in which the spectators' access to diegetic events exceed that of particular characters. However, such scenes or cut-aways do not function in the same way to attest to larger, systemic, or structural socio-economic problems. Rather, they merely allow the spectator to anticipate the painful problems about to befall the protagonists.

28. As noted by John King and others, the nascent film industry adapted many of these canonical novels, including *Amalia* (Argentina, Enrique García Velloso, 1914) and (Argentina, Luis Moglia Barth, 1936); *María* (Colombia, Máximo Calvo Olmedo and Alfredo del Diestro, 1922) and (Mexico, Chano Ureta, 1939); *O Guaraní* (Brazil, Paulo Benedetti, 1912), (Brazil, Vittorio Capellaro, 1916 or 1926), (Brazil, João de Deus, 1920); and *Iracema* (Brazil, Vittorio Capellaro, 1917) and (Brazil, Vittorio Cardineli/Gino Talamo, 1949) during the silent and early sound period as a means to imbue the new medium with cultural legitimacy.

29. Sommer, *Foundational Fictions: The National Romances of Latin America* (Berkeley: University of California Press, 1991), 27.

30. Ibid., 12.

31. Ibid., 48.

32. Thomas Skidmore notes that by 1950, 40 percent of the Brazilian population was urban (vs. 30 percent in 1940) and that an "increasing proportion" of them were children under twelve years of age [*Brazil: Five Centuries of Change*, (New York: Oxford University Press, 1999), 139]—like the protagonists of dos Santos's film. The film's critique anticipated the acceleration of the modernization process under the administration of President Juscelino Kubitschek (1956–61).

33. Hess notes that the neorealist films' interest in the "point-of-view of children" was a means by which they expressed "an intense sympathy for the poor and wretched" ("Neo-Realism and New Latin American Cinema," 106). Traverso makes a different argument, noting that the representation of children in both Italian neorealism and Brazilian "political" films (including *Rio, 40 Graus)* "subverts the Western myth of the innocent child" ["Migrations of Cinema: Italian Neorealism and Brazilian Cinema," in *Italian Neorealism and Global Cinema*, eds. Laura E. Ruberto, et al. (Detroit: Wayne State University Press, 2007), 177, 179–80]—a position I find less convincing.

34. Gunderman ("Entre observación desprendida y dinamización emocional") does a lovely Deleuzian reading of this scene as "excessive" or "purely optic"—in that it does not serve the forward motion of the narrative—by recalling Deleuze's discussion of the child as a recurrent figure in Italian neorealism whose presence allows for a more "open" gaze. I am less persuaded by Gunderman's contention that the scene in *Rio, 40 Graus* avoids sentimentality as a result of "its sparse narration and . . . the poetic potential of the child's gaze." As I have been suggesting, the scene's focalization tactics foster the spectator's attachment to the boy. Rather than being devoid of sentiment, the scene evokes it in a calculating way.

35. For his part, Randal Johnson calls the sequence poignant, as it suggests that "economic repression and marginalization render tenderness impossible" (*Cinema Novo x 5*, 168).
36. As cited in Salem, *Nelson Pereira dos Santos: o sonho possível do cinema brasileiro* (Rio: Nova Frontera, 1987), 95.
37. San Miguel, "Rio, 40 Graus," 76.
38. In his analysis, San Miguel cites this unconvincing resolution as an example of one of the film's weaker moments, along with its one-dimensional caricature of upper-class characters (Ibid., 77).
39. In the case of San Miguel, this posture leads him to overstate the film's radical aesthetics when he likens its editing techniques to those employed by Soviet filmmakers in the early twentieth century, arguing that dos Santos wanted "to provoke a rational response, to generate an idea in the spectator's mind, and not to produce an easy emotional identification" (Ibid., 78).
40. In *Cine, cultura y descolonización*, 147.
41. Ibid., 147. As I have argued elsewhere, Solanas's perspective on the power of film (and, in particular, its emotional efficacy) was strongly influenced by his experience in the advertising industry, where he made over 400 shorts between 1963 and 1966, the year in which he began work on *La hora de los hornos*. The trick, of course, was to use the techniques of advertising (e.g., the artful juxtaposition of imagery, the use of repetition, and graphic clarity) against the capitalist system—that is, to engage the viewer in an immediate, visceral way and "sell" the revolution. See Podalsky, *Specular City: Transforming Culture, Consumption, and Space in Buenos Aires, 1955–1973* (Philadelphia: Temple University Press, 2004), 208–27 and Bernini, "Politics and the Documentary Film in Argentina during the 1960s," *Journal of Latin American Cultural Studies* 13.2 (August 2004), 161, who also notes the influence of advertising on Solanas's work. For an overview of Solanas's early career and a detailed discussion of his films, see Monteagudo, *Fernando Solanas* (Buenos Aires: Centro Editor, 1993). The figure on publicity shorts made by Solanas comes from p. 11.
42. "Hacia un tercer cine," 37.
43. Ibid., 59.
44. "Towards a Third Cinema," in Michael Martin, *New Latin American Cinema. Vol. 1. Theory, Practices, and Transcontinental Articulations* (Detroit: Wayne State University Press, 1997), 55.
45. The template's first two stages might even be useful for understanding the relationship between the more sensational character of Part I and the drier, analytical nature of Part II.
46. In his essay, Alea recognizes how their theories evolved over time and does not offer a simplistic characterization associating Brecht with the technique of (critical) distantiation and Eisenstein with (unthinking) reflexive montage. Alea notes that Brecht did not reject the role of emotion in epic theater; according to Brecht, rather than "combating" emotion, a play should examine it [*La dialéctica del espectador* (La Habana: Cuadernos de la Revista Unión, 1982), 42–43n11]. See also pp. 55–56, where Alea comments on Brecht's use of

identification (and other techniques of traditional theater) in *Mother Courage* (1938), one of his later works; the remarks lead into a synthesis of Alea's argument about the relationship between the German playwright and the Soviet filmmaker.

47. Ibid., 49.
48. Ibid., 46–47.
49. Ibid., 53.
50. Ibid., 48.
51. Ibid., 55.
52. Gutiérrez Alea carefully details these techniques in an appendix to respond to the foreign reception of his film (*La dialéctica del espectador*, 69–71).
53. See Alea's own discussion of the interface between his theoretical and filmic work in the early 1980s in Evora, *Tomás Gutiérrez Alea* (Madrid: Cátedra/ Filmoteca Española, 1996), 48.
54. See López, who notes the difference between the female voice-over reading the legal record "in a cold and mechanical fashion" and the [livelier] voice-over of the male reporter "who sensationalizes the search for José and, later, his petition for a pardon" ["At the Limits of Documentary: Hypertextual Transformation and the New Latin American Cinema," in *The Social Documentary in Latin America*, ed. Julianne Burton (Pittsburgh: University of Pittsburgh Press, 1990), 413). In its double-edged attack on the sensationalist press and the heartless rationality of the law, Littín's film might be considered a precursor to Lourdes Portillo's *Señorita extraviada*, a film discussed in Chapter 5.
55. Ibid., 416
56. See López for a discussion of how the camera positions the spectator (Ibid., 415).
57. *El coraje del pueblo* employs a baby's cry in a similar way in the scene at the Siglo XX mining office. The sequence depicts a fruitless confrontation between a dismissive company bureaucrat and an angry worker over the whereabouts of several missing miners. Infuriated by the official's obfuscating tactics denying the company's involvement in the disappearances, the man becomes increasingly agitated. In this representation using nonprofessional actors, the worker's anger appears less spontaneous than staged as the scene is less concerned with inviting the viewer to share his fury than to consider the unproductive nature of such attempts to dialogue between labor and management. However, the sequence punctuates this restaged encounter with the sound of a baby's unrelenting sobs. Erupting at the end of the argument and continuing on as the worker turns back to the miners' wives to explain the situation, the high-pitched cries channel the primal wrath of the oppressed workers and their families in a way that makes it palpable to viewers.
58. Hart, *A Companion to Latin American Film*, 64.
59. Ibid., 67.
60. Ibid., 66.
61. Ruffinelli, *Patricio Guzmán*, 12. Calling the two films "monuments of the Latin American documentary," Paranaguá also underscores their many

differences [*Cine documental en América Latina* Madrid: Cátedra, 2003), 58, 61].

62. MacBean, "La hora de los hornos," *Film Quarterly* 24.1 (1970), 33. The citation continues: "Again and again, serving as a counterpoint to the neocolonialist reality in Argentina, short powerful quotations from Frantz Fanon force their way onto the screen as if hammered out, letter by letter, by some invisible typewriter, literally chasing from the screen the images of imperialism and proclaiming the urgent need for revolutionary struggle."

63. Bernini, "Politics and the Documentary Film in Argentina during the 1960s," 162. See also Mestman, "The Hour of the Furnaces," in *The Cinema of Latin America*, eds. Alberto Elena et al. (London: Wallflower, 2003), 120.

64. See also Stam, "*La hora de los hornos* and the Two Avant-Gardes," in *The Social Documentary in Latin America*, ed. Julianne Burton (Pittsburgh: University of Pittsburgh Press, 1990), 255 and Monteagudo, *Fernando Solanas*.

65. In its polarized moral vision and its "excessive" displays, one could make the provocative case that *La hora* is melodramatic.

66. It is interesting to note that despite their critique of Western culture, the two filmmakers follow the tenets of continental philosophy in privileging mind over body and in associating the rational with the former and sensation with the latter.

67. Mestman, "The Hour of the Furnaces," 121.

68. Mestman contends that "one of the most singular aspects [of *La hora de los hornos*] was the tendency to use different parts of the film depending on the kind of audience. On many occasions, the first part was exhibited for discussion with intellectuals and middle-class professionals, and the second one for working-class and popular sectors. The third was exhibited much less often" (Ibid., 128).

69. Making a similar connection in the conclusion to his "Entre observación desprendida y dinamización emocional," Gunderman nonetheless characterizes this linkage as a sign that films like *La hora de los hornos* were less politically radical than previously thought since such works do not destabilize the spectator to the extent of time-image cinema such as *Tire dié*, *El mégano*, *Rio 40 Graus*, and *Vidas Secas*.

70. Armstrong, *The Radical Aesthetic*, 13, 86–90.

71. Ibid., 115.

## 2   Thrilling Histories: Replaying the Past in Genre Films

1. Leslie A. Payne, *Unsettling Accounts: Neither Truth nor Reconciliation in Confessions of State Violence* (Durham: Duke University Press, 2008), 9, 182. In 1995, newly elected President Fernando Henrique Cardoso "officially acknowledged the regime's responsibility for past violations and established an indemnity program for victims' families and survivors of military-regime repression" (176). While "[a]ctivists have sought justice in local and regional courts," only

in 2004 did "human-rights violations become a federal offense through a constitutional amendment (9, 180).

2. Payne, *Unsettling Accounts*, 181; Luiz Zanin Oricchio, *Cinema de Novo: Um Balanço Crítico da Retomada* (São Paulo: Estação Libertade, 2003), 104, 119–20. Historian Thomas Skidmore seems to bolster Oricchio's characterization of the larger societal ethos by noting that by the late 1980s, "[b]ookstores that had few new literary works on their shelves now overflowed with books on self-help…rang[ing] from how to succeed in business to how to tolerate your mate" (*Brazil*, 210).

3. *Rojo amanecer* was a top box-office draw in Mexico in 1990. At the time of their release, *Johnny Cien Pesos* (Chile) and *Tango feroz* (Argentina) were "all-time national grossers in their countries'" (Daniel Moore, "Sundance Ever Warm to Latin American Fare," *Variety* March 25–31, 1996, 59). Meanwhile, coproductions *O Que É Isso, Companheiro?, Cidade de Deus,* and *Diarios de motocicleta* enjoyed commercial success both at home and abroad.

4. As Michael Chanan noted in "Latin American Cinema in the 90s," the return to the genre film has been a characteristic of Latin American cinema since the 1980s. Both he and Marvin D'Lugo argue that genre has become an "authorial vehicle" with political goals that include an interrogation of the past, as evident in melodramas like *Camila* (Argentina, María Luisa Bemberg, 1984), musicals like *Danzón* (Mexico, María Novaro, 1992) and *Tangos el exilio de Gardel* (Argentina-France, Fernando Solanas, 1987), and political thrillers like *Tiempo de revancha* (Argentina, Adolfo Aristarain, 1981). D'Lugo sees the "return to recognizable genres" as a means to "compensate foreign audiences for their ignorance of local culture or history" ("Authorship, Globalization, and the New Identity of Latin American Cinema," 113).

5. Director Walter Salles has employed the journey as a central plot structure in his earlier work as well, such as *Terra Estrangeira* and *Central do Brasil.*

6. Likewise, *Crónica de una fuga* includes elements of the thriller. Director Adrián Caetano characterized *Crónica,* right before filming began, as "una película de género *fuga* / "an escape genre-film" ["Es una película inocente y pura," *Clarín* October 23, 2005. http://edant.clarin.com/diario/2005/10/23/espectaculos/c-01076078.htm (accessed April 18, 2006)]. Scholar Gonzalo Aguilar notes that while the New Argentine Cinema does not tend to include genre films per se, it does utilize their "frame[s] of expectations" as "a launching point that ends in often unclassifiable results" [*Other Worlds: New Argentine Cinema* (New York: Palgrave Macmillan, 2008), 100].

7. Michael Chanan argues that such techniques are employed "to bring the past into the present" [*The Cuban Image: Cinema and Cultural Politics in Cuba* (London: BFI/Bloomington: Indiana University Press, 1985), 48]. Timothy Barnard has been one of the few scholars to problematize the NLAC's take on history. He contends that historical films like *La primera carga al machete* turned to the past to avoid talking about the difficulties of the present ["Death Is Not True: Form and History in Cuban Film," in *Mediating Two Worlds:*

*Cinematic Encounters in the Americas*, eds. John King, et al. (London: British Film Institute, 1993), 235–40].

8. The film then cuts to shots of Afro-Cubans running through a forest until they reach a peak. A final graphic title notes that it would be many decades before the "color barrier" would be overcome and that Cubans of all races (among them, Agramonte, Maceo, and Martí) would fight together for their freedom.

9. Martin Rubin has called the thriller a "'metagenre' that gathers several other genres under its umbrella" [*Thrillers* (Cambridge: Cambridge University Press, 1999), 5]. Carroll notes that "[s]uspense is not exactly a genre unto itself, since suspense is an emotion that is often elicited in many other genres" ("Film, Emotion, and Genre," 42).

10. *Thrillers*, 5, 6.

11. Guy Hennebelle argues that thrillers "often play [...] with politics, only using it as an illusory device to give weight to what are, in effect, conventional detective stories" [as described in Scott, *American Politics in Hollywood Film* (Chicago: Fitzroy Dearborn, 2000), 106]. Ian Scott agrees in principle, while noting an exception to the rule in the work of director Oliver Stone.

12. Jameson, *The Geopolitical Aesthetic: Cinema and Space in the World System* (Bloomington: Indiana University Press, 1992), 41. His take on the thriller is slightly different from that of Hennebelle. Although critical of such films' tendency toward emotional appeal, Jameson nonetheless seems to recognize their sociopolitical function.

13. Debates over the historiographical merits and limitations of *JFK* and *Forrest Gump* have not undercut the proclivity to associate Hollywood films with mainstream historical narratives and non-Hollywood films (those made outside the commercial circuit and particularly those made outside the United States and Western Europe) with alternative practices (See the articles in Sobchack, *The Persistence of History* and Landy, *The Historical Film*). Historian Robert Rosenstone does something similar when he draws a clear distinction between mainstream historical films and documentaries like *Glory, Reds,* and *The Civil War* and more experimental works like *Shoah, Potemkin,* and *Black God/White Devil*. Although he is careful not to dismiss the former, he suggests that it is the latter that perform a more radical historiographical operation. See "The Historical Film: Looking at the Past in a Postliterate Age" in *Visions of the Past: The Challenge of Film to Our Ideas of History* (Cambridge: Harvard University Press, 1995). This tendency is evident even in critical works that treat the representation of the past tangentially. Laura Marks's fascinating study *The Skin of the Film* privileges avant garde works by diasporic filmmakers as uniquely suited to access collective memories that attenuate, if not openly question, dominant history.

14. I include *Death and the Maiden* in this comparison because of its concern for history and epistemology—preoccupations that it shares with the other two works that were made in Brazil. As demonstrated later in the essay, Polanski's

film challenges the notion that only those works made in Latin America can speak about the meaningfulness of the dictatorial past in provocative ways.

15. Richard further suggests that the political realm has become simply another site of market logic: "The consensual model of 'democracy of agreements' formulated by Chile's transitional government (1989) signaled the shift from politics as antagonisms—the dramatization of conflict ruled by a mechanism of confrontation—to politics as *transaction*: a formula of pacts and their praxis of negotiation" ("Cites/Sites of Violence," 27). See also Alejandro Kaufman, "Memoria, Horror, Historia," in *Memorias en presente: Identidad y transmisión en la Argentina posgenocidio*, ed. Sergio Guelerman (Buenos Aires: Grupo Editorial Norma, 2001), 15, 20–22, 26 for similar arguments in the case of Argentina.

16. Carroll, "Film, Emotion, and Genre," 42–46.

17. Carroll argues that "[i]n everyday life, we don't normally feel suspense about what happened in the past. I don't feel suspense about the outcome of World War II, since I already know it. Suspense is a posture that we typically adopt to what will happen, not to what has happened" (Ibid., 43).

18. Spielmann, "Intelectuales brasileños 1969–1997. El caso Fernando Gabeira: O que é isso, companheiro?" in *Nuevas perspectives desde/sobre América Latina: El desafío de los estudios culturales*, ed. Mabel Moraña (Santiago, Chile: Cuatro Propio/Instituto Internacional de Literatura Iberoamericana, 2000), 352.

19. Carroll might offer a different explanation. In an earlier article discussing the thrill of a suspense film for viewers that returned to watch it for a second, third, or fourth time, he included a more qualified definition of suspense as "future-oriented." He argued that while an audience member would already know what happens, she or he could still "entertain the thought that the relevant outcome is uncertain or improbable" ["The Paradox of Suspense," in *Suspense: Conceptualizations, Theoretical Analyses, and Empirical Explorations*, eds. Peter Vorderer, et al. (Mahwah, New Jersey: Lawrence Erlbaum Associates, 1996), 87]. This explanation ignores contextual factors that influence viewing practices and pleasures.

20. Fernando's subsequent actions with MR-8 culminating in the kidnapping of the U.S. ambassador (that he himself masterminds) are all aimed to break the censorship and force the military to acknowledge a vibrant resistance movement.

21. The character of Jonas, one of the two more experienced guerrillas who take over the cell, serves as a foil to underscore the relative innocence of the others as his brutal and authoritarian ways suggest parallels to those of the military government. For Oricchio, these characterizations (of pretty girls and evil villains) are evidence of the film's problematic take on urban guerrilla warfare as "a grand adventure" that fails to explore in any depth the militants' motivations (*Cinema de Novo*, 114).

22. The film further intensifies the spectator's anxiety by setting up a number of smaller obstacles. Will the militants be able to correctly identify the

ambassador's limo? After they succeed in pulling Elbrick into a getaway car, will René be able to start the car she is using to follow them?

23. Indeed, the privileging of Elbrick's point of view is one of the most criticized aspects of the film. Spielmann argues that in contrast to Gabeira's book, in the film Elbrick becomes the "narrator subject" and the guerrillas serve as tertiary characters within his story ("Intelectuales brasileños 1969–1997," 355).

24. Ibid., 355–56.

25. Dorfman wrote the play in 1990 during the initial stages of the Chilean redemocratization. See "Final and First Words about *Death and the Maiden*" for a detailed discussion of his motivations for writing the play and his thoughts about its relation to Chilean redemocratization as well as its universal appeal. According to Francisco Javier Millán, the play was a failure when it opened in Chile because society had "blindfolded itself" in order to facilitate the transition to democracy [*La memoria agitada: cine y represión en Chile y Argentina* (Huelva: Fundación Cultural de Cine Iberamericano de Huelva, 2001), 278]. Dorfman himself shares this perspective, as evident in the documentary *A Promise to the Dead: The Exile Journey of Ariel Dorfman* (Canada, Peter Raymont, 2006). In Idelbar Avelar's withering critique of the film version, he offers an alternate explanation, attributing the play's "resounding failure" within Chile to its implausible characterizations of former militants (Paula and Gerardo) and its depiction of a former torturer (Miranda) as "the only one who reasons and is plausible" ["From Plato to Pinochet," in *The Letter of Violence: Essays on Narrative, Ethics, and Politics* (New York: Palgrave Macmillan, 2004), 42–43, 45]. While Avelar correctly identifies many shortcomings of Dorfman/ Polanski's work (particularly for Chilean audiences) resulting from its pursuit of universal appeal, he offers an impoverished understanding of the film's affective dynamics—as evident in his frequent characterizations of the film as melodramatic.

26. Suspense is a key element of numerous Polanski's films, including *Nóz w wodzie / Knife in the Water* (1962), *Rosemary's Baby* (1968), *Chinatown* (1974), and *Frantic* (1988).

27. Ariel Dorfman, "Final and First Words about *Death and the Maiden*," in *Other Septembers, Many Americas: Selected Provocations, 1980–2004* (New York: Seven Stories Press, 2004), 187; Millán, *La memoria agitada*, 276–78, 280.

28. This is a favored interpretation of the negotiated transition toward elected government in Chile whereby General Pinochet remained as the supreme commander of the military forces.

29. Millán, *La memoria agitada*, 281.

30. Dorfman agrees with Nelly Richard's argument about the postdictatorial rationalization of the public sphere in Chile, noting the "alarming fear of conflict [and] the widely accepted supposition that the past never existed" (cited in Ibid., 278).

31. As noted by Millán, Dorfman's play made this even clearer in the final scene at the concert where an enormous mirror was lowered onto the stage to "return the spectator's own image" and invite the public to "reflect upon and position

themselves in relation to the problem of [postdictatorial] reconciliation" (Ibid., 282).

32. Andreas Huyssen, *Twilight Memories: Marking Time in a Culture of America* (New York: Routledge, 1995), 5–7; Vivian Sobchack, "Introduction: History Happens," in *The Persistence of History: Cinema, Television, and the Modern Event.* New York: Routledge, 1996), 4–5.

33. Sobchack, "Introduction: History Happens," 5.

34. Oricchio, *Cinema de Novo*, 114.

35. This is Oricchio's specific critique of Brant's film in *Cinema de Novo*, 109. Interestingly enough, Skidmore notes the explosion in Brazil in the early 1990s of best-selling biographies on leading historic figures from the nineteenth and early-mid-twentieth century. He attributes the popularity of such texts to "a common desire to recapture the past through some unique personality" and to "reach beyond the nightmare of military rule to find the roots of a more authentic Brazil" (*Brazil*, 211).

# 3 Affecting Legacies and Contemporary Structures of Feeling

1. *Ônibus 174* chronicles a crime that turned into a media sensation in June 2000 when a bungled robbery by a poor young man from one of Rio's poorest neighbourhoods turned into a hostage situation that was shown live on Brazilian television. In the documentary, Padilha takes direct aim at numerous institutions, including the police and the media, for their handling of the situation and, at the same time, points to underlying issues (poverty, racism)—all the while questioning viewers about their own complicity as fascinated spectators.

2. Deborah Shaw, "Seducing the Public: Images of Mexico in *Like Water for Chocolate* and *Amores perros*," in *Contemporary Latin American Cinema: Ten Key Films* (London: Continuum, 2003) 54–55, 59–60; and Ignacio Sánchez Prado, "*Amores perros*: violencia exótica y miedo neoliberal" *Casa de las Américas* 240 (1996), 3–6, 9, 13. Claudia Schaeffer agrees that Iñárruti's film swipes at radical political projects—not only those in the past, but also in the present through references to the Ejército Zapatista de la Liberación Nacional (EZLN). However, her interpretation also suggests that the film offers a trenchant commentary on the defunct politics of the PRI ("*Amores perros*: Throwing Politics to the Dogs," in *Bored to Distraction: Cinema of Excess in End-of-the Century Mexico and Spain* (Albany: State University of New York Press, 2003))

3. García Borrero, "Las iniciales de la ciudad," in *Imágenes en libertad: Horizontes latinos*, 51st Festival Internacional de Cine, San Sebastián, 2003), 120–21, and "La utopía confiscada," 185–86; Serra, "La Habana Cotidiana: Espacio Urbano en el Cine de Fernando Pérez," *Chasqui: revista de literatura latinoamericana* 35.1 (2006), 890–2; Mennell, "Dreaming the Cuban Nation: Fernando Perez's *Madagascar*," *Canadian Journal of Latin American and Caribbean Studies* 33.66 (2008), 105–7. Citing Cuban critic Ambrosio Fornet who called the film "an X-ray exposure of the prevailing state of our soul," Ann Marie Stock has argued

that the film "captur[ed] the existential uncertainty...of the Special Period" and reimagined the nation as "unbounded" (*On Location*, 4–6).

4. García Borrero, "La utopía confiscada," 173. In this 2002 essay, he seems to direct his comments toward a younger generation of filmmakers, including Arturo Sotto who emerged in the early 1990s, as well even younger filmmakers like Miguel Coyula, Jorge Molina, and others, who made their first films in the early 2000s. For an alternative interpretation of the newest generation of Cuban filmmakers, see Stock, *On Location*. This debate about contemporary Cuban filmmakers will be explored in greater depth in chapter 4. In his 2003 overview of Pérez's oeuvre written for the San Sebastián film festival, García Borrero argued that Pérez was one of the only contemporary directors to recuperate the radical promise of Cuban filmmakers from the 1960s ("Las iniciales de la ciudad," 115–16, 122).

5. Claudia Schaeffer's chapter on *Amores perros* (in her book *Bored to Distraction* published in 2003, the same year as an earlier version of this chapter appeared in *Screen*) is, to my knowledge, the only other analysis to address this aspect of Iñárruti's film.

6. Others films have demonstrated a similar interest in staging the difference between contemporary youth and the previous generation. *Buenos Aires viceversa* (Alejandro Agresti, Argentina-Netherlands, 1996) examines the subtle effects felt by young adults growing up in the aftermath of dictatorship during a period of rampant consumerism fed by the rapid proliferation of sensationalistic media technologies. The Brazilian films *Ação Entre Amigos* and *Cidade de Deus* both contrast today's youth with earlier generations. The opening of Brant's film includes a brief sequence of former militant Miguel stuck at a stoplight and a young man rushing to clean off his windshield for a few cents. The scene makes a quick but devastating insinuation that the socioeconomic inequalities against which Miguel had militated as a young man still exist.

7. As mentioned in the previous chapter (note 13), this is the case even in the very thoughtful work of historian Robert Rosenstone, who criticizes his colleagues' traditional denunciation of the representation of history in film as oversimplisitic. See "The Historical Film."

8. Raymond Williams, "Structures of Feeling," in *Marxism and Literature* (Oxford: Oxford University Press, 1977), 128–29, 132–33.

9. Thomas Elsaesser, "Subject Positions, Speaking Positions: From *Holocaust, Our Hitler*, and *Heimat* to *Shoah* and *Schindler's List*," in *The Persistence of History: Cinema, Television, and the Modern Event*, ed. Vivian Sobchack (New York: Routledge, 1996), 172.

10. Ibid.,173.

11. Ibid.,173.

12. Ibid.,174.

13. *M. Klein* focuses on a gentile who buys the art collections of Jews fleeing Hitler. Despite the character's "morally suspect behavior," the film encourages the spectator to identify with him up until the moment he is arrested by the

Gestapo and loaded onto a "train with all the Jews who have been rounded up" at which point the "spectator want[s] to say... 'But you've got the wrong man: he isn't a Jew'—until with a sudden shock one realizes that all the people on the train are 'the wrong men' and must acknowledge one's own 'impotence' and 'complicity'" (Ibid.,174–75).

14. As noted in chapter 2, for an incisive analysis of Cuban historical films as well as viewing practices, see Barnard, "'Death Is Not True': Form and History in Cuban Film." See also Marvin D'Lugo's discussion of the way in which Cuban films promote interpretive communities through "dramatised on-screen audiences" in "Transparent Woman: Gender and Nation: Gender and Nation," in *Mediating Two Worlds: Cinematic Encounters in the Americas*, eds. John King, Ana M. López, Manuel Alvarado (London: BFI Institute, 1993).

15. For discussions of the film's representation of masculinity and sexuality, see Hector Amaya "*Amores perros* and Racialised Masculinities in Contemporary Mexico," *New Cinemas: Journal of Contemporary Film* 5.3 (2007) and Orla Juliette Borreye, "The Signficance of the Queer and the Dog in Alejandro González Iñárruti's *Amores perros* (2000): Masculinity at War," *Wide Screen* 1.1 (2009). http://widescreenjournal.org.

16. The extradiegetic rock ballad playing in this later sequence (speaking of a lover's frailty and the need for honesty) provides an ironic counterpoint to what we visually witness.

17. The film initially characterizes El Chivo's past actions as criminal, not political as we hear about them from Leonardo, the corrupt policeman, who tells another character that El Chivo placed a bomb in a commercial center, kidnapped people, and assassinated two policemen.

18. In the end, El Chivo is the only character able to recognize the detrimental effects of systemic violence on basic human relations. The film's critique of revolutionary struggle is particularly noteworthy in the context of contemporary Mexico where the EZLN has, since 1994, offered a highly innovative alternative to the totalizing projects of societal transformation characteristic of radical movements from the 1960s and 1970s.

19. In her reading of the *Amores perros*, Dolores Tierney suggests that what we see on screen –specifically, the differential use of film stocks—is vital for "map[ping] social or emotional differences between characters": "the faster stock used in the first and third stories gives the impression of a realistic, visually authentic, close-up look at poverty and marginalization [...while t]he slower stock used in the second story [...] produces a much less contrasted, more muted, and consequently, much less emotionally realistic representation of the frivolous world of magazine modeling and adultery" ["Alejandro González Iñárruti: Director without Borders," *New Cinemas: Journal of Contemporary Film* 7.2 (2009), 105–6]. These are insightful observations, as is the commentary by G. King about the use of a handheld camera in the first and third episodes to "creat[e] an impression of immediacy and 'heightened emotional proximity'" (106).

20. Williams, "Structures of Feeling," 135.

21. "Preface to the English edition" in *Cinema 2: The Time-Image*, xi.
22. "Throwing Politics to the Dogs," 84, 86, 107. I am less persuaded by Sánchez Prado's argument that the film offers a catalogue of (exclusively) middle-class fears (*"Amores perros,"* 4–5)
23. Here I depart from Williams's theorization of structures of feeling that pointed toward their progressive potential. See Shaw, "Seducing the Public" and Sánchez Prado, *"Amores perros"* for potent critiques of the film's ideological and political limitations that underscore its exclusive focus on the family, its inability to acknowledge larger political or economic structures, and its packaging of Mexico/Mexican culture to appeal to foreign audiences.
24. For an overview of Pérez's work, see Beat Borter, "Moving to Thought: The Inspired Reflective Cinema of Fernando Pérez," in *Framing Latin American Cinema: New Critical Perspectives*, ed. Ann Marie Stock (Minneapolis: University of Minnesota Press, 1997); García Borrero, "Las iniciales de la ciudad"; and Jorge Ruffinelli, *Sueños de realidad: Fernando Pérez, tres décadas de cine* (Madrid: Universidad de Alcalá/Fundación del Nuevo Cine Latinoamericano, 2005).
25. Another is *Mujer transparente* (Cuba, 1990), composed of five shorts, each directed by a different filmmaker. See Arredondo, "From Transparent to Translucid: Cuban Filmmakers in 1990" for a detailed analysis of the ways in which most of the shorts foreground the particularities of women's lives and explore women's agency [*Latin American Literary Review*. 25.49 (1997), 25, 28]. Mennell suggests that *Madagascar* also signals a break in Pérez's own work—away from historical fiction [both *Clandestinos* (Cuba, 1987 and *Hello Hemingway* (Cuba, 1990) are set in 1950s Cuba] and toward a less celebratory view of the revolution. See "Dreaming the Cuban Nation," 92.
26. In an earlier version of this essay (published in Screen), I had misidentified the extradiegetic music as "Con te partirio" / "It's Time to Say Goodbye." I am grateful to Jan Mennell's article for correctly identifying the song as an aria from Puccini's Turandot.
27. This exploration of the cityscape is not entirely new, as it was a recurrent motif in the work of Tomás Gutiérrez Alea at least as far back as his 1968 classic *Memorias del subdesarrollo*. See López, *"Memorias* of a Home: Mapping the Revolution (and the Making of Exiles?)," *Revista Canadiense de Estudios Hispánicos* 20.1 (1995), 5–17. For a fine exploration of urban space in Pérez's larger oeuvre, see Serra, "La Habana Cotidiana."
28. After the end of the Soviet subsidies in the early 1990s, tourism once again, as in prerevolutionary days, became one of the central pillars of the Cuban economy. For a discussion of subsequent urban renovation projects, see Roberto Segre, *América Latina, fin de milenio: Raíces y perspectives de su arquitectura* (La Habana: Artes y Literatura, 1990).
29. In a 1997 article, Stock argues that *Madagascar* explores migrant identities and "the impossibility of locating oneself in place and time" in the late twentieth century—issues that had particular resonance in Cuba given the hardships of the Special Period ["Migrancy and the Latin American Cinemascape: Towards

a Post-national Critical Praxis," *Revista canadiense de estudios hispánicos* 20.1 (1995), 24–27].

30. Both Serra and Mennell suggest that Pérez's work demonstrates ambivalence toward the Revolution. See Serra, "La Habana Cotidiana," 103 and Mennell, "Dreaming the Cuban Nation," 89.

31. Barnard, "'Death Is Not True,'" 235–40.

32. In "La utopia confiscada," García Borrero called "la búsqueda de la emotividad más bien intimista…otro de los síntomas más recurrentes del cine cubano de los noventa" (186–87). For his defense of Pérez's work, see "Las iniciales de la ciudad," 119.

33. In her lovely analysis of contemporary Argentine cinema, Joanna Page offers an eloquent defense of how youngish directors like Adrián Caetano, Bruno Stagnaro, Ana Poliak, Pablo Trapero, and Gustavo Fontán cannily toy with the conventions of realism. See *Crisis and Capitalism in Contemporary Argentine Cinema* (Durham: Duke University Press, 2009), 34–56.

## 4    Alien/Nation: Contemporary Youth in Film

1. Héctor Babenco's *Pixote, A Lei do Mais Fraco / Pixote, The Law of the Weakest* (Brazil, 1981) is a clear antecedent, as is, of course, Luis Buñuel's *Los olvidados / The Young and the Damned* (Mexico, 1950). See João Luiz Vieira, "The Transnational Other: Street Kids in Contemporary Brazilian Cinema," in *World Cinemas, Transnational Perspectives*, eds. Nataša Ďurovičová, et al. (New York: Routledge, 2010) for an analysis of *Rio 40, Graus* and *Pixote* in relation to other "street urchin films" from Brazil and elsewhere.

2. See Beatriz Sarlo, *Escenas de la vida posmoderna*, 18–23, 41–55, 57–73 and her *Tiempo presente; Notas sobre el cambio de una cultura* (Buenos Aires: Siglo XXI, 2001), 79–91. Taken as a whole, Sarlo's essays make a clear distinction between young adults in late-twentieth-century Argentina and earlier generations of youth. While not uncritical of young adults from the 1950s and 1960s, she suggests that they had a much better grasp of history and, thus, were more capable (and willing) to act as agents of social change.

3. My thanks to an anonymous reviewer for informing me about this program.

4. Henry Giroux, *Fugitive Cultures: Race, Violence and Youth* (New York: Routledge, 1996), 10.

5. In the case of Mexico, Televicine's productions are a case in point. Starting in the early 1980s, this branch of media conglomerate Televisa began to produce feature films that combined pop music and entertainers like Luis Miguel, Lucerito, and later Gloria Trevi and Yuri to draw younger viewers. Although the commercial success of such films is uneven, recent statistics point to the importance of young adults as a market sector in Latin America. For a more detailed analysis of the Mexican case, see Podalsky, "De la pantalla: jóvenes y el cine mexicano contemporáneo," *El Ojo que Piensa* 6 (November 2004) (www.elojoquepiensa.udg.mx) and "The Young, the Damned, and the Restless: Youth

in Contemporary Mexican Cinema," *Framework* 49.1 (Spring 2008). In Brazil most cinema-goers are between 14 and 25 years old, and it is this audience that has drawn the interest of global capital like Warner Brothers and Diler Asociados who have collaborated on a number of films starring Xuxa ("Muy caliente: Hollywood majors team up with Latin film producers," *Variety* April 1–7, 2002, A2).

6. There are few critical essays that examine Sapir's film in any depth, although several note the significance of its aesthetic experimentalism. See, for example, Martín Morán, "La ciénaga," in *The Cinema of Latin America*, eds. Alberto Elena, et al. (London: Wallflower, 2003), 237; and Aguilar, *Other Worlds*, 210. For a more substantive discussion of Sapir's work, see Wolf, et. al., "Esteban Sapir," in *60/90 Generaciones: cine argentino independiente*, ed. Fernando Martín Peña (Buenos Aires: MALBA, 2003) and chapter 2 of Raquel Pina's "El sujeto en escena: Huellas de la globalización en el cine argentino contemporáneo," PhD diss., The Ohio State University, 2010, 56–75.

7. See the articles in Fernando Peña's edited volume *60/90 Generaciones: cine argentino independiente* (Buenos Aires: MALBA, 2003) for further comparison of the work of filmmakers from these two eras.

8. Translations provided by author, unless otherwise noted.

9. For some of the earliest coverage of the new independent cinema, see the archives of the online journal *El Amante* (www.elamante.com); Peña's aforementioned volume *Generaciones 60/90*; Horacio Bernades, Diego Lerer, and Sergio Wolf's edited volume *Nuevo cine argentino*; and Adriana Callegaro and Miriam Goldstein, "Cine Argentino, 1998–2000: Universo juvenil y mundo urbano," *Revista de cine* 1 (2001). Gonzalo Aguilar's *Other Worlds* (or *Otros mundos*, the original Spanish-language version from 2006) and Joanna Page's *Crisis and Capitalism in Contemporary Argentine Cinema* offer very fine in-depth studies of Argentine cinema of the 1990s and 2000s that are more theoretically engaged.

10. Pablo Vila, "El rock nacional: género musical y construcción de la identidad juvenil en Argentina," in *Cultura y pospolítica: El debate sobre la modernidad en América Latina*, ed. Néstor García Canclini (México, DF: Consejo Nacional para la Cultura y las Artes, 1991), 255.

11. Ibid., 258. For an account of the period leading up to the dictatorship, see Valeria Manzano, "Sexualizing Youth: Morality Campaigns and Representations of Youth in Early 1960s Buenos Aires," *Journal of the History of Sexuality* 14.4 (October 2005) and "Blue Jean Generation: Youth, Gender and Sexuality in Buenos Aires, 1958–1975," *Journal of the Social History* 42.3 (Spring 2009).

12. Vila, "El rock nacional," 258–59. For an example of the vision of youth promoted by the repressive military government, see the illustration reproduced in Diana Taylor, *Disappearing Acts: Spectacles of Gender and Nationalism in Argentina's Dirty War* (Durham: Duke University Press, 1997), 195.

13. Guillermo O'Donnell cited in Vila, "El rock nacional," 258–59.
14. Ibid., 256.
15. Ibid., 265.
16. See Marcela Jabbaz and Claudia Lozano, "Memorias de la dictadura y transmisión generacional: representaciones y controversias," in *Memorias en presente: identidad y transmisión en la Argentina posgenocidio*, ed. Sergio J. Guelerman (Buenos Aires: Grupo Editorial Norma, 2001), 99 for a summary of such comments and Trigo, "Rockeros y grafiteros: la construcción al sesgo de una antimemoria," in *Memoria colectiva y políticas del olvido: Argentina y Uruguay (1970–1990)*, eds. Adriana J. Bergero, et al. (Rosario, Argentina: Beatriz Viterbo, 1997), 309–10 for an overview of similar critiques of contemporary Uruguayan youth articulated by both those on the right and the left.
17. See, for example, Jabbaz and Lozano, "Memorias de la dictadura y transmisión generacional," and Sergio Guelerman, "Escuela, juventud y genocidio: una interpretación posible," in *Memorias en presente: identidad y transmisión en la Argentina posgenocidio* (Buenos Aires: Grupo Editorial Norma, 2001).
18. Elvira Martorell, "Recuerdos del presente: memoria e identidad. Una reflexión en torno a HIJOS," in *Memorias en presente: Identidad y transmisión en la Argentina posgenocidio*, ed. Sergio Guelerman (Buenos Aires: Grupo Editorial Norma, 2001), 137–38. Beatriz Sarlo provocatively shifts the terms to argue that youth functions as an allegory for today's marketplace, characterized by "rapid circulation and…accelerated obsolescence" (*Escenas de la vida posmoderna*, 43).
19. HIJOS are most well known for their public acts of denunciation staged in front of the homes of individuals presumed to have been part of the Proceso's repressive apparatus who have never been brought to justice. See Kaiser, "*Escraches*: demonstrations, communication and political memory in post-dictatorial Argentina," *Media, Culture & Society* 24 (2002); Martorell, "Recuerdos del presente," and Taylor, "'You are Here': HIJOS and the DNA of performance," *The Archive and the Repertoire: Performing Cultural Memory in the Americas* (Durham: Duke University Press, 2003) for more in-depth analyses.
20. Indeed, they might be reworking notions of public sphere and perhaps of civil society itself. This possibility is mapped out by Paolo Carpignano, et al. in their article on talk shows and "the public mind" where they suggest moving away from the notion of civil society as constituted by institutions—political parties, unions, and so on—toward one "consolidated in the circulation of discursive practices" ["Chatter in the Age of Electronic Reproduction: Talk Televisión and the 'Public Mind'," in *The Phantom Public Sphere*, ed. Bruce Robbins (Minneapolis: University of Minnesota Press, 1993), 119].
21. Wolf, et. al., "Esteban Sapir," 176–78.

22. Joanna Page makes the same observation in *Crisis and Capitalism in Contemporary Argentine Cinema*, 185–86.

23. See also Martín Morán, who mentions the film's disquieting use of off-screen space ("La ciénaga," 236). Page underscores how Martel's films play with the issue of perception, noting that whereas *La ciénaga"* asks "What is seen?", her subsequent film *La niña santa* (Argentina-Italy-Netherlands-Spain, 2004) examines "What is heard?" (*Crisis and Capitalism*, 187).

24. By the end of the film Momi will lose her ability to penetrate the surface of things. Returning from town, she will join her sunglass-clad sister Vero on the pool deck, in a scene reminiscent of the opening tableau of the drunken adults, having failed to see the miraculous appearance of the Virgin on the town's water tower that had attracted so much attention in news reports seen throughout the film.

25. See Martín Morán, who attributes the film's sensuality to the soundtrack ("La ciénaga," 235).

26. Monteagudo, "Lucretia Martel: susurrus a la hora de la siesta," in *Nuevo cine argentino: Temas, autores, estilos de una renovación*, eds. Horacio Bernades, et al. (Buenos Aires: Ediciones Tatanka/FIPRESCI, 2002), 74; translation from original, bilingual volume.

27. Peña, Felix-Didier, Luka, "Lucretia Martel," in *60/90 Generaciones: cine argentino independiente*, ed. Fernando Martín Peña (Buenos Aires: MALBA, 2003),121.

28. Ibid., 122.

29. Ibid., 123.

30. Quintín, "De una generación a otra," 115.

31. Peña, Felix-Didier, Luka, "Lucretia Martel," 123.

32. Martel as cited in Ibid., 123.

33. Feld, *Del estrado a la pantalla: Las imágenes del juicio a los ex comandantes en Argentina* (Madrid: Siglo Veintiuno, 2002), 103–38. Feld notes that reports on former naval officer Adolfo Scilingo appeared in print prior to his appearance on *Hora Clave*—most notably through investigative reporter Horacio Verbitsky's *El vuelo* (1995)—but argues that it was the perpetrator's appearance on television that allowed his testimony to reach a wider public and to rekindle debate (103). See Payne for a detailed discussion of the public confessions of Scilingo and Alfredo Astiz, another former naval officer (*Unsettling Accounts*, 41–105).

34. Feld, *Del estrado a la pantalla*, 107.

35. Kaufman, "Memoria, horror, historia," 17–18, 23; Kaiser, "*Escarches*," 500, 502–3. Feld sees a similar tendency in *ESMA: El día del juicio*, a documentary that aired on Channel 13 in August 1998 and was seen by over three million people. Drawing on archival footage of the 1985 Trial of the Generals (of which only a small portion was televised at that time), the documentary recut the recordings to dramatize the events, included dramatic re-creations, and "utilized emotion as a vehicle to tell the story." One particular scene placed

Emiliano Hueravillo, a young man born in the ESMA in 1977 whose mother had been disappeared, in front of a television screen featuring a close-up of General Massera with a voice-over asking, "When you look at this man, Massera, what do you feel?" (121, 127–29, 131–32).

36. In her analysis of the aforementioned documentary, Feld faults the work for "packaging" emotions about the past into "pre-established formats (the melodrama, the epic, the detective story)." Ibid., 143.

37. Page, *Crisis and Capitalism*, 182, 193.

38. Ibid., 184–85.

39. Stock, *On Location*, 15.

40. Ibid., 17.

41. Ibid., 16, 238. Cristina Venegas dissents here, arguing that "young Cuban filmmakers echo their predecessors' discontent with commercial homogenization and domination, but their quiet concentration on personal digital production is, until now, its own counter-discourse to notions of film contributing to any larger identity or expression" (*Digital Dilemmas*, 144). The discrepancy between these positions may relate, in part, to the filmmakers discussed by Stock and Venegas. While mentioning Cremata and Padrón, Venegas places particular attention on the work of Miguel Coyula, a particularly iconoclastic young filmmaker best known off the island for his film *Red Cockroaches* (United States-Cuba, 2003).

42. Stock, *On Location*, 16.

43. Martha Oneida Pérez, Armando Perryman, Nilza González, Leydi González, Mayra Abréu, "Identidad nacional, organizaciones culturales, y tiempo libre," in *Cuba: Jóvenes en los 90* (Havana: Editorial Abril, 1999), 264–65.

44. María Isabel Domínguez, "La juventud cubana en una época de crisis y reestructuración," in *Cuba, período especial*, ed. José A. Moreno (La Habana: Editorial de Ciencias Sociales, 1998), 226–27.

45. Ibid., 230–31.

46. Ibid., 233–35.

47. Ibid., 240–41.

48. Luis Gómez, "La política cubana de juventud en los 90," in *Cuba: Jóvenes en los 90* (Havana: Editorial Abril, 1999), 120; Oneida Pérez et al., "Identidad nacional...," 258, 262, 264–65; Edgar Romero, et al., "Juventud y valores en los umbrales del siglo XXI," in *Cuba: Jóvenes en los 90*. Havana: Editorial Abril, 1999), 359–60.

49. Romero, et al. "Juventud y valores...," 335–36, 338–39; Gómez, "La política cubana...," 123, 140–41; Oneida Pérez et al., "Identidad nacional...," 256.

50. Gómez, "La política cubana...," 140–41; Romero et al., "Juventud y valores...," 340–41.

51. Domínguez, "La juventud cubana...," 242

52. Romero, et al., "Juventud y valores...," 345, 347.

53. The imagery of the original Spanish phrase (literally translatable as "Don't flit around like a butterfly, work") becomes significant later on when butterflies begin to appear on screen.

54. The inclusion of the telenovela provides one of the film's funniest and sharpest critiques of the stagnancy of Cuba's audiovisual productions and their calcified notion of youth. Coming on right before Professor Cruzado's show, the telenovela features an old nun with wrinkled features who cries out about the impossibility of love even as throws herself against the dapper young hero, dressed in nineteenth-century garb. The setting and the age difference of the two protagonists recall Humberto Solás's *Cecilia* (1982), which featured the forty-year-old Daisy Granados (b. 1942) in the title role of the teenage mulata and the much younger Spanish actor Imanol Arias (b. 1956) as her lover. The allusion is particularly noteworthy as Granados herself appears in *Nada* as Carla's vicious boss, the rigid Cunda Severo.

55. García Borrero, "La utopía confiscada," 176.

56. Ibid., 173, 177–78.

57. For a more thorough analysis of *Viva Cuba* and a detailed description of the many obstacles the filmmakers had to overcome to make the film, see Stock, *On Location*, 149–69. A similarly sentimental view of young children can be found in Pavel Giroud's *La edad de la peseta / The Awkward Age* (Cuba-España-Venezuela, 2006)

58. Aram Vidal (b. 1981) is another Cuban filmmaker whose work deals with the subjectivities of youth in a manner that appears to be less traditional. *De Generación / De-generation* or *Of the Generation* (2006) examines the lives of young people in their twenties and thirties living in Cuba, and his subsequent documentary short *Ex Generación* (2009) looks at the experiences of young Cubans who have left the island for Mexico. I am indebted to an anonymous reviewer for pointing me to this work. For more on Vidal, see Stock, *On Location*, 243–47.

59. For a more detailed discussion of Sánchez's work and its influence on younger filmmakers and established directors like Fernando Pérez, see Stock, *On Location*, 49–56.

60. Ryan Moore, " '... And Tomorrow Is Just Another Crazy Scam': Postmodernity, Youth, and the Downward Mobility of the Middle Class," in *Generations of Youth: Youth Culture and History in Twentieth-Century America*, ed. Joe Austin (New York: New York University Press, 1998), 253.

61. Ibid., 259–61.

62. Ibid., 254–55.

63. Lawrence Grossberg, "The Political Status of Youth and Youth Culture," in *Adolescents and Their Music: If It's Too Loud, You're Too Old*, ed. Jonathon S. Epstein (New York: Garland, 1994), 35, 40, 43; also cited in Moore, " '... And Tomorrow Is Just Another Crazy Scam'," 265.

64. Moore, " '... And Tomorrow Is Just Another Crazy Scam'," 259–60.

65. Kathleen Newman, "Cinemas of Solitude after the Lettered City," unpublished paper presented at the annual conference of the Latin American Studies Association (LASA), Dallas, March 2003.

66. Moore, " '... And Tomorrow Is Just Another Crazy Scam,' " 261.

67. Ibid., 261.

## 5 Migrant Feelings: Global Networks and Transnational Affective Communities

1. Bruno, *Atlas of Emotion*, 7, 251.
2. Indeed, as might be apparent, the road film is a defining characteristic of the films of contemporary Brazilian auteur Walter Salles as well as a recurrent trope in the oeuvre of Mexican director Alfonso Cuarón (if we can consider *Children of Men* a type of road film).
3. My comments are indebted to Gilberto Blasini's pioneering work on the Latin American road film.
4. Examples of travelling Latin American filmmakers who have worked in Hollywood include Cuban director Ramón Peón as well as Mexicans Emilio Fernández and Alfonso Arau. Those who work(ed) in Europe include Argentines Rodolfo Kuhn (Germany) and Fernando Solanas (France and Spain) and Chilean Raoul Ruiz (France). Others left their countries to work elsewhere in Latin America; one remarkable case from the "golden age" was Argentine filmmaker Carlos Hugo Christiansen who directed important films in his homeland of Argentina as well as in Venezuela and Brazil.
5. Deborah Shaw also discusses this possibility ["*Babel*: A Hollywood World Cinema Text," Paper presented at the annual meeting of the Society of Cinema and Media Studies, Los Angeles, California, March 17–21, 2010), 2].
6. Lauren Berlant, "Introduction: Compassion (and Withholding)," in *Compassion: The Culture and Politics of Emotion* (New York: Routledge, 2004), 7.
7. See Elizabeth Swanson Goldberg, "Splitting Differences: Global Identity Politics and the Representation of Torture in the Counterhistorical Dramatic Film," in *Violence and American Cinema*, ed. J. David Slocum (New York: Routledge, 2001) for a critique of how this dynamic is evident in earlier films, including *Salvador* (1987) and *Beyond Ragoon* (United States-UK, John Boorman, 1995).
8. See Catherine Grant, "Camera solidaria" *Screen*, 38.4 (1997) for an analysis of two analogous films made slightly earlier: *La amiga / The Female Friend* (Argentina-West Germany, Jeanine Meerapfel, 1989) and *Un muro de silencia / Black Flowers: A Wall of Silence* (Argentina-Mexico-UK, Lita Stantic, 1993). Her discussion suggests that the two films offer a more self-reflexive depiction of suffering-in-relation, than do the works by U.S. and British male directors studied by Swanson Goldberg.
9. Appadurai, "Topographies of the Self: Praise and Emotion in Hindu India," in *Language and the Politics of Emotion*, eds. Catherine A. Lutz and Lila Abu-Lughold (Cambridge: Cambridge University Press 1990), 94.
10. Released in over 1,251 theaters, *Babel* earned a total of US\$135,330,182 worldwide. See http://www.boxofficemojo.com/movies/?id=babel.htm.
11. Besides director-producer Portillo, the production crew included Kyle Kibbe (cinematographer), José Araujo (sound recordist), Celeste Carrasco Moreno (production manager), three camera assistants, and two production assistants See http://www.lourdesportillo.com/senoritaextraviada/credits.html.

12. For reviews of *Babel*, see Andrew Tracy ["Babel." *Cinemascope: Expanding the Frame of International Cinema* 28, http://www.cinema-scope.com/cs28/cur_tracy_babel.html (accessed on July 27, 2009)] and Leslie Felperin ["Babel," *Sight and Sound* 17.2 (2007)] as well as those discussed in Shaw, "Babel." For *Señorita extraviada*, see Navarro, "Who Is Killing the Young Women of Juárez: A Filmmaker Seeks Answers," *The New York Times* August 19, 2002. http://www.nytimes.com/2002/08/19/movies/who-is-killing-the-young-women-of-juarez-a-filmmaker-seeks-answers.html?scp=2&sq=senorita%20extraviada&st=cse (accessed on August 23, 2009).

13. Fregoso, "Introduction: Tracking the Politics of Love," in *Lourdes Portillo: The Devil Never Sleeps and Other Films* (Austin: University of Texas Press, 2001), 8–9.

14. See Kathleen Newman and B. Ruby Rich, "Interview with Lourdes Portillo (1990)," in *Lourdes Portillo: The Devil Never Sleeps and Other Films*, ed. Rosa Linda Fregoso (Austin: University of Texas Press, 2001), 50–51, 60–61.

15. Sergio de la Mora notes that Portillo's work departs from the "cold, analytic, rational revolutionary rhetoric" visible in the work of directors and critics of the NLAC. See "Terrorismo de género en la frontera México-EUA: asesinato, mujeres y justicia en *Señorita extraviada* (Lourdes Portillo, 2001)," August 2003 http://www.elojoquepiensa.udg.mx (accessed on July 11, 2009).

16. See Rosa Linda Fregoso, "Introduction: Tracking the Politics of Love" for more on Portillo's contention that "[p]olitics is about your heart" (7).

17. The table places individual sequences in chronological order according to location and charts the *approximate* temporal relationship of events taking place in different locations.

18. Other scholars locate the melodramatic nature of Iñarruti and Arriaga's films in their kinship with the telenovela (including the censure of the rich and "victimism") and their overwrought emotion. See Paul Julian Smith, *Amores perros* (London: British Film Institute, 2003), 38–49; Michael Stewart, "Irresistible Death: *21 Grams* as Melodrama," *Cinema Journal*, 47.1 (2007), 49–50; Vaidovits, "La levedad del ser"; and Lida, "Unos gramos más."

19. Melodrama is ideologically conservative, as it typically works to realign the social order. At the same time, as noted by many feminist scholars, in the process of restoring that order, it can also showcase some of the contradictions or limitations of that order. For more detailed discussion of these issues, see the articles in Christine Gledhill's *Home Is Where the Heart Is*.

20. Williams, "Melodrama Revisited," 48.

21. Martín Barbero, "Memory and Form in the Latin American Soap Opera," in *To be continued…Soap Operas Around the World*, ed. Robert C. Allen (London: Routledge, 1995), 277.

22. Williams, "Melodrama Revisited," 69–70.

23. Moretti, cited in Ibid., 70

24. Ibid., 71.

25. Ibid., 49.

26. In her argument about the relative complexity of melodramatic pathos, Williams draws on the work of Christine Gledhill who has argued that "if a melodramatic character appeals to our sympathy, it is because pathos involves us in assessing suffering in terms of our privileged knowledge of its nature and causes. Pathos is thus 'intensified by the misrecognition of a sympathetic protagonist because the audience has privileged knowledge of the "true" situation.'" (Gledhill, "The Melodramatic Field," 45–46 as cited in Williams, 49.)

27. An extended discussion of the narrative set in Japan is not possible given the parameters of this chapter. However, it will be useful to briefly comment on the staging of recognition and reconciliation in that plotline. In one of the sequences set in Chieko's apartment, after she inexplicably takes off all of her clothes, places his hand upon her breast, and begins kissing him, Lt. Mamiya responds by offering her his coat and then embracing her as she breaks down and sobs. The reasons behind her emotional outpouring are not entirely clear (and thus may not invite the same type of pathetic release from the viewer). However, the detective's small gesture suggests that he (correctly) interprets Chieko's actions not as a sign of perversity but as a call for help. Contrasting his actions not only to those of other policemen but also to the Japanese dentist (who, in an earlier sequence, responds to Chieko's sexual advances with horror), the film seems to hold up and celebrate his act of compassion.

28. For example, as Richard screams at a Moroccan officer about the delay in getting an ambulance to take his bleeding wife to a hospital, it becomes evident that it is the result of political maneuvering, whereby the U.S. government insists upon sending in a U.S. helicopter to "rescue" the couple.

29. Drawing on the pioneering book *Televisión y Melodrama* (1992) by Jesús Martín Barbero and Susana Muñoz, Ana López notes that "Mexican *telenovelas* are notorious for their weepiness, extraordinary Manichean vision of the world, and lack of specific historical referents" ["Our Welcomed Guests: Telenovelas in Latin America," in *To be continued... Soap Operas Around the World*, ed. Robert C. Allen (London: Routledge, 1995), 261]. Basing his analysis on the typology offered by Argentine communications scholar Nora Mazziotti (2005), Mexican communications scholar Guillermo Orozco Gómez points to the Mexican telenovela's valuation of the spoken word (traceable to its "strong roots in the *radionovela*); tendency to focus almost exclusively on a love story; disinterest in sensuality, eroticism, and politics; and underlying Christian morality that positions suffering as the basis of redemption ["La telenovela en México: ¿de una expresión cultural a un simple producto para la mercadotecnia?" *Comunicación y Sociedad* Nueva época 6 (July–December 2006), 19–24].

30. Chieko is depicted as a much more sophisticated teenager (in a media-saturated urban setting) who knowingly commits transgressive, exhibitionist acts (pulling off her underwear to flash a boy; opening her legs to the dentist; stripping off her clothes in front of Lt. Mamiya). Yet, the subplot about her mother's suicide helps to cast her actions in light of that psychological trauma and thus attenuate her moral culpability.

31. The film also accentuates Amelia's underlying goodness by situating Santiago, her feckless nephew, as her foil. Unlike Amelia, Santiago appears to be motivated by more self-serving desires—by drinking excessively, by fleeing from the border guard, and by abandoning Amelia and the children in the desert.

32. Andrea Noble argues that "the kinds of narrative structure that characterize melodrama are similarly to be found as central components in the rituals of the Catholic religion that arrived in the 'New World' with the Spanish invasion and revolve around sin, suffering, abnegation and punishment" [*Mexican National Cinema* (London: Routledge, 2005), 100]. It is important to underscore the performative nature of religious rituals, such as pilgrimages, processions, and passion plays, wherein the suffering body is staged for onlookers.

33. In establishing a parallel between the blurred figure of the official in the foreground and the ghostly visage of Vice President Dick Cheney (in a photograph on a wall in the background), the initial over-the-shoulder shot positions Amelia as sandwiched between two draconian officials symbolizing the overpowering force of the U.S. government. While the placement of the camera align us with the perspective of the law, the depiction of the distressed Amelia as the only character who is in focus upsets that alignment.

34. Williams, "Melodrama Revisited," 67.

35. Olga Nájera Ramírez, "Unruly Passions: Poetics, Performance, and Gender in the Ranchera Song," in *Chicana Feminisms: A Critical Reader*, ed. Gabriela Arredondo (Durham: Duke University Press, 2003), 185.

36. Ibid., 188, 199.

37. Ibid., 186, 188.

38. Ibid., 187.

39. Williams, "Melodrama Revisited," 55.

40. In speaking about melodrama as "a peculiarly democratic and American form," Williams points to 1) its utopian, "wish-fulfilling impulse towards the achievement of justice" (Ibid., 48); 2) its Calvinist understanding of virtue (55); and 3) its tendency to heroicize the victim (83n15).

41. Elsaesser, "Tales of Sound and Fury: Observations on the Family Melodrama," in *Home Is Where the Heart Is: Studies in Melodrama and the Woman's Film*, ed. Christine Gledhill (London: BFI, 1987), 49.

42. Orozco Gómez, "La telenovela en México," 15, citing Martin-Barbero and Muñoz, *Televisión y melodrama*.

43. Berlant, "Introduction," 1, 5.

44. Clearly, I'm speaking generally. The works of scholars such as Peter Stearns offer a much more nuanced discussion of the history of emotions in the United States.

45. In this way, my argument here also counters critics who suggest that *Babel* relies on and promotes the universality of human emotions. In his review for the *New York Times*, A. O. Scott contends that "Iñárritu's own visual grammar tries to [...] suggest a common idiom of emotion present in certain immediately recognizable gestures and expressions" ("Emotion Needs No Translation," *New*

*York Times* October 27, 2006). Scholar Deborah Shaw argues that the film cannot divest itself of a tourist gaze (despite the director's Third World-ist pretensions) and criticizes its reliance on "melodramatic structures" as mechanisms that help to conceal unequal power structures ("*Babel*: A Hollywood World Cinema Text," 5, 9–13).

46. Martín Barbero, "Memory and Form in the Latin American Soap Opera," 276.

47. Orozco Gómez argues that the disconnected narratives and increased number of scenes per episode have turned contemporary Mexican telenovelas into publicity spots. It is noteworthy that he dates the origin of this "fifth stage" of the Mexican telenovela to 2000, the same year in which Iñárruti and Arriaga's *Amores perros* (a film known for its fractured story, fast pace, and the influence of advertising) premiered. See "La telenovela en México," 30–32.

48. Rosa Linda Fregoso has argued forcefully that the murders should not be explained *merely* in terms of globalization, but rather as the result of a variety of factors, including the reconfiguration of the Mexican state ["Towards a Planetary Civil Society," in *meXicana Encounters: The Making of Social Identities on the Borderlands* (Berkeley: University of California Press, 2003), 8, 17–20]. Given Fregoso and Portillo's close working relationship, it is no surprise that *Señorita extraviada* also ultimately favors this multifactor interpretation (as noted near the end of my analysis of the film). Nonetheless, this opening sequence is absolutely fundamental to framing globalization as *the* key element behind either the murders themselves or the incapacity of the Mexican state to find those responsible.

49. de la Mora, "Terrorismo de género…"; Alejandro Enríquez, "Lourdes Portillo's *Señorita extraviada*: The Poetics and Politics of Femicide," *Studies in Latin American Popular Culture* 23 (2004), 129, 131; Fregoso, "Toward a Planetary Civil Society," 26.

50. While underscoring some of these same characteristics (namely, the film's interest in provoking an emotional response in the viewer as well as its use of recreations), Alejandro Enríquez argues that *Señorita extraviada* positions itself as a detective story (Ibid., 125–28).

51. See Fregoso, "Interview with Lourdes Portillo (1994), in *Lourdes Portillo: The Devil Never Sleeps and Other Films* (Austin: University of Texas Press, 2001); Fregoso, "Sacando los trapos al sol (airing dirty laundry) in Lourdes Portillo's Melodocumentary, *The Devil Never Sleeps*," in *Redirecting the Gaze: Gender, Theory, and Cinema*, ed. Diana Robin (Albany: State University of New York Press, 1999), 312, 314, 324; and Yvonne Yarbro-Bejarano, "Ironic Framings: A Queer Reading of the Family (Melo)drama in Lourdes Portillo's *The Devil Never Sleeps / El Diablo Nunca Duerme*," in *Lourdes Portillo: The Devil Never Sleeps and Other Films*, edited by Rosa Linda Fregoso (Austin: University of Texas Press, 2001), 106–9.

52. As Yarbro-Bejarano notes about *El Diablo*, the "tongue-in-cheek detective framings ironize the filmmaker's search for the truth (someone to 'frame'). The

highly charged extreme aesthetic of melodrama frames her subjects' *own* versions of the truth in the interviews, as well as provincial understandings of history" (Ibid., 107).

53. Kevin Glynn, *Tabloid Culture: Trash Taste, Popular Power, and the Transformation of American Television* (Durham: Duke University Press, 2000), 97.

54. Ibid., 72.

55. John Langer, *Tabloid Television: Popular Journalism and the "Other News"* (London: Routledge, 1998), 9; 152–53.

56. Ibid., 154.

57. Enríquez, "Lourdes Portillo's *Señorita extraviada*," 128–29.

58. Carlos Monsivais, *Los mil y un velorios* (Mexico, D.F.: Patria, 1994), 9–10.

59. Ibid., 11.

60. Lerner, *The Shock of Modernity: Crime Photography in Mexico City* (Mexico City: Turner, 2007), 10, 44

61. Ibid., 25.

62. Ibid., 31, 48.

63. Ibid., 48.

64. Ibid., 44–45.

65. Ibid., 48

66. Ibid., 37.

67. Ibid., 80.

68. Ibid., 71, 73.

69. Ibid., 82. See 90–91 for two sample covers.

70. The mediational role played by the *nota roja* in the first decades of the twentieth century would continue in subsequent periods. It is perhaps not surprising that a "new milestone in the increasingly gory scramble for the attention of the public" was reached in 1950 with the establishment of *Alarma!* (Lerner,101). After all, it was precisely in the 1950s that an urbanizing Mexico began to experience the effects of its second wave of modernization initiated a decade earlier with the shift away from an agricultural-based economy toward industrialization. Almost sixty years later, in an era marked by globalization, the tabloid remains popular with an online version called *Nueva Alarma*.

71. Daniel Hallin, "*La Nota Roja*: Popular Journalism and the Transition to Democracy in Mexico," in *Tabloid Tales: Global Debates over Media Standards*, eds. Colin Sparks, et al. (Lanham, MA: Rowman & Littlefield, 2000), 267.

72. Ibid., 269.

73. Ibid., 279.

74. Ibid., 272.

75. Ibid., 267–68, 278. Hallin notes that *Ciudad desnuda* reached a 30 percent market share before Televisa introduced its rival program, *Fuera de la ley* (269). Although both shows were canceled in 1992 as a result of governmental pressure, their rapid replacement by similar programs suggests the continuing commercial viability of the format.

76. My reading draws on the insights of previous scholars such as Sergio de la Mora who argues that the film "works as a vehicle to stimulate cross-border

solidarity" ("El Terrorismo de género...."). For her part, Fregoso contends that the film helps to promote a "planetary civil society"—in part by employing "religious symbolism and iconography subversively" ("Towards a Planetary Civil Society," 25–26).

77. See chapter 1, note 3 for more on this distinction.

78. Carl Gutiérrez-Jones, *Rethinking the Borderlands: Between Chicano Culture and Legal Discourse* (Berkeley: University of California Press, 1995), 149. In his discussion of trauma in Mexican society, Gutiérrez-Jones relies on Octavio Paz's famous book-length essay *El laberinto de la soledad* (1950).

79. Ibid., 148.

80. Ibid., 156–58.

81. Ibid., 153, 159–62.

82. Ibid., 153–54. According to Gutiérrez Jones, Anglo practices can be traced to the early colonial period when the Puritans began to regulate funeral practices and contain grief in ways that were deemed less socially divisive than in previous social practices of mourning (145–46). If Puritan traditions contributed to the Anglo-American containment of grief, another shift occurred in the post–World War II period when mourning practices were further sublimated by shifting the locus of articulation to legal institutions (146–47). According to Gutiérrez Jones, in the post–World War II period, it became more socially acceptable to address feelings of injury and loss by seeking redress through legal channels where the rational(izing) language of the law supplanted sensorial enactments of grief. His discussion of this shift is underdeveloped. However, his suggestion that Anglo society began to further "contain" the public expression of emotion during the twentieth century coincides with the arguments of historian Peter Stearns, who attributes this gradual change to shifting gender and familial dynamics; the growth of consumer society; and the rise of managerial bureaucracies, among other things.

83. Ibid., 153–54, 193n34.

84. For a lovely analysis of how this film draws on Mexican cultural traditions (including a pre-Colombian understanding of death associated with the Aztecs), see Kathleen Newman, "Steadfast Love and Subversive Acts: The Politics of *La Ofrenda: The Days of the Dead*," in *Visible Nations: Latin American Cinema and Video*, ed. Chon A. Noriega (Minneapolis: University of Minnesota Press, 2000).

85. For more on these tactics, see Diana Taylor, *Disappearing Acts: Spectacles of Gender and Nationalism in Argentina's Dirty War*.

86. Appadurai, "Topographies of the Self," 93.

87. Catherine Grant makes a similar argument in relation to U.S.-made "solidarity" films about Nicaragua and El Salvador from the 1980s and their potential interest for Central American refugees living in the United States, as well as for those participating in international solidarity movements against the repressive governments in the southern cone and Central America (1997, 312).

88. Enríquez, "Lourdes Portillo's *Señorita extraviada*," 123–24, 134–35.

89. My survey reviewed sixty comments posted on http://www.nytimes.com/ between October 27, 2006, and February 19, 2009. Of the sixty people who posted comments during that period, approximately twenty-two identified themselves in their signature line as from the United States, three from Latin America, two from Canada, one from Stockholm, and one from India. Thirty-one reviewers did not self-identify according to a particular country.

90. A handful of reviewers offered a more honed interpretation of the film's politics as a critique of U.S. politics.

91. Shaw, "*Babel*: A Hollywood World Cinema Text," 7, 11. For her part, Tierney defends the director's credentials as an independent filmmaker and the way in which *Babel* makes the inequalities between classes and between countries visible; she nonetheless notes the "conservatism of its ending" ("Alejandro González Iñárruti," 114).

# Works Cited

Aguilar, Gonzalo. *Other Worlds: New Argentine Cinema*. New York: Palgrave Macmillan, 2008.

Ahmed, Sara. *The Cultural Politics of Emotion*. New York: Routledge, 2004.

Alvaray, Luisela. "National, Regional, and Global: New Waves of Latin American Cinema" *Cinema Journal* 47.3 (Spring 2008): 48–65.

Amaya, Hector. "*Amores perros* and racialised masculinities in contemporary Mexico." *New Cinemas: Journal of Contemporary Film* 5.3 (2007): 201–16.

Appadurai, Arjun. Fear of Small Numbers: An Essay on the Geography of Anger. Durham: Duke University Press, 2006.

———. "Topographies of the self: Praise and emotion in Hindu India," in *Language and the Politics of Emotion*, edited by Catherine A. Lutz and Lila Abu-Lughold, 92–112. Cambridge: Cambridge University Press, 1990.

Armstrong, Isobel. *The Radical Aesthetic*. Oxford: Blackwell, 2000.

Arredondo, Isabel. "From Transparent to Translucid: Cuban Filmmakers in 1990." *Latin American Literary Review*. 25.49 (1997): 25–41.

Avelar, Idelbar. "From Plato to Pinochet." In *The Letter of Violence: Essays on Narrative, Ethics, and Politics*. New York: Palgrave Macmillan, 2004.

———. *The Untimely Present: Posdictatorial Latin American Fiction and the Task of Mourning*. Durham: Duke University Press, 1999.

Ayala Blanco, Jorge. "González Iñárruti y el neotremendismo chafa." *El Financiero-Cultural*, June 19, 2000, 108.

Barnard, Timothy. "Death Is Not True: Form and History in Cuban Film." In *Mediating Two Worlds: Cinematic Encounters in the Americas*, edited by John King, Ana López, and Manuel Alvarado, 230–41. London: British Film Institute, 1993.

Batlle, Diego. "From Virtual Death to the New Law: The Resurgence." In *New Argentine Cinema: Themes, Auteurs and Trends of Innovation / El Nuevo cine argentino: temas, directores y estilos de una renovación*, edited by Horacio Bernades, Diego Lerer, and Sergio Wolf, 17-27. Buenos Aires: Tatanka/FIPRESCI, 2002.

Bauman, Zygmunt. *Liquid Fear*. Cambridge: Polity, 2006.

———. *Liquid Times: Living in an Age of Uncertainty*. Cambridge: Polity, 2007.

Benjamin, Walter. "The Work of Art in the Age of Mechanical Reproduction." In *Film Theory and Criticism*, edited by Leo Braudy and Marshall Cohen, 665–85. 7th ed. New York: Oxford University Press, 2009.

Bennett, Jill. *Empathic Vision: Affect, Trauma, and Contemporary Art*. Stanford: Stanford University Press, 2005.

Bentes, Ivana. "The *sertão* and the *favela* in contemporary Brazilian film." In *The New Brazilian Cinema* edited by Lúcia Nagib, 121–37. London: IB Tauris, 2003.

Berlant, Lauren. "Introduction: Compassion (and Withholding)." In *Compassion: The Culture and Politics of Emotion*. New York: Routledge, 2004.

Bernades, Horacio, Diego Lerer, and Sergio Wolf, eds. *New Argentine Cinema: Themes, Auteurs and Trends of Innovation / El Nuevo cine argentino: temas, directores y estilos de una renovación*. Buenos Aires: Tatanka/FIPRESCI, 2002.

Bernini, Emilio. "Politics and the Documentary Film in Argentina during the 1960s." *Journal of Latin American Cultural Studies* 13.2 (August 2004): 155–70.

Borreye, Orla Juliette. "The Significance of the Queer and the Dog in Alejandro González Iñárruti's *Amores perros* (2000): Masculinity at War." *Wide Screen* 1.1 (2009). http://widescreenjournal.org

Borter, Beat. "Moving to Thought: The Inspired Reflective Cinema of Fernando Pérez." In *Framing Latin American Cinema: New Critical Perspectives*, edited by Ann Marie Stock, 141–61. Minneapolis: University of Minnesota Press, 1997.

Bruno, Guiliana. *Atlas of Emotion: Journeys in Art, Architecture, and Film*. New York: Verso, 2002.

Burton, Julianne, ed. *Cinema and Social Change: Conversations with Filmmakers*. Austin: University of Texas Press, 1986.

Callegaro, Adriana and Miriam Goldstein. "Cine Argentino, 1998–2000: Universo juvenil y mundo urbano." *Revista de cine* 1 (2001): 59–62.

Carpignano, Paolo, Robin Andersen, Stanley Aronowitz, and William DiFazio. "Chatter in the Age of Electronic Reproduction: Talk Televisión and the 'Public Mind." In *The Phantom Public Sphere*, edited by Bruce Robbins, 93–120. Minneapolis: University of Minnesota Press, 1993.

Carr, Jay. "With violent "Amores perros,' a stunning directorial debut." *The Boston Globe* April 13, 2001, D6.

Carroll, Noel. "Affect and the Moving Images." In *The Philosophy of Motion Pictures*, 147–91. Malden, MA: Blackwell, 2008.

———. "Film, Emotion, and Genre." In *Passionate Views: Films, Cognition, and Emotion*, edited by Carl Platinga and Greg Smith, 21–47. Baltimore: Johns Hopkins University Press, 1999.

———. "The Paradox of Suspense." In *Suspense: Conceptualizations, Theoretical Analyses, and Empirical Explorations*, edited by Peter Vorderer, Hans J. Wulff, and Mike Friedrichsen, 71–91. Mahwah, NJ: Lawrence Erlbaum Associates, 1996.

Cartwright, Lisa. *Moral Spectatorship: Technologies of Voice and Affect in Postwar Representations of the Child*. Durham: Duke University Press, 2008.

Caruth, Cathy. *Unclaimed Experience: Trauma, Narrative, and History.* Baltimore: Johns Hopkins University Press, 1996.

Chanan, Michael. *The Cuban Image: Cinema and Cultural Politics in Cuba.* London: BFI/Bloomington: Indiana University Press, 1985.

———. "Latin American Cinema in the 90s. Representational Space in Recent Latin American Cinema." *Estudios interdisciplinarios de América Latina y el Caribe* 9.1 (1998): 111–20.

———. "Rediscovering Documentary: Cultural Context and Intentionality." In *The Social Documentary in Latin America*, edited by Julianne Burton, 31–47. Pittsburgh: University of Pittsburgh Press, 1990.

Colina, Enrique and Daniel Díaz Torres. "Ideología del melodrama en el viejo cine latinoamericano." *Cine Cubano* 73/74/75 (1972): 14–26.

Cvetkovich, Ann. *An Archive of Feeling: Trauma, Sexuality, and Lesbian Public Cultures.* Durham: Duke University Press, 2003.

Damasio, Antonio. *Descartes' Error: Emotion, Reason and the Human Brain.* New York: Grosset/Putnam, 1994.

De la Mora, Sergio. "Terrorismo de género en la frontera México-EUA: asesinato, mujeres y justicia en *Señorita extraviada* (Lourdes Portillo, 2001)" August 2003. http://www.elojoquepiensa.udg.mx. Accessed on July 11, 2009.

Deleuze, Gilles. *Cinema 2: The Time-Image*, translated by Hugo Tomlinson and Robert Galeta. Minneapolis: University of Minnesota Press, 1989 [1985].

——— and Félix Guattari. "Percept, Affect and Concept." In *The Continental Aesthetic Reader*, edited by Clive Cazeaux, 465–87. London: Routledge, 2000.

Dika, Vera. *Recycled Culture in Contemporary Art and Film: The Uses of Nostalgia.* Cambridge: Cambridge University Press, 2003.

D'Lugo, Marvin. "Amores perros." In *The Cinemas of Latin America*, edited by Alberto Elena and Mariana Díaz López, 221–29. London: Wallflower Press, 2004

———. "Authorship, globalization, and the new identity of Latin American cinema: From the Mexican 'ranchera' to Argentinian 'exile'." In *Rethinking Third Cinema*, edited by Anthony R. Guneratne and Winal Dissanayake, 103–25. New York: Routledge, 2003.

———. "Transparent Woman: Gender and Nation." In *Mediating Two Worlds: Cinematic Encounters in the Americas*, edited by John King, Ana M. López, Manuel Alvarado, 279–90. London : BFI Institute, 1993.

Domínguez, María Isabel. "La juventud cubana en una época de crisis y reestructuración." In *Cuba, período especial*, edited by José A. Moreno. La Habana: Editorial de Ciencias Sociales, 1998.

Dorfman, Ariel. "Final and First Words about Death and the Maiden." In *Other Septembers, Many Americas: Selected Provocations, 1980–2004.* New York: Seven Stories Press, 2004.

Douglas, Ann. *The Feminization of American Culture.* New York: Knopf: 1977.

Elena, Alberto and Mariana Díaz López, eds. *The Cinemas of Latin America.* London: Wallflower Press, 2004.

Elsaesser, Thomas. "Subject Positions, Speaking Positions: From *Holocaust, Our Hitler*, and *Heimat* to *Shoah* and *Schindler's List*." In *The Persistence of History: Cinema, Television, and the Modern Event*, edited by Vivian Sobchack, 145–83. New York: Routledge, 1996.

———. "Tales of Sound and Fury: Observations on the Family Melodrama." [1972]. In *Home Is Where the Heart Is: Studies in Melodrama and the Woman's Film*, edited by Christine Gledhill, 43–69. London: BFI, 1987.

Enríquez, Alejandro. "Lourdes Portillo's *Señorita extraviada*: The Poetics and Politics of Femicide." *Studies in Latin American Popular Culture* 23 (2004): 123–36.

"Es una película inocente y pura." *Clarín* October 23, 2005. http://edant.clarin.com/diario/2005/10/23/espectaculos/c-01076078.htm. Accessed April 18, 2006.

Evora, José Antonio. *Tomás Gutiérrez Alea*. Madrid: Cátedra/Filmoteca Española, 1996.

Falicov, Tamara. "Argentina's Blockbuster Movies and the Politics of Culture under Neoliberalism, 1989–98." *Media, Culture & Society* 22.3 (2000): 327–42.

———. The Cinematic Tango: Contemporary Argentine Film. London: Wallflower, 2007.

———. "Latin America: How Mexico and Argentina Cope and Cooperate with the Behemoth of the North." In *The Contemporary Hollywood Film Industry*, edited by Paul McDonald and Janet Wasko, 264–76. Malden, MA: Blackwell, 2008.

Feld, Claudia. *Del estrado a la pantalla: Las imágenes del juicio a los ex comandantes en Argentina*. Madrid: Siglo Veintiuno, 2002.

Felperin, Leslie. "Babel." *Sight and Sound* 17.2 (2007): 41–42.

Franco, Jean. "Obstinate Memory: Tainted History." In *The Decline and Fall of the Lettered City: Latin America in the Cold War*. Cambridge: Harvard University Press, 2002.

Fregoso, Rosa Linda. "Interview with Lourdes Portillo (1994)." In *Lourdes Portillo: The Devil Never Sleeps and Other Films*, 40–47. Austin: University of Texas Press, 2001.

———. "Introduction: Tracking the Politics of Love." In *Lourdes Portillo: The Devil Never Sleeps and Other Films*, 1–23. Austin: University of Texas Press, 2001.

———. "Sacando los trapos al sol (airing dirty laundry) in Lourdes Portillo's Melodocumentary, *The Devil Never Sleeps*." In *Redirecting the Gaze: Gender, Theory, and Cinema*, edited by Diana Robin and Ira Jaffe, 307–29. Albany: State University of New York Press, 1999.

———. "Toward a Planetary Civil Society." In *meXicana Encounters: The Making of Social Identities on the Borderlands*, 1–29. Berkeley: University of California Press, 2003.

Garber, Marjorie. "Compassion." In *Compassion: The Culture and Politics of Emotion*, edited by Lauren Berlant, 15–27. New York: Routledge, 2004.

García Borrero, Juan Antonio. "Las iniciales de la ciudad." In *Imágenes en libertad: Horizontes latinos*. 51$^{st}$ Festival Internacional de Cine, San Sebastián, 2003.

———. "La utopia confiscada (De la gravedad del sueño a la ligereza del realismo)." In *La edad de herejía (Ensayos sobre el cine cubano, su crítica y su público)*. Santiago de Cuba: Editorial Oriente, 2002.

Giroux, Henry. *Fugitive Cultures: Race, Violence and Youth*. New York: Routledge, 1996.

Gledhill, Christine, ed. *Home Is Where the Heart Is: Studies in Melodrama and the Woman's Film*. London: BFI, 1987.

Glynn, Kevin. *Tabloid Culture: Trash Taste, Popular Power, and the Transformation of American Television*. Durham: Duke University Press, 2000.

Gómez, Luis. "La política cubana de juventud en los 90." In *Cuba: Jóvenes en los 90*. Havana: Editorial Abril, 1999.

Gormley, Paul. *The New-Brutality Film: Race and Affect in Contemporary Hollywood Cinema*. Bristol: Intellect, 2005.

Grant, Catherine. "Camera solidaria." *Screen*, 38.4 (1997): 311–28.

Grossberg, Lawrence. "The Political Status of Youth and Youth Culture." In *Adolescents and Their Music: If It's Too Loud, You're Too Old*, edited by Jonathon S. Epstein, 25–46. New York: Garland, 1994.

Guelerman, Sergio. "Escuela, juventud y genocidio: una interpretación posible." In *Memorias en presente: identidad y transmisión en la Argentina posgenocidio*, 35–64. Buenos Aires: Grupo Editorial Norma, 2001.

Gunderman, Christián. "Entre observación desprendida y dinamización emocional: algunos comentarios sobre los Nuevos Cines latinoamericanos en Argentina, Brasil y Cuba." *Estudios Interdisciplinarios de América Latina y el Caribe*. 22.1 (2007). http://www1.tau.ac.il/eiai. Accessed on December 29, 2009.

———. "The Stark Gaze of the New Argentine Cinema: Restoring Strangeness to the Object in the Perverse Age of Commodity Fetishism." *Journal of Latin American Cultural Studies* 14.3 (2005): 241–61.

Gutiérrez Alea, Tomás. "Beyond the Reflection of Reality." In *Cinema and Social Change: Conversations with Filmmakers*, edited by Julianne Burton, 151–31. Austin: University of Texas Press, 1986.

———. *La dialéctica del espectador*. La Habana: Cuadernos de la Revista Unión, 1982.

Gutiérrez-Jones, Carl. *Rethinking the Borderlands: Between Chicano Culture and Legal Discourse*. Berkeley: University of California Press, 1995.

Hallin, Daniel. "*La Nota Roja*: Popular Journalism and the Transition to Democracy in Mexico." In *Tabloid Tales: Global Debates over Media Standards*, edited by Colin Sparks and John Tulloch, 267–84. Lanham, MA: Rowman & Littlefield, 2000.

Hardt, Michael. "Foreword: What Affects Are Good For." In *The Affective Turn: Theorizing the Social*, edited by Patricia Ticineto Clough and Jean Halley, ix–xiii. Durham: Duke University Press, 2007.

Hart, Stephen. *A Companion to Latin American Film*. Woodbridge, UK: Tamesis. 2004.

Herlinghaus, Hermann. "Affectivity beyond 'Bare Life': On the Non-Tragic Return of Violence in Latin American Film." In *A Companion to Latin American*

*Literature and Culture*, edited by Sara Castro-Klaren, 584–601. Malden, MA: Blackwell, 2008.

Hess, John. "Neo-Realism and New Latin American Cinema: *Bicycle Thieves* and *Blood of the Condor*." In *Mediating Two Worlds: Cinematic Encounters in the Americas*, edited by John King, Ana López, and Manuel Alvarado, 104–18. London: BFI, 1993.

Hopenhayn, Martín. *Ni apocalípticos ni integrados: aventuras de la modernidad en América Latina*. México: Fondo de Cultura Económica, 1994.

———. *No Apocalypse, No Integration: Modernism and Postmodernism in Latin America*, translated by Cynthia Margarita Tompkins and Elizabeth Rosa Horan. Durham: Duke University Press, 2001.

Huyssen, Andreas. *Twilight Memories: Marking Time in a Culture of America*. New York: Routledge, 1995.

Jabbaz, Marcela and Claudia Lozano. "Memorias de la dictadura y transmisión generacional: representaciones y controversias." In *Memorias en presente: identidad y transmisión en la Argentina posgenocidio*, edited by Sergio J. Guelerman, 97–131. Buenos Aires: Grupo Editorial Norma, 2001.

Jameson, Frederic. "The Cultural Logic of Late Capitalism." In *Postmodernism or The Cultural Logic of Late Capitalism*. Durham: Duke University Press, 1991.

———. *The Geopolitical Aesthetic: Cinema and Space in the World System*. Bloomington: Indiana University Press, 1992.

Johnson, Randal. *Cinema Novo x 5: Masters of Contemporary Brazilian Film*. Austin: University of Texas Press, 1984.

———. "Departing from *Central Station*: Notes on the Reemergence of Brazilian Cinema." In *The Brazil e-Journal* (a publication of the Brazilian Embassy in Washington, DC), http://www.brasilemb.org/br_ejournal/cinebras.htm. Accessed on September 28, 2000.

Kaplan, E. Ann and Ban Wang, eds. *Trauma and Cinema: Cross-Cultural Explorations*. Hong Kong: Hong Kong University Press, 2004.

Kaiser, Susana. "*Escarches*: Demonstrations, Communication and Political Memory in Post-dictatorial Argentina." *Media, Culture & Society* 24 (2002): 499–516.

Kaplan, E. Ann and Ban Wang. "Introduction: From Traumatic Paralysis to the Force Field of Modernity." In *Trauma and Cinema: Cross-Cultural Explorations*. Hong Kong: Hong Kong University Press, 2004.

Kaufman, Alejandro. "Memoria, horror, historia." In *Memorias en presente: Identidad y transmission en la Argentina posgenocidio*, edited by Sergio Guelerman, 11–34. Buenos Aires: Grupo Editorial Norma, 2001.

Keating, Patricia. "The Fictional Worlds of Neorealism." *Criticism* 45.1 (Winter 2003): 11–30.

Kennedy, Barbara. *Deleuze and Cinema: The Aesthetics of Sensation*. Edinburgh: Edinburgh University Press, 2000.

King, John. *Magical Reels*. London: Verso, 2000 [1990].

Kosofsky Sedgwick, Eve. *Touching Feeling: Affect, Pedagogy, Performativity*. Durham: Duke University Press, 2003.

Kun, Josh. *Audiotopia: Music, Race, and America*. Berkeley, University of California Press, 2005.

LaCapra, Dominick. *Writing History, Writing Trauma*. Baltimore: Johns Hopkins University Press, 2001.

Langer, John. *Tabloid Television: Popular Journalism and the "Other News."* London: Routledge, 1998.

Lerner, Jesse. *The Shock of Modernity: Crime Photography in Mexico City*. Mexico City: Turner, 2007.

Lida, David. "Unos gramos más." *Reforma-Cultural*, November 30, 2003, 7.

López, Ana. "At the Limits of Documentary: Hypertextual Transformation and the New Latin American Cinema." In *The Social Documentary in Latin America*, edited by Julianne Burton, 403–32. Pittsburgh: University of Pittsburgh Press, 1990.

———. "*The Battle of Chile*: Documentary, Political Process, and Representation." In *The Social Documentary in Latin America*, edited by Julianne Burton, 267–87. Pittsburgh: University of Pittsburgh Press, 1990.

———. "Cuba." In *The Cinema of Small Nations*, edited by Mette Hjort and Duncan Petrie, 179–97. Edinburgh: Edinburgh University Press, 2008.

———. "*Memorias* of a Home: Mapping the Revolution (and the Making of Exiles?)." *Revista Canadiense de Estudios Hispánicos* 20.1 (1995): 5–17.

———. "Our Welcomed Guests: Telenovelas in Latin America." In *To be continued…Soap Operas Around the World*, edited by Robert C. Allen, 256–75. London: Routledge, 1995.

Lorenzano, Sandra. "Contrabando de la memoria." *Escrituras de sobrevivencia: narrativa y dictadura*. México, D.F.: Universidad Autónoma, 2001.

MacBean, James Roy. "La Hora de los Hornos." *Film Quarterly* 24.1 (1970): 31–43.

Manzano, Valeria. "Blue Jean Generation: Youth, Gender and Sexuality in Buenos Aires, 1958–1975." *Journal of the Social History* 42.3 (Spring 2009): 657–76.

———. "Sexualizing Youth: Morality Campaigns and Representations of Youth in Early 1960s Buenos Aires." *Journal of the History of Sexuality* 14.4 (October 2005): 433–61.

Marcel, Mario. "La Generación Pendiente." *Nueva Sociedad* 76 (1985): 43–51.

Marks, Laura U. *The Skin of the Film: Intercultural Cinema, Embodiment, and the Senses*. Durham: Duke University Press, 2000.

Martin, Michael, ed. *New Latin American Cinema. Vol. 1 Theory, Practices, and Transcontinental Articulations*. Detroit: Wayne State University Press, 1997.

———. *New Latin American Cinema. Vol. 2. Studies of National Cinemas*. Detroit: Wayne State University Press, 1997.

Martín Barbero, Jesús. *Al sur de la modernidad: comunicación, globalización, y multiculturalidad*. Pittsburgh: Instituto Internacional de Literatura Iberoamericana, Universidad de Pittsburgh, 2001.

———. "La ciudad que median los miedos." In *Espacio urbano, comunicación y violencia en América Latina*, edited by Mabel Moraña, 19–35. Pittsburgh: Instituto Internacional de Literatura Iberoamericana, 2002.

———,. "Mediaciones urbanas y nuevos escenarios de comunicación." In *Las ciudades latinoamericanas en el nuevo [des]orden mundial*, edited by Patricio Nava y Marc Zimmerman, 73–84. Mexico: Siglo XXI, 2004.

———. "Memory and Form in the Latin American Soap Opera." In *To be continued... Soap Operas Around the World*, edited by Robert C. Allen, 276–84. London: Routledge, 1995.

———and Sonia Muñoz. *Televisión y melodrama*. Bogotá: Tercer Mundo, 1992.

Martín Morán, Ana. "La ciénaga." In *The Cinema of Latin America*, edited by Alberto Elena and Mariana Díaz López, 231–39. London: Wallflower, 2003.

Martorell, Elvira. "Recuerdos del presente: memoria e identidad. Una reflexión en torno a HIJOS." In *Memorias en presente: Identidad y transmisión en la Argentina posgenocidio*, edited by Sergio Guelerman, 133–70. Buenos Aires: Grupo Editorial Norma, 2001.

Masiello, Francine. *The Art of Transition: Latin American Culture and Neoliberal Crisis*. Durham: Duke University Press, 2001.

Massumi, Brian. *Parables for the Virtual: Movement, Affect, Sensation*. Durham: Duke University Press, 2002.

Mazziotti, Nora. "Modelos y tendencias hegemónicas en las telenovelas latinoamericanas: un recorrido por las principales estéticas." M.A. thesis, Universidad Autónoma de Barcelona, 2005.

Melche, Julia Elena. "Entre amores y perros." *Reforma-Magazzine*. June 25, 2000, 15.

Mennell, Jan. "Dreaming the Cuban Nation: Fernando Perez's *Madagascar*." *Canadian Journal of Latin American and Caribbean Studies* 33.66 (2008): 89–107.

Mestman, Mariano. "The Hour of the Furnaces." In *The Cinema of Latin America*, edited by Alberto Elena and Marina Díaz López, 119–29. London: Wallflower, 2003.

Millán, Francisco Javier. *La memoria agitada: cine y represión en Chile y Argentina*. Huelva: Fundación Cultural de Cine Iberamericano de Huelva, 2001.

Mitchell, Elvis. "From Mexico, 3 Stories and an Array of Lives United by a Car Wreck." *New York Times*, October 5, 2000. E5

Monsiváis, Carlos. "Lo local y lo global." *Público*, October 21, 2001, 21.

———. *Los mil y un velorios*. Mexico, D.F.: Patria, 1994.

———. *Mexican Postcards*. Translated and introduced by John Kraniauskas. London: Verso, 1997.

Monteagudo, Luciano. *Fernando Solanas*. Buenos Aires: Centro Editor, 1993.

———. "Lucretia Martel: susurrus a la hora de la siesta." In *New Argentine Cinema: Themes, Auteurs and Trends of Innovation / Nuevo cine argentino: Temas, autores, estilos de una renovación*, edited by Horacio Bernades, Diego Lerer, and Sergio Wolf, 69–78. Buenos Aires: Ediciones Tatanka/FIPRESCI, 2002.

Moore, Daniel. "Sundance ever warm to Latin American fare." *Variety* March 25–31, 1996: 59

Moore, Ryan. "'...And Tomorrow Is Just Another Crazy Scam': Postmodernity, Youth, and the Downward Mobility of the Middle Class." In *Generations of*

*Youth: Youth Culture and History in Twentieth-Century America*, edited by Joe Austin and Michael Nevin Willard, 253–71. New York: New York University Press, 1998.

"Muy caliente: Hollywood majors team up with Latin film producers." *Variety* April 1–7, 2002, A2.

Nagib, Lucia, ed. *The New Brazilian Cinema*. London: I.B. Tauris/Centre for Brazilian Studies/Oxford University Press, 2003.

Nájera-Ramírez, Olga. "Unruly Passions: Poetics, Performance, and Gender in the Ranchera Song." In *Chicana Feminisms: A Critical Reader*, edited by Gabriela Arredondo, et al., 184–227. Durham: Duke University Press, 2003.

Navarro, Mireya. "Who Is Killing the Young Women of Juárez: A Filmmaker Seeks Answers." *The New York Times* August 19, 2002. http://www.nytimes. com/2002/08/19/movies/who-is-killing-the-young-women-of-juarez-a-filmmaker-seeks-answers.html?scp=2&sq=senorita%20extraviada&st=cse. Accessed on August 23, 2009.

Newman, Kathleen and B. Ruby Rich. "Interview with Lourdes Portillo (1990)." In *Lourdes Portillo: The Devil Never Sleeps and Other Films*, edited by Rosa Linda Fregoso, 48–73. Austin: University of Texas Press, 2001.

———. "Steadfast Love and Subversive Acts: The Politics of *La Ofrenda: The Days of the Dead*." In *Visible Nations: Latin American Cinema and Video*, edited by Chon A. Noriega, 285–301. Minneapolis: University of Minnesota Press, 2000.

Noble, Andrea. *Mexican National Cinema*. London: Routledge, 2005.

Oneida Pérez, Martha, Armando Perryman, Nilza González, Leydi González, and Mayra Abréu. "Identidad nacional, organizaciones culturales, y tiempo libre." In *Cuba: Jóvenes en los 90*. Havana: Editorial Abril, 1999.

Orozco Gómez, Guillermo. "La telenovela en México: ¿de una expresión cultural a un simple producto para la mercadotecnia?" *Comunicación y Sociedad* Nueva época 6 (July–December 2006): 11–35.

Oricchio, Luiz Zanin. *Cinema de Novo: Um Balanço Crítico da Retomada*. São Paulo: Estação Liberdade, 2003.

Page, Joanna. *Crisis and Capitalism in Contemporary Argentine Cinema*. Durham: Duke University Press, 2009.

Paranagua, Paulo Antonio. "Cuban Cinema's Political Challenges." In *New Latin American Cinema. Vol. 2: Studies of National Cinemas*, edited by Michael T. Martín, 167–90. Detroit: Wayne State University Press, 1997.

———, ed. *Cine documental en América Latina*. Madrid: Cátedra, 2003.

Patton, Paul, ed. *Deleuze: A Critical Reader*, Oxford, UK: Blackwell, 1996.

Payne, Leslie A. *Unsettling Accounts: Neither Truth nor Reconciliation in Confessions of State Violence*. Durham: Duke University Press, 2008.

Peña, Fernando Martín, ed. *60/90 Generaciones: cine argentino independiente*. Buenos Aires: MALBA, 2003.

———, Paula Felix-Didier, Ezequiel Luka, and Gabriel Bobillo. "Lucretia Martel." In *60/90 Generaciones: cine argentino independiente*, edited by Fernando Martín Peña, 116–25. Buenos Aires: MALBA, 2003.

Pick, Zuzana. "Social Inquiry and *Los inundados*." In *The New Latin American Cinema: A Continental Project*. Austin: University of Texas Press, 1993.

Pina, Raquel. "El sujeto en escena: Huellas de la globalización en el cine argentino contemporáneo." PhD diss., The Ohio State University, 2010.

Platinga, Carl and Greg Smith, eds. *Passionate Views: Films, Cognition, and Emotion*. Baltimore: Johns Hopkins University Press, 1999.

Podalsky, Laura. "Affecting Legacies: Historical Memory and Contemporary Structures of Feeling in *Madagascar* and *Amores perros*." *Screen* 44.3 (Autumn 2003): 277–94.

———. "De la pantalla: jóvenes y el cine mexicano contemporáneo." *El Ojo que Piensa* 6 (November 2004) (www.elojoquepiensa.udg.mx).

———. "Migrant Feelings: Melodrama, *Babel*, and Affective Communities." *Studies in Hispanic Cinemas* 7.1 (Spring 2011).

———. "Out of Depth: The Politics of Disaffected Youth and Contemporary Latin American Cinema." In *Youth Culture in Global Cinema*, edited by Timothy Shary and Alexandra Seibel, 109–30. Austin: University of Texas Press, December 2006.

———. *Specular City: Transforming Culture, Consumption, and Space in Buenos Aires, 1955–1973*. Philadelphia: Temple University Press, 2004.

———. "The Young, the Damned, and the Restless: Youth in Contemporary Mexican Cinema." *Framework* 49.1 (Spring 2008).

Probyn, Elspeth. *Blush: Faces of Shame*. Minneapolis: University of Minnesota Press, 2005.

Quintín. "De una generación a otra: ¿hay una línea divisoria?" In *New Argentine Cinema: Themes, Auteurs and Trends of Innovation / Nuevo cine argentino: Temas, autores, estilos de una renovación*, edited by Horacio Bernades, Diego Lerer, and Sergio Wolf, 111–17. Buenos Aires: Ediciones Tatanka/FIPRESCI, 2002.

Rich, B. Ruby. "An/Other View of New Latin American Cinema." *Iris* 13 (1991): 5–28.

Richard, Nelly. "Cites/Sites of Violence: Convulsion of Sense and Official Routines." In *Cultural Residues: Chile in Transition*. Minneapolis: University of Minnesota Press, 2004.

———. "El drama y sus tramas: memoria, fotografía y desaparición." In *Espacio urbano, comunicación y violencia en América Latina*, edited by Mabel Moraña, 195–202. Pittsburgh: Instituto Internacional de Literatura Iberoamericana, 2002.

Roccio, Vincent. *Cinema of Anxiety: A Psychoanalysis of Italian Neorealism*. Austin: University of Texas Press, 1999.

Romero, Edgar, Matilde Molina, Lidia González, Rosa T. Rodríguez, and Liliana Rodríguez. "Juventud y valores en los umbrales del siglo XXI." In *Cuba: Jóvenes en los 90*. Havana: Editorial Abril, 1999.

Rosenstone, Robert. "The Historical Film: Looking at the Past in a Postliterate Age." In *Visions of the Past: The Challenge of Film to Our Ideas of History*. Cambridge: Harvard University Press, 1995.

Rotker, Susana, ed. *Citizens of Fear: Urban Violence in Latin America.* Rutgers University Press, 2002.

Rubin, Martin. *Thrillers.* Cambridge: Cambridge University Press, 1999.

Ruffinelli, Jorge. *Sueños de realidad: Fernando Pérez, tres décadas de cine.* Madrid: Universidad de Alcalá/Fundación del Nuevo Cine Latinoamericano, 2005.

———. *Patricio Guzmán.* Madrid: Cátedra/Filmoteca Española, 2001.

Sadlier, Darlene. "Nelson Pereira dos Santos's *Cinema de lágrimas.*" In *Latin American Melodrama: Passion, Pathos, and Entertainment.* Urbana: University of Illinois Press, 2009.

Salem, Helena. *Nelson Pereira dos Santos: o sonho possível do cinema brasileiro.* Rio de Janeiro: Nova Frontera, 1987.

San Miguel, Helidoro. "Rio, 40 Graus." In *The Cinema of Latin America,* edited by Alberto Elena and Mariana Díaz López, 71–79. London: Wallflower, 2003.

Sánchez Prado, Ignacio. "Amores perros: violencia exótica y miedo neoliberal." *Casa de las Américas* 240 (1996).

Sarlo, Beatriz. *Escenas de la vida posmoderna: Intelectuales, arte y videocultura en la Argentina.* Buenos Aires, Ariel, 1994.

———. *Instantáneas: medios, ciudad y costumbres en el fin de siglo.* Buenos Aires: Ariel, 1996.

———. *Tiempo presente: Notas sobre el cambio de una cultura.* Buenos Aires: Siglo XXI, 2001.

Schaefer, Claudia. "*Amores perros*: Throwing Politics to the Dogs." In *Bored to Distraction: Cinema of Excess in End-of-the Century Mexico and Spain.* Albany: State University of New York Press, 2003.

Schumann, Peter B. *Historia del cine latinoamericano.* Buenos Aires: Legasa, 1987.

Scott, A. O. "Emotion Needs No Translation," *New York Times* October 27, 2006.

Scott, Ian. *American Politics in Hollywood Film.* Chicago: Fitzroy Dearborn, 2000.

Segre, Roberto. *América Latina, fin de milenio: Raíces y perspectives de su arquitectura.* La Habana: Artes y Literatura, 1990.

Serra, Ana. "La Habana Cotidiana: Espacio Urbano en el Cine de Fernando Pérez." *Chasqui: revista de literatura latinoamericana.* 35.1 (2006): 88–105.

Shaw, Deborah. "*Babel*: A Hollywood World Cinema Text." Paper presented at the annual meeting of the Society of Cinema and Media Studies, Los Angeles, California, March 17–21, 2010.

———. "Seducing the Public: Images of Mexico in *Like Water for Chocolate* and *Amores perros.*" In *Contemporary Latin American Cinema: Ten Key Films.* London: Continuum, 2003.

Skidmore, Thomas E. *Brazil: Five Centuries of Change.* New York: Oxford University Press, 1999.

Smith, Greg. *Film Structure and the Emotion System.* Cambridge: Cambridge University Press, 2003.

Smith, Murray. *Engaging Characters: Fiction, Emotion, and the Cinema.* Oxford: Clarendon Press, 1995.

Smith, Paul Julian. *Amores perros.* London: British Film Institute, 2003.

Sobchack, Vivian. "Introduction: History Happens." In *The Persistence of History: Cinema, Television, and the Modern Event*. New York: Routledge, 1996.

Solanas, Fernando and Octavio Gentino. *Cine, cultura y descolonización*. Buenos Aires: Siglo Veintiuno, 1973.

———. "Hacia un tercer cine." In *Hojas de cine: testimonios y documentos del nuevo cine latinoamericano* Vol. I. México, D.F.: Fundación Mexicana de Cineastas : SEP : Universidad Autónoma Metropolitana, c1988.

Sommer, Doris. *Foundational Fictions: The National Romances of Latin America*. Berkeley: University of California Press, 1991.

Spielmann, Ellen. "Intelectuales brasileños 1969–1997. El caso Fernando Gabeira: O que é isso, companheiro?" In *Nuevas perspectives desde/sobre América Latina: El desafío de los estudios culturales*, edited by Mabel Moraña, 351–57. Santiago, Chile: Cuatro Propio/Instituto Internacional de Literatura Iberoamericana, 2000.

Stam, Robert. "*La hora de los hornos* and the Two Avant-Gardes." In *The Social Documentary in Latin America*, edited by Julianne Burton, 251–66. Pittsburgh: University of Pittsburgh Press, 1990.

Stearns, Peter. *American Cool: Constructing a Twentieth Century Emotional Style*. New York: New York University Press, 1994.

Stewart, Michael. "Irresistible Death: *21 Grams* as Melodrama," *Cinema Journal*, 47.1 (2007): 49–69.

Stock, Ann Marie. "Migrancy and the Latin American Cinemascape: Towards a Post-national Critical Praxis." *Revista canadiense de estudios hispánicos* 20.1 (1995): 19–29.

———. *On Location in Cuba: Street Filmmaking during Times of Transition*. Chapel Hill: University of North Carolina Press, 2009.

Swanson Goldberg, Elizabeth. "Splitting Differences: Global Identity Politics and the Representation of Torture in the Counterhistorical Dramatic Film." In *Violence and American Cinema*, edited by J. David Slocum, 245–70. New York: Routledge, 2001.

Taylor, Diana. *Disappearing Acts: Spectacles of Gender and Nationalism in Argentina's Dirty War*. Durham: Duke University Press, 1997.

———. "'You Are Here': HIJOS and the DNA of performance." In *The Archive and the Repertoire: Performing Cultural Memory in the Americas*. Durham: Duke University Press, 2003.

Ticineto Clough, Patricia and Jean Halley, eds. *The Affective Turn: Theorizing the Social*. Durham: Duke University Press, 2007.

Tierney, Dolores. "Alejandro González Iñarruti: Director without Borders." *New Cinemas: Journal of Contemporary Film*. 7.2 (2009): 101–17.

Tompkins, Jane. *Sensational Designs: The Cultural Work of American Fiction, 1790–1860*. New York: Oxford University Press, 1985.

Tracy, Andrew. "Babel." *Cinemascope: Expanding the Frame of International Cinema* 28. http://www.cinema-scope.com/cs28/cur_tracy_babel.html. Accessed July 27, 2009.

Traverso, Antonio. "Migrations of Cinema: Italian Neorealism and Brazilian Cinema." In *Italian Neorealism and Global Cinema*, edited by Laura E. Ruberto and Kristi M. Wilson, 165–86. Detroit: Wayne State University Press, 2007.

Trigo, Abril. "Rockeros y grafiteros: la construcción al sesgo de una antimemoria." In *Memoria colectiva y políticas del olvido: Argentina y Uruguay (1970–1990)*, edited by Adriana J. Bergero and Fernando Reati, 305–34. Rosario, Argentina: Beatriz Viterbo, 1997.

Vaidovits, Guillermo. "La levedad del ser." *El Informador-Espectáculo*, November 23, 2003.

Venegas, Cristina. *Digital Dilemmas: The State, the Individual, and Digital Media in Cuba*. New Brunswick: Rutgers University Press, 2010.

Vieira, João Luiz. "The Transnational Other: Street Kids in Contemporary Brazilian Cinema." In *World Cinemas, Transnational Perspectives*, edited by Nataša Ďurovičová and Kathleen Newman, 226–43. New York: Routledge, 2010.

Vila, Pablo. "El rock nacional: género musical y construcción de la identidad juvenil en Argentina." In *Cultura y pospolítica: El debate sobre la modernidad en América Latina*, edited by Néstor García Canclini, 231–71. México, DF: Consejo Nacional para la Cultura y las Artes, 1991.

Whissel, Karen. "Tales of Upward Mobility: The New Verticality and Digital Special Effects." In *Film Theory and Criticism*, edited by Leo Braudy and Marshall Cohen, 7th ed., 834–52. Oxford: Oxford University Press, 2009.

Williams, Linda. "Melodrama Revised." In *Refiguring American Film Genres: History and Theory*, edited by Nick Browne. Berkeley: University of California Press, 1998. 42–88.

Williams, Raymond. "Structures of Feeling." In *Marxism and Literature*. Oxford: Oxford University Press, 1977.

Wolf, Sergio. "Las estéticas del nuevo cine argentino: el mapa es el territorio." In *New Argentine Cinema: Themes, Auteurs and Trends of Innovation / Nuevo cine argentino: Temas, autores, estilos de una renovación*, edited by Horacio Bernades, Diego Lerer, and Sergio Wolf, 29-48. Buenos Aires: Ediciones Tatanka/FIPRESCI, 2002.

——, Carlos Salgado, and Raúl Escobar."Esteban Sapir." In *60/90 Generaciones: cine argentino independiente*, edited by Fernando Martín Peña, 174–83. Buenos Aires: MALBA, 2003.

Woodward, Kathleen. "Calculating Compassion." In *Compassion: The Culture and Politics of Emotion*, edited by Lauren Berlant, 59–86. New York: Routledge, 2004.

Yarbro-Bejarano, Yvonne. "Ironic Framings: A Queer Reading of the Family (Melo) drama in Lourdes Portillo's *The Devil Never Sleeps / El Diablo Nunca Duerme*." In *Lourdes Portillo: The Devil Never Sleeps and Other Films*, edited by Rosa Linda Fregoso, 102–18. Austin: University of Texas Press, 2001.

# Index